Petra Kuenkel, Silvine Gerlach, Vera Frieg

Working with Stakeholder Dialogues

Key Concepts and Competencies for Achieving Common Goals
a practical guide for change agents from public sector, private sector and civil society

Collective Leadership Institute

The German Library's bibliographical information: The German Library has recorded this publication in the German National Library's catalogue; detailed information can be accessed via http://d-nb.de

Kuenkel, Petra
Gerlach, Silvine
Frieg, Vera
Working with Stakeholder Dialogues – Key Concepts and Competencies for Achieving Common Goals. A practical guide for change agents from public sector, private sector and civil society

Publishing and production: Books on Demand GmbH, Norderstedt, Germany.
Editing: Angela Voges, Cape Town
Book layout and setting: buchgestaltung.de
Cover: Marco Sarich & Thomas Weiß – triple-spin.com

A publication of the Collective Leadership Institute
www.collectiveleadership.com

ISBN: 978-3-8391-8302-1

ACKNOWLEDGEMENTS

In the spirit of Collective Leadership, this handbook outlines a framework and brings forth examples of what can be made possible when a diverse group of individuals with a common interest come together and work jointly toward a common goal of sustainable development. We would like to acknowledge and thank the various contributors who not only helped develop the content of this publication, but also helped take this book from the drawing board and into reality.

Much of the knowledge contained in this book has been gained from the combined experience of participants from the Collective Leadership Institute's workshops series entitled "Working with Stakeholder Dialogues". As of the date of publication of this book, we now count over 400 alumni from over 50 countries, and active in the public and private sectors as well as civil society. Without the extensive experience and insight of these individuals, this book would not have been possible.

Although we hope that we have provided Stakeholder Dialogue practitioners with a substantially new approach to making cross-sector collaboration work for sustainability, we are aware that most new ideas have been touched or thought through by other people, too. We believe that there is always a history of conceptual thought. We are grateful for the inputs the Collective Leadership Institute's concept of Stakeholder Dialogue had from Minu Hemmati. We also acknowledge the inspiration we have received from the works of Bill Isaacs, Peter Garrett, Otto Scharmer and Adam Kahane. Our Dialogic Change model has roots in their approach to change. The model is based on our ample experience in Stakeholder Dialogue, but in developing it, we have also been considering the wide-ranging conceptual contribution of the Partnering Initiative.

Thanks also go to the entire Collective Leadership Institute team who supported the development of the concepts, methods, and tools developed over the last 5 years and tirelessly worked on getting all the details of a publication in place. A special thanks to Andrew Aitken, who translated much of the content and managed the last phase of this project and to Kristiane Schäfer, who continuously reminded us of need to consider private sector requirements in Stakeholder Dialogues.

Many thanks also go to Dave Bond for proofreading the countless drafts while on 3 different continents, and of course Glenda Wildschut for her invaluable contribution to shaping our model of engagement, and constantly reminding us of the spirit of UBUNTU. Special thanks to Angela Voges in Cape Town, our editor, who subjected this text to rigorous scrutiny and contributed greatly to improving its overall quality.

We are particularly grateful to the German Development Cooperation (GIZ, Deutsche Gesellschaft für Internationale Zusammenarbeit GmbH) who supported the development of the practical guide and provided a substantial number of case examples.

CASE EXAMPLES

Most case examples in this practical guide have been developed in cooperation with the Program Capacity Development for Partnerships with the Private Sector (CDP) of the Deutsche Gesellschaft für Internationale Zusammenarbeit (GIZ) GmbH which, since 1999, has implemented over 1.200 partnerships with the private sector on behalf of the German Federal Ministry for Economic Cooperation and Development (BMZ). Through the concept of CDP, GIZ passes on its expertise and experience in joint development projects to institutions in developing and transition countries and emerging economies. The advisory and training approach communicates the appropriate know-how to local partner organizations, enabling them to fulfill the role of the public partner in cooperation with the private sector. It is aligned to the specific needs of the partner concerned and focuses on three types of Cooperation: Development Partnerships, Public Private Partnerships (PPP) and Stakeholder-Dialogues. The expertise required is conveyed in individually tailored training measures and in-process advisory services.

List of case Examples:

1. Sustainable and joint use of land and resources in the Croatian Adriatic coastal region*
2. Public and private sector cooperation and capacities in the area of Vitamin A food fortification*
3. Corporate Social Responsibilities and social standards in China*
4. Strengthening the capacity of local government in South Africa*
5. The National Development Council (NEDLAC) in South Africa
6. African Cashew Alliance
7. The Global Reporting Initiative (GRI)*
8. Common Code for the Coffee Community (4C)*
9. The Ethical Trading Initiative (ETI)
10. Namibian Ministry for Agriculture, Water and Forestry*
11. Land-restitution claim in the community of Makuleke in South Africa
12. National Labor Programs on Safety and Health at Work
13. Sertão initiative
14. Public Service Reform Program, South Africa*
15. Promotion of competitiveness of Senegalese small and medium sized enterprises (SMEs)*
16. Worldwide Enhancement (WE) of Social Quality*
17. Advancing legal and social equality for women in Bangladesh*
18. The Common Code for the Coffee Community (4C): Phase 1*
19. The Common Code for the Coffee Community (4C): Phase 2*
20. The Common Code for the Coffee Community (4C): Phase 3*
21. The Common Code for the Coffee Community (4C): Phase 3*

22. The Common Code for the Coffee Community (4C): Phase 4*
23. Key success factor 1: High-level and cooperative support in 4C*
24. Key success factor 2: African Cashew initiative(ACi) *
25. Key success factor 3: Development of Cambodian land policy declaration *
26. Key success factor 4: Development of Cambodian land policy declaration*
27. Key success factor 5: The Common Code for the Coffee Community (4C)*
28. Key success factor 6: The Common Code for the Coffee Community (4C)*
29. Key success factor 7: development program to promote the competitiveness of Senegalese small and medium sized enterprises (SMEs)*
30. Key success factor 8: African Cashew initiative*

**These projects are supported by the Deutsche Gesellschaft für Internationale Zusammenarbeit (GIZ) on behalf of the German Federal Ministry for Economic Cooperation and Development (BMZ)*

TABLE OF CONTENTS

PREFACE

Social, economic and environmental sustainability requires a change in the human mindset. It also requires innovation, inventiveness, and, above all, people who are not only inspired by the potential of sustainability but who are willing to implement change at all levels of the global society. But it also requires that we acquire new competencies: the ability to bring about change collectively, on a broad scale.

The challenges of sustainability have reached the entire globalized world. Our success – or failure – in moving towards a more sustainable way of living on this planet affects everybody: societies' global interdependency is palpable when it comes to issues of sustainability. Currently, we face a lack of dialogue and collaborative leadership skills, an absence of collective responsibility for a globally sustainable future and an inability to create and implement solutions jointly beyond sectors, institutions, national societies and cultures. There is still too little awareness of this interdependency and the need for joint action towards sustainability. Constituencies and sectors within one country often work in isolation of each other and sometimes in competition. Too few leaders anchor their action in the concern for the greater good. This has resulted in an inability to jointly find long term and sustainable solutions to the challenges humankind is facing.

However, our globalized world needs innovation for sustainability based on people's ability to think together, to cooperate across sectors, nations and cultures, and to mutually respect differences. In our view, the capacity for constructive, result-oriented dialogue and value-based collaboration is at the core of humankind's ability to master challenges such as climate change, poverty, economic justice, energy security, resource management, peace, and population growth, among others.

Working towards a more sustainable world requires bringing together differing worldviews and balancing conflicts of interests for **responsible business, people-oriented public services and a strong civil society**. Solving the complex challenges arising from globally linked problems, conflicts, economic disparities and the effects of climate change increasingly calls for result-oriented collaboration between the public sector, private sector and civil society. This requires new competencies for globally and locally responsible leaders: we need to generate change initiatives towards sustainability that can be supported collectively by all parties involved. Solutions to current and future challenges can only be initiated and implemented jointly by many different actors in global and local society. A proactive approach to taking individual and collective responsibility for a more sustainable future also includes developing the human capacity to engage heart and mind more consciously for the common good.

The different actors in global society need to communicate respectfully, in a way that shows that they appreciate each other, despite serious differences in opinion. We need to enable people from various backgrounds to see the world through different lenses, yet also to begin to see the whole. We need to create opportunities for people to develop a deeper sense of possibility for future sustainable action. We need to build trust-based stakeholder relationships and increase our ability to communicate and partner with multiple stakeholders.

Such a collaborative approach can become the norm in the daily business of mastering the challenges of sustainable development: poverty, injustice, climate change, resource management, technological development, political participation, green technologies, energy security, peace-building, social cohesion, healthcare, diversity management, sustainability standards, public-private partnerships for development, democratization, education, sustainable economic development and good governance. We can implement the collective action that is required to overcome the challenges lying ahead for humankind.

The Common Code for the Coffee Community Association (4C) was founded in 2006 and represents an international strategic alliance for sustainability and responsible supply chain management in the coffee sector. It developed out of a cross-sector partnership between three stakeholder groups – Coffee Trade and Industry, Coffee Producer Organizations and International Civil Society Organizations. The 4C association is a remarkable example for the creation of a global community that has joined forces to continuously improve the social, environmental and economic conditions for the people making their living with coffee.

> *"Here was a growing community of people who had voluntarily decided to join a movement of sustainable business practices: company representatives, leaders of coffee cooperatives, coffee farmers, researchers, and activists from civil society, presidents of coffee federations, lawyers, and sustainability managers. These were people who would not necessarily talk to one another, they would not get to know each other under normal business circumstances. The initiative for more sustainable coffee production drew people together whose lives and worldviews differed in the extreme. […] The participants in the coffee initiative would have all agreed that it was a strenuous process, but not only did it make sense, it was great fun. Back home they promoted the business value of sustainability engagement, explained the marketing advantages of sustainable coffee, expressed their concerns that this would really benefit small coffee farmers, and presented the benefits of an ambitious public-private development project. […] Despite all the repeated political fights and contradictory positions, people felt that there was a climate of responsibility for the future."* [1]

If more people knew how this was possible, we would have a greater chance of being more in tune with the potential of human evolution, as we become more in tune with our ability to sense a sustainable future and are equipped with the skills to implement necessary changes. We would have a greater chance of bringing forward humanity's capacity to build a sustainable world. We could trust that collective intelligence is possible, we could collectively see more easily what needs doing and we could more actively take on the work of changing the world to become a more livable planet for all.

Stakeholder Dialogues can become a bridge between the individual's capacity to tune into sustainable action and the procedures, structures and methodologies that need to be collectively applied to change our societal and global systems towards increased sustainability. Stakeholder Dialogues cultivate innovation, inventiveness, pragmatism, integration and the ability to implement initiatives jointly. So, Stakeholder Dialogues are a global learning field: if we begin to master the art of processing difference into progress, we have taken a decisive step beyond the pattern of fragmentation that is currently so much a feature of our globalized world.

[1] ***Kuenkel 2008: 204-205***

At the core of Stakeholder Dialogues is the principle of **collective leadership**.

Collective Leadership for sustainability is the capacity of a group of leaders to contribute to a more sustainable future through assuming joint and flexible leadership in service of the common good. It takes place by various individuals on a collective scale towards the larger and integrated goal of economic, social and environmental sustainability. **At the core of collective leadership is the human capacity to dialogue and transform differences into progress: it enables the transcendence of self-centered views – a pre-requisite to successfully addressing the challenges of globalization and sustainability.**

Only a dialogic way of change towards sustainability creates commitment and the willingness of all to find innovative solutions to today's challenges. When co-creation of the future is more consciously understood as a collective task, active engagement for a sustainable future follows – by individuals, organizations and political actors. A climate of collective leadership arises. Hence, Stakeholder Dialogues create passion for change: they open a gateway for emotional commitment to creating a better future together.

In this sense, this practitioner's guide to **Working with Stakeholder Dialogues** is an important contribution to sustainability, as it provides you with the core methodology for creating collaborative change in a climate of collective leadership. Stakeholder Dialogues can become a vital contribution to making our world more sustainable – as a key methodology for finding solutions to complex challenges in the area of sustainability, new forms of governance as well a global learning and innovation processes.

Whether they fail or succeed depends less on a rigid instrument, or a blueprint sequence of action, than it does on our ability to learn the art of creating a space in which collective intelligence can emerge: **the art of respectfully processing differences into progress.** But as with all of the arts, there are skills we need to develop to succeed and to bring our gifts to the world – we need to know when and how to use dialogue, and when and how to take action.

We need to know effective ways of engaging stakeholders to ensure that collective knowledge, individual experience and expertise are harvested sufficiently. We need to be familiar with methodologies that generate productive and outcome-oriented dialogue around complex social, political and environmental issues. We need to attend to the factors that enable a sense of ownership and subsequent commitment to implementation. We need to broaden our strategic abilities and implementation skills in using Stakeholder Dialogues for initiatives that require collective action. We need to know when to attend to differences and when to attend to consensus-building. We need to develop our ability to sense when open dialogue is required and when to consolidate agreements. Therefore, we need **essential tools for the successful implementation of result-oriented Stakeholder Dialogues.**

This practical guide is based on experiences with successful Stakeholder Dialogues and includes the experience of a few hundred alumni that have taken part in the educational programs of the Collective Leadership Institute. It focuses on understanding success factors in Stakeholder Dialogues. It also helps you to develop your competence in assessing when to apply the Stakeholder Dialogue approach. It will enhance your skills in initiating and implementing Stakeholder Dialogue processes successfully. And it introduces you to the key elements of Stakeholder Dialogues: how to prepare, implement and evaluate them.

INTRODUCTION

WORKING WITH STAKEHOLDER DIALOGUES

Stakeholder Dialogues are a methodology for designing and implementing consultation and cooperation in complex change processes that require different interest groups to be included and integrated. Well-structured Stakeholder Dialogues can create and cultivate ownership of change towards sustainability.

Stakeholder Dialogues are increasingly used as an important tool for sustainable development initiatives, adaptation to climate change, strengthening economic development, social dialogue and efforts to achieve the Millennium Development Goals (MDGs). Many global and societal actors have discovered and further developed this approach to collaborate with different stakeholders, to find solutions to complex challenges and to implement solutions collectively. Dialogue is often the right path to take to ensure that solutions are based on different perspectives and competencies.

> **➲ What are stakeholders?**
>
> Stakeholders are people or institutions that have an interest in a particular course of development, or a particular decision, either as individuals or as representatives of a group. This includes people who influence a decision, who are key players in implementation, or who are affected by the development.

The intention of stakeholder participation is, in essence, dialogic: to get people from different walks of life and with different perspectives into a conversation that will lead to a practical outcome. Dialogue allows one to integrate different perspectives, standpoints and interests into planning and implementation processes.

In dialogic terms, Stakeholder Dialogues are guided conversations that ensure that people with different viewpoints and sometimes contradictory interests exchange (world)views. The most important common feature of Stakeholder Dialogues are structured conversations about certain issues of common interest or concern between people

- from different sectors and constituencies;
- with different perspectives and points of view; and
- with different interests.

These conversations improve planning and decision-making, solve problems, contribute to finding innovative solutions, or to designing and implementing joint interventions for change. Stakeholder Dialogues are a vital stepping stone in achieving a common goal, and are therefore often embedded in a short-term or long-term societal or global change process. **Ideally, Stakeholder Dialogues lead to a practical outcome that could not have been achieved otherwise and that can more easily be implemented because all stakeholders involved experience a higher degree of ownership.**

INTRODUCTION

In high-quality Stakeholder Dialogues, differences, sometimes even conflicts, hold the potential for innovative solutions and can achieve goals that ultimately benefit all.

This can lead to

- trust-building between different stakeholders;
- future-oriented and constructive cooperation between different societal actors;
- innovative solutions to existing economic or social challenges;
- a higher quality and broader acceptance of decisions;
- ownership of and commitment to implementing agreed-upon results;
- collective responsibility for change;
- credible change endeavors;
- sustainable outcomes; and
- long-lasting cooperation structures.

Stakeholder Dialogues often chart unknown territory. Different forms of organizations with subsequently different internal structures, mandates, purposes, values and decision-making procedures meet in a common space, often for the first time. Different, sometimes contradicting, world-views need to be mutually understood and mediated. Different forms of planning need to be negotiated. Different dialogue expectations need to be managed. When people of various backgrounds decide to move into such output-oriented constructive dialogue, they need to develop their communicative competence. This is greatly supported by dialogue facilitators, dialogue coordinators or stakeholder brokers: people who understand the different worlds, earn the trust of the different stakeholders and are able to move between the worlds. Successful Stakeholder Dialogue facilitators know how to design and facilitate effective communication processes.

Stakeholder Dialogues are not a tool for unilateral communication, for conveying information to stakeholders, for example. They are only appropriate if the implementation of change is envisaged, or an authentic stakeholder contribution to a decision, a planning process, a strategy, or the design of an initiative is welcomed. The duration of Stakeholder Dialogues can vary, depending on what target results have been set and how deep the engagement and cooperation between the stakeholders in the dialogue needs to be. Well-designed Stakeholder Dialogues can result in partnerships or long-term stakeholder processes, such as cooperation for conflict resolution, standards development, regional development, or public-private dialogues for improved business environments. They can take place on the macro, meso or micro level of the (global) society, depending on the expected outcome and the stakeholders involved. They can also cover a wide range of content areas, such as

- finding innovative solutions to existing economic or social challenges;
- developing strategies for adapting to or mitigating climate change;
- improving policies and regulation;
- implementing government regulations;
- implementing cross-sector partnerships for development;
- improving the delivery of public services;
- improving the management of natural resources;

- integrating disadvantaged groups into economic development;
- creating an enabling environment for economic development; or
- improving responsible value chains.

Stakeholder Dialogues can be implemented in different forms and with various levels of engagement. They are not 'one size fits all' solutions to achieving lasting impact, but are ways of creating common ground for change. They need to be designed flexibly, depending on the issue, the objective, the participants, the time available and many other factors. Nonetheless, the following aspects are crucial for designing and implementing Stakeholder Dialogues successfully:

- creating a context of trust and continuity to enable the partners and stakeholders to engage in open and honest communication;
- being aware of the important role that dialogue coordinators or stakeholder facilitators play;
- integrating the tangible goals of the Stakeholder Dialogue into a frame, including the overall objectives and a joint vision (sustainable development, for example);
- making sure that the objectives and the goals of the Stakeholder Dialogue match the existing interests of the participating stakeholders and their respective organizations;
- being prepared to understand the different codes of conduct and value systems of the various sectors involved, and being open to these codes and systems; and
- establishing feedback mechanisms between direct participants of the Stakeholder Dialogue and indirect participants ('influencers', 'constituencies').

Stakeholder Dialogues seek to establish true exchange and trust. They are rooted in the principles of transparency and participation, and they recognize the relevance of equity and accountability in interpersonal interaction and communication. Hence, the concept of Stakeholder Dialogues is based on values and principles that need to underlie the planning of every Stakeholder Dialogue, regardless of its structure or level of engagement, and should be guarded throughout the entire implementation process.

The value base of Stakeholder Dialogues is given on pages 18 and 19.

The value base of Stakeholder Dialogues[2]

Being transparent and accountable	For individuals and institutions, accountability means being responsible for one's actions and their consequences. Decision-makers in the public, private and civil sector thus become answerable to the people taking a stake in their decisions. For their decisions and actions to be legitimate, a broad range of opinions and interests needs to be considered and integrated into the decision-making process. This also requires setting up transparent communication procedures. Accountability means that those affected by decisions can inquire about the decision-making process, thus making it comprehensible and traceable.
Ensuring equity	Stakeholder Dialogues value and consider the contributions of all stakeholder groups equally. This requires consensus-building based on a participatory process with balanced representation, engagement and integration of the relevant stakeholder groups. Tolerance, mutual respect, overcoming stereotyping, and the willingness to reach consensus is indispensible in this process, which allows the voices of those who may be weakly represented in existing position-finding and decision-making procedures to be heard.
Focusing on the contribution to the common good	The particular value that Stakeholder Dialogues can add to programs, projects and other forms of joint undertakings is to reach better decisions and more sustainable solutions by considering a wider range of opinions, interests, experiences and competencies. Making a Stakeholder Dialogue effective means ensuring that its focus lies on solution-finding and implementation. This is achieved by consulting a broader range of stakeholders and developing decisions, recommendations and actions that find broad support. It fosters participants' commitment and leadership because they identify with the dialogue process and therefore play a decisive role in its implementation, and as multipliers. Throughout the dialogue process, the contribution to the common good, or the 'bigger picture', needs to be palpable.
Fostering collective leadership	To be effective, results that are developed in an equitable and participatory process need to be implemented through collective leadership. Stakeholder Dialogues foster the development and advancement of partnerships and networks between stakeholders. They increase fruitful exchange, collective action, mechanisms for shared power and collective responsibility.
Ensuring reliable processes	Engaging in a stakeholder process needs the trust of all participants – not only mutual trust, but also trust in the possibility of jointly working towards a common goal, and trust in the process of walking this way together. To build this trust, stakeholders need to be able to rely on a process design, implementation and facilitation that provides for predictable engagement, iterative procedures, transparent planning and a comprehensive system in which each participant knows where and when they can take part in the process.

[2] Inspired by and adapted from: Hemmati 2002

The value base of Stakeholder Dialogues[3]

Being open to iterative learning	Stakeholder Dialogues can contribute to the emergence of collective intelligence and innovative solutions. To live up to this potential, they need to be designed and implemented with awareness of collective human communication processes. Beyond discussing the subject matter and defending points of view, participants need to adopt a learning attitude. This cultivates an atmosphere for new ideas and solutions to emerge that would not have evolved otherwise. It requires the individual participants of a Stakeholder Dialogue to be open to, and willing to learn from, each other, to be self-reflective and to allow for change in their own perspectives. It also requires an openness to venture into the unknown that true equity, participation and consensus-building can promise.
Cultivating consensus-building	Decisions reached by consensus strengthen the ownership that participants develop for results and their implementation. To enable consensus-building, the process design needs to ensure appropriate communication architecture within the Stakeholder Dialogues system. The principles of participation, ownership, inclusiveness and collaborative leadership require a process within the Stakeholder Dialogue where agreements can be reached jointly in meetings specifically designed for this purpose.
Ensuring participation and engagement	To create ownership of Stakeholder Dialogues among the participants, they need to participate and actively engage all relevant stakeholders. All actors need to be brought together. Resources such as information need to be made equally accessible to all. It is important to find ways of including stakeholders who may usually be kept outside of position-finding and decision-making processes, such as people with less academic education, less organized stakeholders, or people with few financial means. Inclusiveness strengthens the credibility and legitimacy of a process, since its outputs and outcomes are based on broader stakeholder involvement.
Respecting legitimacy	For all participants to engage in Stakeholder Dialogues and their outcomes, they need to be legitimate. Concretely, this implies that the dialogue needs to be designed and implemented in an accountable, transparent and equitable way and that the initiators or conveners have a sufficient mandate to hold the dialogue. Dialogue process and participating stakeholders need to be perceived as legitimate by those involved, but also by non-participating stakeholders.

[3] ***Inspired by and adapted from: ebd***

How to use this book

Stakeholder Dialogues require very conscious leadership: it can be a challenge to deal with the diversity of cultures, interests and goals among stakeholders. Similarly, it may require leadership confidence to overcome an initial lack of trust between people from different stakeholder groups, particularly if some of them have stronger influence than others. Successfully implementing Stakeholder Dialogues therefore requires multilevel skills development. For the result-oriented implementation of Stakeholder Dialogues, **instruments and tools** are essential, as well as a good understanding of what is required in which phase of a Stakeholder Dialogue.

The knowledge and understanding of background **concepts** places the actual implementation of Stakeholder Dialogues into a larger context of the management of change in complex human systems.

For the sensitive and successful design of Stakeholder Dialogues, we need a high degree of **process competence** that enables us to know when informal engagement processes are required, when workshops need to be held, when to attend to emotional issues and when to create the structure for tangible outcomes.

Stakeholder Dialogues are an attempt to change an existing status quo. To do this successfully, we need to understand the context in which the particular stakeholder initiative takes place: the complex system that is built around the particular issue at stake. We need to understand what can foster or prevent change. **System awareness** is a prerequisite for the initiation of Stakeholder Dialogues, and remains an important skill throughout their implementation.

The most important 'tools' for Stakeholder Dialogues are the people who initiate, implement, support and facilitate them. To increase the likelihood of positive impact, Stakeholder Dialogue facilitators need a high degree of **self-awareness.** They need to know their own preferences, strengths and weaknesses. They need to be able to reflect their leadership role and be open to continuous learning.

Self-awareness	Awareness of ourselves is an essential element in the implementation of Stakeholder Dialogues.
System awareness	An understanding of the system (the field we are intervening in or operating in) and its dynamic is crucial for the successful implementation of Stakeholder Dialogues.
Process competence	Process competence is a key success factor for the design and implementation of Stakeholder Dialogues
Concepts	Concepts are important for understanding the potential and limitations of Stakeholder Dialogues.
Instruments, tools	Instruments and tools are useful and important for planning and implementing Stakeholder Dialogues.

The guidebook **Working with Stakeholder Dialogues** touches on all these levels of skill development.

Chapter 1 gets you started by exploring the field of Stakeholder Dialogues. It explains when Stakeholder Dialogues are the appropriate approach to take and what forms of Stakeholder Dialogues exist. It also gives you an insight into the characteristics of the three main societal stakeholder groups, namely the public sector, private sector and civil society.

Chapter 2 introduces you to the **Dialogic Change Model**[4] that shows the different phases of Stakeholder Dialogues and helps you to understand what is required in each phase. It provides a guided approach to the preparation and implementation of Stakeholder Dialogues.

Chapter 3 takes you deeper into the understanding of dialogue, and into the abilities that Stakeholder Dialogue facilitators need.

Chapter 4 invites you to reflect and equips you with an approach to monitor the key factors of successful Stakeholder Dialogues.

Chapter 5 offers you resources providing you with conceptual background on Stakeholder Dialogues as an approach to change. It gives you a deeper knowledge of engagement processes – an important prerequisite for making Stakeholder Dialogues work.

Chapter 6 equips you with a variety of tools that are helpful for working with Stakeholder Dialogues. It provides assessment tools, diagnostic and implementation tools.

In the appendix, you will find links and literature.

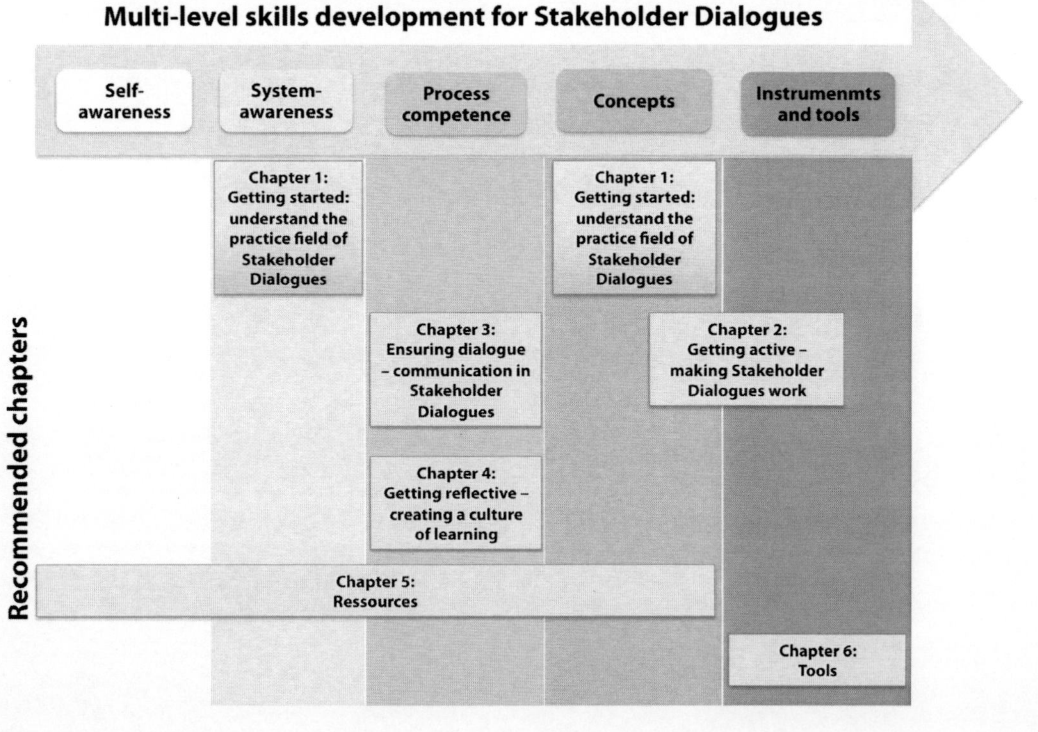

[4] Developed by the Collective Leadership Institute

GETTING STARTED – UNDERSTANDING THE ACTION FIELD OF STAKEHOLDER DIALOGUES

GETTING STARTED – UNDERSTANDING THE ACTION FIELD OF STAKEHOLDER DIALOGUES

Stakeholder Dialogues can be applied in a variety of settings, for diverse reasons, at different levels of global society, initiated by different stakeholder groups and implemented in different forms. What they have in common is:

- the **value base**: an underlying assumption that participation and engagement, accountability and mutual respect, constructive collaboration and openness to different perspectives lead to better solutions;
- the **larger goal**: an underlying assumption that achieving consensus for sustainable action – no matter how small or large – is always a contribution to sustainability and the future of humankind;
- the **dialogic approach**: an underlying assumption that a dialogic way of change leads to solutions that last better and guarantees that all aspects of an issue are integrated into the change envisaged; and
- the **methodology**: an underlying assumption that understanding the core methodology for implementing Stakeholder Dialogues enables you to apply tools and instruments, system interventions and process competence successfully in a variety of settings.

1.1 Understanding why and when to work with Stakeholder Dialogues

Ideally, Stakeholder Dialogues lead to practical outcomes that could not have been achieved otherwise and that can be implemented more easily because all stakeholders involved can see the 'bigger picture' of the issue at stake and can experience a higher degree of ownership for the results that the process achieved. High-quality Stakeholder Dialogues create a climate for **trust, commitment and collective intelligence**. When they are based on recognizing diverse opinions and consensus-building processes, they can lead to improved implementation of initiatives, projects, or change endeavors.

Stakeholder Dialogues bring different interest groups into a new form of communication together. In the beginning, this may feel unfamiliar and sometimes uncomfortable for participants. But experience shows that people catch up with a true dialogic exchange very easily. Differences in points of view become more constructive, if discussed in a space of respect and acknowledgement. Consensus becomes more authentic if differences have been properly explored. Exchanging experiences becomes outcome-focused if stakeholders can see the bigger picture of an issue. Solutions become easier to find when the emotional connection to a larger goal is maintained. Decision-making is more credible if it is based on authentic listening to differing perspectives. Implementation-steering becomes easier if there is a sense of collective responsibility for change.

Well-designed Stakeholder Dialogues ensure that:

- all stakeholders involved can see the full picture by listening, and opening up to different perspectives;
- different interests, points of view and levels of power are equally represented;
- there is as much transparency of interests as possible;
- trust is created;
- a common goal can be agreed on; and
- implementation activities are jointly designed

Why are Stakeholder Dialogues a promising approach?[5]

The quality of decision-making improves	Drawing together expertise and perspectives from a number of disciplines and areas of work can lead to an improved understanding of the situation, the challenges ahead and better solutions. Through Stakeholder Dialogues, the **quality** that goes into recommendations or decision-making improves tremendously.
Creativity and innovation prevail	Diversity, if brought into the structured setting of a dialogue, can unfold its potential for increased **creativity and innovation**.
The credibility of planning and decisions is higher	Recommendations or decisions made in a participatory setting have a higher degree of **credibility**. Including stakeholders in consultation and decision-making lends credibility to any decision because it is based on a wider range of inputs and balanced interests. Collaborating across interest groups is not easy, but the result of identifying common ground, building trust and aligning behind an issue of common concern often pays off. This can create results that are more likely to be regarded as legitimate than efforts that are undertaken by one stakeholder group alone. The more transparently stakeholder inputs are integrated into decision-making, the greater the credibility of a Stakeholder Dialogue.
The likelihood of implementation increases	True participation generates a stronger sense of ownership and responsibility for the process. This leads to a **higher likelihood of implementation**: people help to implement the future when they have had the chance to be part of its design. Hence, stakeholder engagement done in the right way can be a cornerstone for success in implementation. Outcomes developed in a Stakeholder Dialogue are likely to be more appropriate and based on broader commitment.
Information is disseminated	The involvement of different stakeholder groups helps to convey a particular issue of concern to a broader range of people. The different stakeholder constituencies will transfer the information to their institutions, organizations and support groups. Wider **dissemination** of a particular change initiative's goal is an important feature of Stakeholder Dialogues.
Cross-sector relationships become more collaborative	Stakeholder Dialogues improve people's capacity not only to see the wider picture or broaden their narrow position: they also help people to cooperate with stakeholders they normally would avoid, not know, or at least not collaborate with. Hence, a structured dialogue helps to improve the social cohesion and thus the **quality of cross-sector relationships** – an important prerequisite for tackling the challenges of sustainable development.

[5] inspired by and adapted from: Hemmati, 2002

Why are Stakeholder Dialogues a promising approach?

The outreach increases	Change processes, decisions and implementation procedures often touch upon the interest of stakeholders who do not actively participate in the process, but who nevertheless are concerned with the developments of the issue at stake (for example, depending on the concern, the interested public, communities or political leaders involved with the issue). Well-designed Stakeholder Dialogues include **outreach** and provide information to constituencies during decision-finding and for implementation. This creates trust in those steering the dialogue, and generates broad acceptance of the process and its outcomes – also beyond those who are actively involved in implementing the dialogue.
The problem-solving capacity of complex systems increases	Strategic learning requires the synergy of different perspectives, expertise and competences. Stakeholder Dialogues integrate experiences and knowledge. This generates points of view that are often new and innovative. So, they have a fast learning pace and a high **problem-solving capacity**.
Stalemates and conflicts can be overcome	Through active involvement in Stakeholder Dialogues, participants can fathom out and implement options for future developments jointly. This changes and broadens the stakeholders' perspectives and opens up new possibilities for action. This opening often helps to **overcome standstill and conflicts**.
Results become more robust and sustainable	Cooperation processes produce long-lasting results if the integration of different points of view, interests and perspectives is guaranteed. Stakeholder Dialogues bring different perspectives together, thereby leading to decisions with which all participants can identify. Implementing these decisions generates more **sustainable and robust results** that will also survive the minor obstacles and conflicts that might occur throughout the process.

Stakeholder involvement also bears risks: it could lead to an undue increase of influence of a certain stakeholder group; a lack of transparency towards the public; or a reputational risk from suboptimal processes. Other obstacles that can slow down the dialogue process and endanger its results include: the use of stereotypes to label members of stakeholder groups; competition and intolerance; opposing priorities; insufficient sensitivity towards, and understanding of, the 'worlds' of the other stakeholders; or, simply, unrealistic expectations of what stakeholders can achieve in the time available to them. In addition, the different sectors involved can sometimes turn out to be incompatible. Or, external obstacles such as an unfavorable political framework or a lack of funding can shipwreck the Stakeholder Dialogue.

These risks and obstacles can be mitigated by:

- selecting the appropriate form of Stakeholder Dialogue; and
- ensuring a high-quality management of the stakeholder engagement process and of the implementation of the Stakeholder Dialogue.

GETTING STARTED

Stakeholder dialogues can be a pragmatic approach to successful consultation and collaboration. They are the methodology of choice, if results need to be achieved in a complex context, when different actors need to work together to make a profound difference.

When are Stakeholder Dialogues the right approach to take?

When inspiration for change is required	If the change is clearly needed, but none of the stakeholders actively takes the initiative to bring it about.
When different perspectives need to be integrated	If a change of a status quo is wanted, but different stakeholders have very different stances about direction, objectives and modes of delivery.
When problem-solving requires innovation and collective intelligence	If challenges occur that cannot be addressed by the means, experience, expertise or power of one particular stakeholder group.
When broad acceptance is required	If the implementation of a measure or regulation ensuring sustainability requires the understanding and acceptance of many different stakeholders.
When only joint implementation will lead to success	If the implementation of a project, an initiative or a service delivery depends on the support of and collaboration with different stakeholders.

➲ *Chapter 6, Tools: 6.1. Assessing the potential for Stakeholder Dialogues, page 156*

Stakeholder Dialogues can cover a wide spectrum of forms and levels of engagement. They can be conducted in different settings and for different reasons. Stakeholders can develop consultative dialogues on policy development to include joint decision-making and implementation of practical solutions, although the exact nature of any such process will depend on the issue, its objectives, participants, scope and timelines. So, Stakeholder Dialogues come in different forms. Each situation, issue or problem prompts the need for stakeholder initiators to design a process specifically suited to their abilities, circumstances and expected results.

Stakeholder Dialogues are suitable for situations in which dialogue is possible and where at least a minimum of listening, reconciling interests and integrating viewpoints into joint strategy development seems appropriate and within reach. There is no single appropriate way for all kinds of concerns. Stakeholder Dialogues can take place on different levels of global society, depending on the expected outcome and the stakeholders involved.

At which levels can Stakeholder Dialogues take place?

Global/ international	***International*** ***Stakeholder Dialogues take place when a solution to a problem cannot be found within one country, when the problem requires internationally active stakeholder groups, or representatives from a variety of countries, to become involved. These usually aim at finding agreements that can then be applied to all participating countries. International Stakeholder Dialogues, particularly those that include official government representation, often need to take place in a very formal environment with rigid protocol. They are sometimes prone to political interventions and depend on government–government relationships.***	The **Kyoto Protocol** is an international protocol to the United Nations Framework Convention on Climate Change (UNFCCC). It targets combatting global warming by reducing greenhouse gas emissions. The signatory states of Annex 1 commit to enact national policies and measures that help reduce the emission of greenhouse gases in their respective countries. Furthermore, the protocol foresees the joint implementation of the protocol as well as the usage of the clean development mechanism and emission trading. The Kyoto Protocol, first adopted in 1997, is based on a year-long process of stakeholder negotiations between national governments. ➲ **http://unfccc.int/kyoto_protocol/items/2830.php** The **World Commission on Dams** (WCD) is an independent international research body focusing on environmental, social and economic impacts of the global development of large dams. Based on their studies, the WCD develops guidelines, standards and policy recommendations on the development of future dams. The Commission is composed of members of civil society, academia, industry, professional associations and government. They all act as individuals, not as representatives of the organizations or governments they work for. ➲ **www.dams.org**
	If international Stakeholder Dialogues are focused on specific issues that only affect particular target groups, or are initiated and led by private-sector or non-governmental organizations, they often are more focused on implementation and less prone to political intervention.	The **Forest Steward Council** (FSC) is a non-profit multi-stakeholder organization working to promote sustainable forest management, e.g. through the application of an FSC sustainability standard. The members participate on a voluntary basis. The FSC serves its members as a platform for the exchange and implementation of their accreditation system. It has set up a governance system with equal representation and say from different stakeholder groups (civil society, private sector, public sector). The governance body meets at regular intervals to decide on the further development of the organization. ➲ **www.fsc.org**

At which levels can Stakeholder Dialogues take place?

Regional/ international	***Stakeholder Dialogues on the* regional level *require the collaboration of government or private and civil-society actors beyond the borders of one country. This can, for example, take place to enhance economic and social development in a region. It is often strongly led by governments.***	The **Comprehensive African Agricultural Development Program** (CAADP), a sub-component of the New Partnership for Africa's Development NEPAD is a set of values and principles for the reform of national agro-political reform programs. On national level the government leads the CAADP-process, integrating the CAADP stakeholder approach and respective principles into national policies for agrarian reform. The process development, its implementation and further development are based on continuous consultancy of other agro-politically relevant stakeholders from the very beginning such as academia, producers and industry. The reform programs developed based on the CAADP principles are consolidated in a national CAADP compact and are mandatory for the respective governments. ➲ **www.nepad.caadp.net**
	Stakeholder Dialogues that take place in more than one country, but involve the public sector less, or that focus on very specific issues, such as a value chain or a specific conservation topic, have often a strong focus on implementation. Collaboration is required to achieve an agreed outcome.	The **African Cashew Alliance** is an emerging stakeholder platform promoting the processing of raw cashews, increasing the income of African farmers and promoting the consumption of cashew nuts globally. It supports the development of country-specific cashew policy agendas in 10 member countries and facilitates the exchange of information and best practices on cashew processing. It also assists its members in promoting the African cashew industry in national and international markets. ➲ **www.africancashewalliance.com**

At which levels can Stakeholder Dialogues take place?

National	**National level Stakeholder Dialogues** ***can cover many different topics. They are often led by government if the goal, for example, is to develop national strategies, review or develop policies, or implement a new regulation. Stakeholder Dialogues initiated by government often need to take place in a very formal environment with rigid protocol. If Stakeholder Dialogues are initiated by one government ministry, an internal governmental alignment process is crucially important.***	In the context of an adaption to climate change, the **Tunisian government** holds an open Stakeholder Dialogue inviting stakeholders from the private sector and civil society in order to listen to concerns and receive consultative input for the development of a national strategy on climate change adaptation.
	Stakeholder Dialogues at national level can also be initiated by non-governmental organizations and supported by international development cooperation.	**China CSR Map** is a stakeholder platform which aims to promote CSR in China through sharing and open exchange of information on the spectrum of CSR activities implemented in the country. As an online-registry it lists CSR-practitioners from public, civil and private sector as well as international organizations and their respective projects. The initiative was spurred by the realization that although there is considerable discussion and activities around CSR in China, it is often difficult to find concrete information on which organizations are undertaking what activities. ➲ **www.chinacsrmap.org**
Subregional/local	***Stakeholder Dialogues within one country focusing on implementation can take place in a particular subregion, if the region is affected by the issue at stake.***	The '**Provincial Public Private Dialogue**' (PPPD) in the People's Democratic Republic of Lao seeks to improve the provincial business and investment climate by setting up an institutionalized, transparent dialogue process in which the public and the private sector jointly identify and solve issues at provincial level. The Stakeholder Dialogue was installed to ensure broad-based economic growth in the country. Main focus of PPPD is a better implementation of existing laws and regulations at provincial level on the one hand, and providing the private sector at provincial level with a communications channel for inputs to the drafting of laws and regulations at central level on the other hand.
	Stakeholder Dialogues can take place at a local level (within a municipality or a district, for example) if the issue at stake is restricted to the locality.	In order to support the **value chain development of vegetable and fruits in the Siem Rap Province, Cambodian** institutions created an ongoing stakeholder forum with the function of facilitating regular exchange between all involved actors in the value chain.

1.2 Understanding different forms of Stakeholder Dialogues

Depending on the issues at stake, on the role of Stakeholder Dialogue initiators and the purpose of the dialogue process, Stakeholder Dialogues can be implemented in different forms. If consultation is at the forefront, once-off stakeholder workshops or a sequence of stakeholder workshops can integrate different viewpoints into planning or decision-making. If collaboration and joint implementation is at the forefront, regular stakeholder meetings become part of an overall strategy for implementation and cooperation.

One can distinguish broadly between two underlying purposes of Stakeholder Dialogues:

- Stakeholder Dialogues that are geared towards **consultation**: the structured integration of viewpoints and interests from different stakeholders; and
- Stakeholder Dialogues that have a stronger focus on **collaborative implementation:** the collaboration of different stakeholders to achieve a jointly agreed goal.

In consultative Stakeholder Dialogues, the role of stakeholders is to contribute their expertise, their viewpoints and their experiences. What happens with the input or with recommendations is the responsibility of the leading Stakeholder Dialogue initiator. In cooperative Stakeholder Dialogues, stakeholders are often more active in the joint steering of an implementation process. With a strong focus on implementation, the commitment to collaborate and to take joint responsibility for outcomes and success increases. Stakeholders move from being observers to being active in achieving results.

DIFFERENT FORMS OF STAKEHOLDER DIALOGUES

From stakeholder consultation to cooperation and implementation

Within the two broad distinctions are various forms of Stakeholder Dialogues that may overlap in their features, but that can be distinguished as follows:

Consultative Stakeholder Dialogues	Singular stakeholder consultation
	Regular stakeholder consultation
	Institutionalized stakeholder consultation
	Stakeholder platform (exchange)
Stakeholder Dialogues focused on collaboration and implementation	Stakeholder initiatives
	Stakeholder platforms (management of implementation)
	Stakeholder partnerships

A key success factor for dialogue coordinators is their ability to assess which **form of Stakeholder Dialogue** is appropriate in a situation, and to determine the best possible way to engage stakeholders and to achieve tangible outcomes. On the basis of such an assessment, they can then design and facilitate an effective and result-oriented dialogue process.

The choice of a form of Stakeholder Dialogue depends on what needs to be achieved. In many cases, stakeholder engagement has the primary purpose of consultation – with the aim of ensuring sufficient input for planning or decision-making. Programs or development initiatives requiring collaboration between different stakeholder groups can use several forms of Stakeholder Dialogues. They can also, over time, develop into very targeted cooperation projects. Some initiatives are designed from the outset to ensure collaborative implementation. But even when stakeholders decide to cooperate closely towards an agreed-upon objective with defined deliverables, they may want to use a stakeholder consultation process as part of their implementation design. So, the different forms are distinct, and there are typical situations in which one form is the most recommended path to take, but they are also connected and can develop into each other.

➲ *Chapter 6, Tools: 6.2. Choosing the appropriate form of Stakeholder Dialogue, page 160*

The following paragraphs explain the distinct features of the different forms of Stakeholder Dialogues and are illustrated with examples.

Singular stakeholder consultation

Timeframe	1–3 days
Feature	Event/workshop/conference to get input from different stakeholders

If an initiative, a project or program, a company or a government body intends to build its planning, progress review or impact monitoring on the feedback of relevant stakeholders, a singular stakeholder consultation can take place in the form of a one- to three-day stakeholder event. Such events can raise awareness of a particular issue of common concern, or increase the interest of stakeholder groups in the potential for future collaboration. The focus here is on consultation, generating interest or exchanging experiences. The challenge in singular stakeholder consultations lies in creating events that go beyond conveying information. Only true interest in the different viewpoints of stakeholders will lead to constructive dialogues.

● The **Croatian Ministry for Environment** initiated a stakeholder consultation process to ensure a sustainable and joint use of land and resources in the Croatian Adriatic coastal region. The project's core-team organized a stakeholder workshop offering the diverse interest groups, such as local administration, fishermen, representatives from the tourism industry and other local SMEs the opportunity to exchange ideas and experience on integrated coastal zone management and obtain their input on the sustainable usage of the coastal area.

● A development partnership between the **German development cooperation and the chemical group BASF** aims at strengthening existing public and private sector cooperation and capacities in the area of Vitamin A food fortification. For the implementation of joint efforts in Tanzania, they invited all relevant stakeholders to a Stakeholder Dialogue workshop. The purpose was to explore the common ground for collaboration in a national action plan for food fortification.

Sequence of regular stakeholder consultation

Timeframe	Several 1–3-day events/meetings/workshops
Feature	Consultative stakeholder events leading to a specific outcome

Initiatives that require sustained consultation between different stakeholders, such as in policy development or review, or in the form of a stakeholder forum accompanying an implementation process as a kind of 'sounding board', can take place as a sequence of regular events (from one to three days, several times over a period of one or two years). Feedback and input that is requested from the different stakeholders is then integrated into an implementation process for which the initiator of the Stakeholder Dialogue is responsible. The purpose of regular consultation is to improve, for example, the development of policy, to design a participatory implementation strategy, or to ensure regular feedback for the implementation of a specific initiative. Regular stakeholder consultations have become an essential element of good governance implementation. They ensure that policy decisions, the development and implementation of regulations and public sector planning achieves not only higher quality, but broader consent. This is because stakeholders can raise their concerns, bring in their expertise and experiences and highlight missing aspects of the planning or implementation process. Often, regular stakeholder consultations have a specific outcome, such as the development of a national strategy on a certain topic, for example the implementation planning for a regulatory measure, or the planning for regional development.

● A Round Table initiative which held several meetings to discuss issues of **Corporate Social responsibility and social standards in China**, supported dialogue and the exchange of information between the participating actors. In addition, the repeated interaction led to an increased awareness about the topic and to the identification of concrete measures and their possible implementations.

● To strengthen the capacity of local government, a joint project between the **Department of Cooperative Governance and Traditional AFFAIRS (COGTA)** in South Africa and the German development cooperation aims to stimulate dialogue processes on three levels: on a national level (between the state and private actors), on a local level (between public and private actors), and on national, regional and local levels (between representatives of government organizations and the private sector). The approach includes regular Stakeholder Dialogue meetings.

Institutionalized Stakeholder Consultation

Timeframe	Ongoing, following public planning procedures
Feature	Government-led stakeholder consultation embedded in regulations

Governments, intergovernmental organizations or regional organizations committed to good governance may want to make stakeholder consultation part of their regulatory, implementation or planning procedures. In this case the Stakeholder Dialogue becomes an institutionalized feature: as long-term dialogue structures between the public and private sector to ensure an enabling economic environment, or as statutory agreements on how to involve different stakeholders in planning procedures, such as development planning or environmental impact assessments. The institutionalized stakeholder consultation procedure can be the result of positive experiences in preceding stakeholder consultation processes, such as stakeholder forums for the ongoing review of strategic planning processes. It can also be part of the constitution, or the result of societal or international pressure groups forcing a public sector actor to integrate different stakeholder views to maintain peace. As institutionalized Stakeholder Dialogues are convened following a regulatory procedure, the convening and participating stakeholders may lose the sense of urgency that is typical in other Stakeholder Dialogues. The challenge lies in breathing life into this form of Stakeholder Dialogue and in keeping the purpose and need for stakeholder consultation high on the agenda of decision-makers.

● **The National Development Council (NEDLAC) in South Africa** is an institutionalized Stakeholder Dialogue between the state, private businesses, unions and small communities. This institutionalized dialogue exemplifies and reviews the socio-economic dimension of the South African societal transition and healing process. Within the context of this dialogue, participants discuss draft legislation and strategic decisions. In this way, participation and right of say have been institutionalized on a high level.

Stakeholder Platform (exchange)

Timeframe	Ongoing, taking place for as long as the exchange is relevant, regular meetings
Feature	Regular meetings, exchange of experience, development of joint recommendations, opportunity for networking, advocacy for joint interest

Stakeholders can come together to form an exchange platform, if an issue of common concern affects stakeholders or they have an interest in learning, exchanging experiences or advocating for a particular purpose. Such platforms are often driven by a political or development agenda. The dialogue platform can develop its own identity, and even become an institution (e.g. an association – this may be the case particularly in value-chain development). Or, it can remain a loose structure – sometimes called a round table – where stakeholders meet to report on their activities about a specific topic, to exchange experiences and to learn from each other. Such platforms can be initiated by the public sector, the private sector or civil society, but most often this is a form in which private-sector stakeholders take a particular interest. Either the advocacy purpose or the loose network structure gives actors from the private sector an opportunity to engage in an initiative without commitments that are too binding. In many cases, stakeholder platforms develop recommendations for certain actions, address them to one stakeholder group (e.g. government), or convey them to their own organizations (e.g. corporate social responsibility initiatives). Stakeholder platforms stay alive for as long as there is a sense of urgency to deal with certain issues. The challenge lies in keeping the relevance alive and ensuring that the platform's existence has the desired effect.

● As a stakeholder platform the **African Cashew Alliance** is an emerging organization that promotes the processing of raw cashews, increases the income of African farmers and promotes the global consumption of cashew nuts. It supports the development of country-specific cashew policy agendas in 10 member countries and facilitates the exchange of information and best practices for cashew processing. It also assists its members by promoting the African cashew industry in national and international markets. The African Cashew Alliance works with National Committees in the each member country. These committees are composed of all relevant actors in the cashew value chain, and include government representatives.
➲ **http://www.africancashewalliance.com/**

● The **Global Reporting Initiative (GRI),** an international, multi-stakeholder effort to achieve consensus about voluntary reporting of the economic, environmental and social impacts of business. It is dedicated to enhancing the comparability and credibility of sustainability-reporting practices worldwide. The GRI incorporates the active participation of business, accounting, human rights, environmental, labor and government organizations.

➲ **www.globalreporting.org**

Stakeholder Initiatives

Timeframe	Ongoing until solution is found, regular stakeholder meetings
Feature	Cross-sector initiative to solve complex problems, to develop joint policy and/or standards, or to achieve jointly agreed-upon objectives (often national, regional or international in scope)

Stakeholder initiatives are implementation-focused cross-sector initiatives aiming to solve complex problems and to develop strategies, policies or sustainability standards jointly. Stakeholders join and collaborate to achieve an agreed-upon goal within an agreed-upon timeframe. Sometimes, projects or programs are designed as stakeholder initiatives from the start. In this case, actors from different stakeholder groups (often public/private or private/civil society groups) come together to implement planned activities and monitor results jointly. Stakeholder initiatives can also be the result of stakeholder consultation processes that evolved towards a focus on implementation, and where participating stakeholders see the need to enter into more structured cooperation. The characteristic of this form of Stakeholder Dialogues is the joint intention to bring about lasting change, with the subsequent joint responsibility for success or failure. This implies that a stakeholder initiative needs to set up agreed-upon procedures for decision-making (usually consensual), monitoring and evaluation. So, the initiative requires applying project-management instruments. The more complex a stakeholder initiative is (in other words, if it has a national, regional or international scope), and the more stakeholders it involves, the more it requires governance and representation mechanisms that all participating stakeholders agree on. Stakeholder initiatives often have steering structures (e.g. steering committees) and a project secretariat that is responsible for communication, implementation and preparation of stakeholder events. Such initiatives require high-quality process management, good communication and visible implementation results to keep a complex group of stakeholders aligned behind the common goal.

● The **Common Code for the Coffee Community (4C)**, is a basic sustainability standard for green coffee production. It has been developed by a group of international stakeholders: coffee producers from all major coffee-producing countries, trade and industry in coffee and international NGOs joined the stakeholder initiative and came together as a steering committee to develop the standard and to decide on the conditions of its application.

➲ **www.4c-coffeeassociation.org**

● **The Ethical Trading Initiative (ETI)**, is an alliance of companies, NGOs and trade unions committed to identifying and promoting ethical trade jointly. It focuses on good practice in the implementation of a code of conduct for labor standards, including the monitoring and independent verification of compliance with ethics codes as standards for ethical sourcing.

➲ **www.ethicaltrade.org**

Stakeholder Platform (management of implementation)

Timeframe	Ongoing as long as joint task is required, regular stakeholder meetings
Feature	Joint management of implementation

Stakeholder platforms can also be focused on implementation: stakeholders as members of such a platform come together at regular intervals to review the management of a particular issue of common concern, adjust future planning and revise implementation strategies. Often, such a stakeholder platform functions as a long-term steering structure. Members of the platform represent certain constituencies or expertise. Typical examples for implementation-focused stakeholder platforms are water basin management committees in integrated water resource management. Here, the platform is often composed of different stakeholders, sometimes including the affected communities. Its task is bridging the gap between government interventions, donor interventions and local communities to design appropriate strategies to address water issues. However, an implementation-focused stakeholder platform can also be the result of a stakeholder initiative or stakeholder consultation process: it may serve the purpose of carrying on with what the Stakeholder Dialogues have already achieved and of ensuring stakeholder perspectives in implementation review or coordination of implementation.

● In a project to develop sustainable water usage, the **Namibian Ministry for Agriculture, Water and Forestry** is working to develop sustainable control of water catchment areas through integrated water source management. For this purpose, committees consisting of representatives from the public and private sectors, civil society and NGOs have already been established in two locations. Their duty is to clear up issues and questions regarding water management in cooperation with state water authorities.

● After the end of the apartheid, the **community of Makuleke in South Africa** filed a land-restitution claim against the northern part of the Kruger National Park (KNP). The issue was solved by means of a Stakeholder Dialogue and a mediation process, and involved various government bodies, NGOs, and international development organizations. With the establishment of a joint management board for the contracted inclusion of the restituted land in the national park between the Makuleke community and South African National Parks management, the dialogue partners created a platform to work jointly on implementation points.

Stakeholder implementation partnerships

Timeframe	Temporary according to project agreement, regular review workshops
Feature	Cross-sector implementation project to achieve agreed-upon objectives, joint management of implementation

Stakeholder Dialogues can lead to more concrete cooperation projects implemented by different stakeholders. Such partnerships can be the result of stakeholders realizing that in complex projects, stakeholders from different societal sectors can only implement solutions jointly. This requires additional steps towards an increased commitment to collaborate. Often, stakeholder partnerships manage large budgets, require professional project management and need to set up monitoring and evaluation procedures right from the start. As they are run like projects, they face pressure to implement and report accomplishments and to hold to agreed-upon objectives and milestones. Each of the stakeholder partners has to fulfill an agreed role and is responsible for implementing certain aspects of the project. If the complexity of the partnership requires it, stakeholder partnerships can be managed by a project secretariat. The challenge of stakeholder partnerships lies in balancing and reconciling different expectations of speed and success. Often, actors from very different organizational cultures (for example, from the public sector, development agencies, the private sector, or NGOs) need to work closely and to develop a mutual understanding of their procedural requirements and their mode of operation. Stakeholder partnerships implementing complex projects may require consultative Stakeholder Dialogue events to include relevant stakeholders beyond the actual members of the partnership, to raise awareness, or to receive feedback to adjust implementation strategies.

● A stakeholder partnership between **Volkswagen (VW), the International Labor Organization (ILO) and the German development cooperation** had the common goal of collectively implementing National Labor Programs on Safety and Health at Work in three countries with emerging economies – Brazil, Mexico and South Africa. In addition, a core element of the project was the implementation of Occupational Safety and Health (OSH) measures among VW's suppliers. These practical experiences at the enterprise level were fed into the process of developing national Safework Programs. Thereby, on the basis of ILO conventions, it was envisaged between July 2004 and December 2008 to harmonize political norms and operational practice.

➲ **www.ilo.org/safework**

● The **Sertão initiative** in northeast **Brazil** works to support small farmers' communities in adapting to the challenges of climate change. For this purpose, the initiative identifies opportunities to increase people's income in that particular region. The cooperation of different local actors such as local communities, small and medium-sized enterprises and small farmers facilitates options for action and technical solutions to secure local food supply jointly. The same approaches are being applied to tackle the issue of reducing CO^2 emissions. The projects' scope has been expanded to national level. Due to the great success of the initiative, there are also ambitions to achieve implementation on an international level.

➲ **www.adaptasertao.net/en**

Overview: Different forms of Stakeholder Dialogues – summary of features, purposes and application

CONSULTATIVE STAKEHOLDER DIALOGUES

Form	*Feature*	*Purpose*	*recommended for*
Singular Stakeholder Consultation	Stakeholder event (from information to authentic consultation)	To raise stakeholders' interest in or awareness of a particular issue To get feedback from different stakeholders about a specific issue	• Policy input • Strategy input • Research input • Planning input • Exchange of experience
Sequences of Regular Stakeholder Consultation	Consultative Stakeholder events leading to a specific outcome	To let stakeholders participate in a development or decision-making process, or to exchange experiences among stakeholders	• Policy development • Policy review • Planning review • Strategy review • Stakeholder recommendations are integrated into results
Institutionalized Stakeholder Consultation	Government-led stakeholder consultation embedded in regulations	To regulate input by stakeholders on certain issues of policy or planning development (as part of good governance)	• Institutionalized policy review • Institutionalized planning review • Regulated stakeholder participation in planning • Stakeholder representation follows regulated rules
Stakeholder Platform (Exchange)	Regular coming together of different stakeholders for an exchange of experience	To develop joint recommendations, to use the opportunity to meet different stakeholders, to ensure advocacy for stakeholder interests	• Representation of stakeholders in organized body • Stakeholder advocacy • Regular exchange of lessons learned • Advocacy for political or economic development agenda

Overview: Different forms of Stakeholder Dialogues – summary of features, purposes and application

STAKEHOLDER DIALOGUES FOCUSED ON COLLABORATION AND IMPLEMENTATION

Form	*Feature*	*Purpose*	*recommended for*
Stakeholder Initiative	Cross-sector initiative to solve complex problems, to develop joint policy and/or sustainability standards or to achieve agreed-upon implementation objectives	To develop and implement new approach, voluntary standards, new policy, complex project jointly	Complex project management through: • Joint implementation steering • Creating joint responsibility for change and results • Joint monitoring and evaluation • Joint decision-making Stakeholder Initiatives often require: • Governance mechanisms • Agreed-upon steering structure (steering committee, executive committee)
Stakeholder Platform (Implementation)	Joint management of implementation regarding an issue of common concern	To ensure joint management of complex tasks by different stakeholders	• Voluntary coming together of different stakeholders to improve management of certain task
Stakeholder Partnership	Cross-sector implementation project to achieve agreed-upon objectives	To achieve specific project results with complementary resources in specific timeframe	Collaborative implementation projects and strategic alliances requiring: • Joint implementation planning • Joint implementation of activities • Joint monitoring of results • Joint responsibility for success • Joint decision-making • Management structures in place • Often require formal contracts

1.3 Understanding cross-sector settings

Stakeholders can be broadly divided into three societal groups:

- **The public sector;**
- **Civil society; and**
- **The private sector.**

Not all stakeholders fit clearly into these divisions. For example, donor organizations sometimes represent government, but can also be large civil-society organizations. Research organizations may belong to the civil-society sector or to the public sector. However, in the context of Stakeholder Dialogues, these divisions help to understand the motivation for, or reluctance to, engage in Stakeholder Dialogues.

➲ *Chapter 5, Resources: 5.11 Understanding the need to engage different stakeholder groups differently, page 147*

Within each of the three stakeholder groups, there are important differences that also need to be taken into account: large international corporations often have different interests than small companies; local NGOs have a different outlook on certain subjects than large international NGOs; and national and provincial government institutions are not always aligned. A stakeholder analysis begins with looking at who is particularly important for bringing a change endeavor forward, who has the power and capacity to influence progress, who has specific expertise, and who will be most interested in change, but may be less influential. For an effective Stakeholder Dialogue approach, a thorough stakeholder analysis is therefore a crucial starting point.

➲ *Chapter 6, Tools: 6.3. Stakeholder Analysis, page 168*

Beyond this broad distinction, of course, there are many reasons why stakeholders may want to enter into a dialogue or why they may be skeptical or resistant to join. In preparing an approach to a complex initiative, project or program by using a Stakeholder Dialogue approach, it is important to understand the differences between stakeholders, to respect their particular interests and to become aware of the dynamic that may exist between different stakeholders. The next sections give an overview over the interests, concerns and motivations of the three different stakeholder groups.

COMMON INTERESTS BETWEEN SECTORS

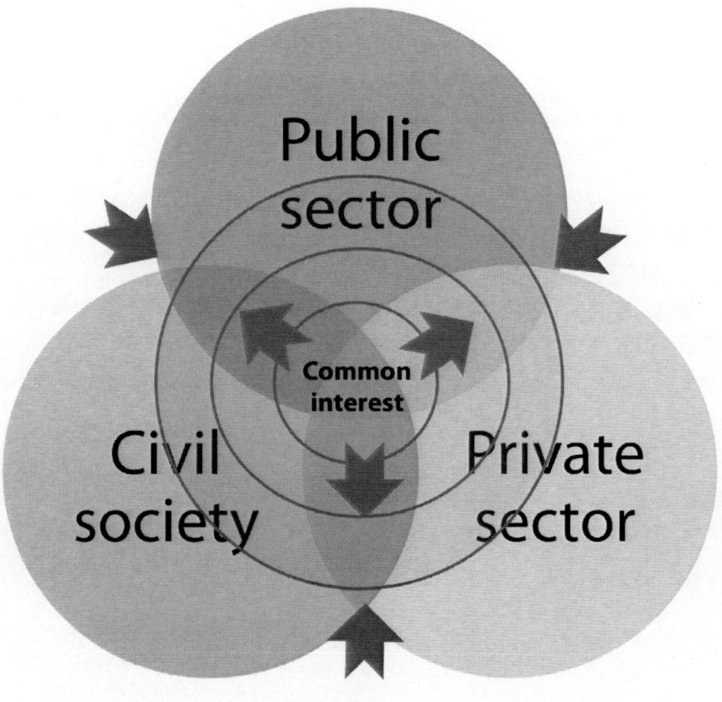

1.3.1 The public sector

The public sector's rationale is guided by the rights-orientation of law and order, the regulation of access to common resources and service delivery to citizens. Designing and enforcing rules and regulations, and complying with internal procedures, is fundamental to the work of public-sector organizations. They often follow a more bureaucratic approach, that is driven by adherence to tradition, processes, procedures, structures and mechanisms. The result is a more conservative and not necessarily innovative milieu that is not always open to change. This is reflected in the decision-making culture of the public sector: it is sometimes slow, administrative, hierarchical, loyal to regulations and procedures, and rigid in protocol. Decision-making follows the political approach (e.g. democratic) and can include regulated internal and external consultation of stakeholders. The core principle is acting on behalf of the common good.

The public sector, with its different institutions on the national, provincial and local level, has in general a common interest, a similar motivation and approach to administration and service delivery. However, even with a similar mission there may be differences in interest between different government departments or between government institutions at national, provincial and local level. There can be differences in specific interests and sometimes challenges in communication between government agencies at different levels: municipalities are not always entirely aligned with their provincial administration, or the provincial administration is not fully aligned with the national government. Even among national or provincial government, ministries or departments often cautiously defend their territory. Their interests are not always the same – especially when it comes to allocating resources. Different line ministries can be in fierce competition. Some Stakeholder Dialogues, therefore, may require internal government dialogues and alignment first, before the wider group of stakeholders can be engaged.

The motivation of the public sector to engage in Stakeholder Dialogues lies in the opportunity to create a broader base for public policy and regulations. Another benefit of Stakeholder Dialogues for the public sector is an increased efficiency in the implementation of public and developmental service delivery through regular feedback from stakeholders. Public-sector-supported or -initiated Stakeholder Dialogues can enhance consensual policy development, the development of standards and broad compliance with regulations. Aside from the benefits of getting involved in a Stakeholder Dialogue, there are also risks involved: for the public sector, it is the risk of losing power, for example by talking to more radical groups or by supporting certain private-sector companies too much.

● The goal of the Public Service Reform Program, a joint undertaking between the **South African Department of Public Service and Administration**, the German development cooperation and other South African governmental partners, is to enhance the efficiency and effectiveness of public service delivery in three South African provinces. This entails improving structures and systems as well as administrative justice procedures – particularly for formerly disadvantaged citizens. The core of the program's approaches is to strengthen the coordinating role of the government in public service provision. For this reason, various government departments, research and educational institutions, as well as civil society organizations increasingly need to work together in harmonizing regulatory frameworks, in ensuring the implementation of development strategies, and in monitoring the impact of service delivery.

1.3.2 The private sector

The private sector's core motivation is growth and business opportunities, so profit orientation is at the forefront. Stakeholders from the private sector are predominantly guided by their company strategy, and are highly motivated to be loyal to the business. They depend on performance indicators and stock-exchange analysts. Efficiency and strategic purpose is critical to their decisions, and they always have to argue the business case. The private sector needs to be innovative and often creative. This leads to a fast, short-term, impatient decision-making model, which is participatory in some cases and hierarchical in others, depending on the organizational culture. At the core of decision-making is loyalty to the business case.

It is important to consider that there are differences between business associations and individual companies, between companies in developed and in developing countries, and between privately owned, stock-listed companies, or public companies. The interests of large companies differ from those of small and medium-sized companies. While large companies are often well organized, small and medium companies are usually less organized, particularly in developing countries. Therefore, they have greater difficulty in speaking with a single voice, in public–private dialogues, for example. The least organized private-sector 'companies' are in the informal sector. This is often a very important stakeholder group, but has little capacity to organize itself and to voice its concerns.

● The **Senegalese Ministry of Finance** sees the promotion of competitiveness of Senegalese small and medium sized enterprises (SMEs) and the development of capacity in the microfinance sector in Senegal as key to the development of the country. An important aspect of the program is the initiation of a Public-Private Dialogue (PPD) between governmental institutions and private sector business associations on SME promotion in the West African State. This dialogue process is to provide a "creative space" for SME stakeholders to discuss options, targets as well as collaborate on implementation measures.

The motivation to engage in Stakeholder Dialogues often lies in being able to influence the business environment (for example, in Stakeholder Dialogues with the public sector), to access new markets, to reduce investment risks, or to gain reputation through participating in Stakeholder Dialogues. Multinational companies' interest in Stakeholder Dialogues is often driven by the motivation to be among the leading companies in Corporate Social Responsibility.

For reasons of reputation or risk management, the private sector can also initiate company-specific Stakeholder Dialogue to improve its relationship with stakeholders or customers. Such a form of exchange can be very important for a company to get feedback from customers and other stakeholders for environmentally or socially responsible strategies, or innovative product development. Collaboration with actors along a value chain can be another reason for joining or initiating Stakeholder Dialogues. This can contribute to long-term or short-term market development, as well as to risk and compliance management.

● **Worldwide Enhancement (WE) of Social Quality** is a stakeholder partnership between the German coffee roaster and consumer-goods company Tchibo and the German development cooperation which aims to improve the acceptance and implementation of social standards in supplier companies in Bangladesh, Thailand and China. The approach combines the dialogue that is taking place along the entire value chain with operational qualification measures for the implementation of labor and social standards in the workplace.

➲ **www.we-socialquality.com**

For the private sector, the benefit of Stakeholder Dialogues can turn into a risk if nothing follows from the Stakeholder Dialogue and the company or the association is accused of only paying lip service to stakeholder engagement. Another risk may lie in the fact that Stakeholder Dialogues require the investment of time, so the top management could see them as economically inefficient.

1.3.3 Civil society

Civil society organizations can include a wide variety of groups, such as national or international NGOs, women's groups, indigenous peoples' groups, farmers, unions, researchers, community organizations, and so on. These organizations represent different kinds of societal interests, groups and subcultures. Civil society organizations are indispensable for protecting, advocating and supporting justice, such as social and environmental protection or economic and social fairness and the prevention of social exclusion. These organizations support and further the participation and inclusion of underrepresented groups.

Civil society stakeholders can represent a diversity of interests, but often have similar rationales. Not-for-profit organizations in particular usually have a strong value orientation. They advocate on behalf of weaker groups, voiceless groups or the environment. Civil society organizations often expose the perceived misbehavior of the private and public sector, such as the abuse of law or malpractice and excesses. They often act through campaigning, awareness raising, education and capacity building.

Not all civil society organizations have similar goals and rationales: there are wide differences among them, with interests that are sometimes contradictory. Environmental NGOs focus on different concerns to human rights or social NGOs. National NGOs often have different interests and a different agenda to international NGOs. Globally active NGOs often have their funding base in developed countries, and depend on maintaining their constituents' interests. They may have a more ambivalent relationship with public sector. NGOs in developing countries often have a strong focus on development, empowerment and capacity–building, and like to work closely with the country's public-sector, and, sometimes, private-sector organizations. However, there are also national NGOs opposing government policies who may not want to enter into a structured dialogue with the public sector. Community development organizations focus on the local area, and often represent the interests of the population in a particular geographical area. International NGOs can be supporters of development and function as donor organizations for smaller development-oriented NGOs or community development organizations.

Due to civil-society organizations' heterogeneity, their participatory approach and their resource shortages, they are often characterized by slow, participatory and democratic decision-making models, or have an analytical approach when decisions are largely based on research findings. The core element of decision-making in these groups is a loyalty to the group's values and principles.

● In **Bangladesh** a number of national NGOs work together closely with the **Ministry of Women and Children** in advancing legal and social equality for women. Despite existing constitutional rights, in reality women still suffer from discrimination and physical violence. A national strategy targets the awareness enhancement in different societal groups (religious leaders, local and traditional judiciary, police, educators) on women's situation in the country as well as the acceptance and enforcement of their rights. The model projects implemented in this context target improving the delivery of justice to women through capacity building, institutional development and dialogue/advocacy. They integrate different stakeholders from civil society such as community councils, community courts, journalists, teachers, Imams, communal interest groups as well as national and international NGOs.

Civil society organizations' motivation to engage in Stakeholder Dialogues is the possibility of influencing public and private actors towards their value based goals, of changing societal and global structures of inequity or disparity, or of improving their target group's situation. In Stakeholder Dialogues, these groups also see the chance for additional opportunities for advocacy and higher efficiency and effectiveness in implementing societal (or global) goals (social developmental, environmental protection, human rights, and so on).

However, participation in a Stakeholder Dialogue can be a risk, particularly for international NGOs focusing on advocacy and campaigning: it may pose the danger of losing acceptance among their members and constituencies that give them financial support and legitimacy. People may see the dialogue as a form of collaboration with the very organization or stakeholder group against which the NGO is advocating. Being part of the dialogue may mean a loss of face, and, subsequently, a loss of financial support. This may undermine the NGO's ability to campaign and advocate.

Overview: Navigating the interests of different stakeholder groups

Stakeholder group	*Rationale*	*Decision-making and organizational culture*	*Motivation to engage in Stakeholder Dialogues*	*Potential risks for engaging in Stakeholder Dialogues*
Public sector	***Guard the rule of law, ensure access to resources, deliver services*** • Rights-orientation of law and order • Access, Information, Stability, Legitimacy • Designing and enforcing rules and regulations • Service delivery • Acting on behalf of the common good	• Slow, bureaucratic, hierarchical, political • Internal consultation processes are key • Loyal to law and order • Keeping to traditions, processes, procedures, structures • Not necessarily innovative • Protocol important	• Opportunity to establish broader platforms to promote and implement regulations or voluntary behavior for the common good (i. e. standards, codes of conduct) • Greater efficiency in the implementation of government regulations, public services, the management of public resources, or large infrastructure projects • Opportunity to create a broader base for necessary regulations or restrictions	• Danger of loss of reputation: • when talking to more radical groups, or • by supporting certain private-sector companies too much • Withdrawal of mandate for engagement in Stakeholder Dialogues from hierarchy
Private sector	***Grow and seek business opportunities*** • Profit orientation, loyal to the business case • Guided by company strategy • Depend on performance indicators, stock-exchange analysts • Efficiency and strategic purpose at the forefront	• Fast, short-term, impatient decision-making • Participatory or hierarchical, depending on the organizational culture • Loyal to the business model • Innovative • Differences between business associations (often in MSPs) and individual companies; between businesses in developed and developing countries; between privately owned and public companies	• Advocacy for enabling business environment • Reputation management • Compliance management • Customer relationship management • Long-term or short-term market development • Risk management	• Danger of not being able to argue the business case • Danger of being accused of lip service, if nothing follows from the Stakeholder Dialogue

Overview: Navigating the interests of different stakeholder groups

Stakeholder group	*Rationale*	*Decision-making and organizational culture*	*Motivation to engage in Stakeholder Dialogues*	*Potential risks for engaging in Stakeholder Dialogues*
Civil society	***Ensure social and environmental rights, development*** • Reacts to injustice and concerns of overall society, provokes attention • Ethical orientation, value orientation • Advocacy on behalf of voiceless (vulnerable) groups, the environment, etc. • Exposing perceived misbehavior of other sectors (private, public), watchdog, whistle-blower • Campaigning	• Slow, participatory (due to heterogeneity, participatory approach, few resources) • Analytical: research as core element of decision-making • Loyal towards the values and principles of the organization • Loyal towards constituencies	• Influence the private sector and government – beyond campaigning and charity • Additional opportunities for advocacy • Higher efficiency and effectiveness in implementing organizational goals (social, developmental, environmental, human rights, etc.)	• Danger of losing reputation among constituencies for talking with the enemy’ • Loss of face, being perceived as sell-outs by members • Internal conflicts • Loss of rationale: campaigning, advocacy • Danger of cooption • Loss of financial support

GETTING ACTIVE – MAKING STAKEHOLDER DIALOGUES WORK

GETTING ACTIVE – MAKING STAKEHOLDER DIALOGUES WORK

At the beginning of a Stakeholder Dialogue is always an intention to change or improve an issue of common concern, solve a problem or tackle a challenge together. People, not necessarily institutions, create ideas and intentions, which have most often undergone a process of development based on conversations with several other people. Usually, only a small group of people can see the future possibility, and trust that Stakeholder Dialogues are the appropriate way to approach, engage and commit. Every official launch of a Stakeholder Dialogue has its own specific history that, ideally, is already a history of learning. But it is also a history of chance encounters, paired with strategic planning – the process and its impact cannot always be steered completely. Working with Stakeholder Dialogues most often are stories of courageous and passionate people committing to making a difference for the common good.

But even when courage and passion is strong, having background knowledge of the methodology for implementing Stakeholder Dialogues will help to achieve the desired results. Success depends, to a large extent, on the quality of the process. Regardless of whether the Stakeholder Dialogue is a singular consultation event, a stakeholder initiative or a long-term implementation partnership, every Stakeholder Dialogue requires a sequence of planning, implementation and review steps. Because they are an intervention into a complex system of actors, they require a very conscious process and communication design.

Stakeholder Dialogues provide a space for people to think together, a space that – if created in the right way – can help collective intelligence to emerge, can pave the way for collective responsibility in implementation, or can offer grounds for true social innovation. So, they must become more than just a meeting of different stakeholders, more than an entertaining event and more than a conference for networking. Well-designed Stakeholder Dialogues create a commitment for change. To meet these expectations, they require a well-designed process architecture. The term 'architecture' is important because the design of processes and communication creates a space not unlike the structural space of an architect-designed building: some buildings make people feel comfortable, while others may have the opposite effect.

Process architecture refers to the design of the overall preparation, implementation and review process of a Stakeholder Dialogue. This can be a sequence of informal and formal communication events that bring stakeholders together into a structured conversation and are designed to lead to a desired outcome. Stakeholders often have different opinions and world views, or, at times, standpoints that may even be controversial. The process architecture can be seen as a guiding structure, almost like a balustrade that keeps the complex set of actors relatively stable and within a frame of action that everybody understands. It helps to prevent chaos, but allows enough freedom for the different forms of communication that Stakeholder Dialogues require. The more difficulties, conflicts and differences of interest that can be expected among stakeholders, the more structure the process architecture needs to provide. It gives all actors the minimum degree of certainty that a Stakeholder Dialogue in a complex and uncertain environment requires: for the initiators and conveners as much as for the participating stakeholders. It helps the participants to develop a sense of cohesion, gives orientation, and safeguards against unhelpful interventions. Process architecture includes communication design: internal and external communication, as well as the actual design of events, meetings and workshops.

What is process architecture in Stakeholder Dialogues?

Process architecture	The design of the overall preparation, implementation and review process of a Stakeholder Dialogue: the sequence of informal and formal communication events (meetings, workshops, conferences, etc.) that bring stakeholders together into a structured conversation, and that are designed to lead to a desired outcome.

Key elements

Reliability	What has been agreed upon in terms of meeting schedules should happen as planned; if delays or obstacles occur, the stakeholder groups need to be transparently informed of the reasons for these.
Joint agreements	Form and sequence of meetings and events needs to be planned together, or at least agreed upon by the key stakeholders.
Flexibility based on collective reflection	Although flexibility seems to contradict reliability, this does not need to be the case – process architectures need to be reviewed in a structured way and adjusted accordingly. Changes need to be transparently communicated and justified.

The underlying intent of process architecture is to enhance dialogic conversations: the **ability to think together** among people who matter and for whom the issue matters. This can become a fertile ground for collective intelligence. How these conversations take place depends on the situation, the context, and the people involved.

The form that the process architecture takes will depend on the phase of the Stakeholder Dialogue: preparation requires different process architecture than implementation. As the success of Stakeholder Dialogues hinges on result-oriented processes, it helps to distinguish different phases that require different sequences of actions. To know what is appropriate at specific times, it is important to develop methodological know-how that is built on process and change-management experience; a good understanding of the dialogical approach; and interest in self-reflection. Bringing actors together who have different backgrounds and interests into a Stakeholder Dialogue requires developing an affinity for dealing with diversity, as well as a willingness to develop communication and change-management skills.

2.1 The Dialogic Change Model

The **Dialogic Change Model**[6] suggested here allows for result-oriented, structured planning and implementation of a Stakeholder Dialogue in four phases. It has been developed over time based on experience with successfully implemented Stakeholder Dialogues. It supports and observes the underlying principles of successful Stakeholder Dialogues.

Guiding questions for each of the four phases will help initiators, as well as the participating actors, to steer a result-oriented process. The checklist will support project teams with planning and implementation. Dividing Stakeholder Dialogues into four phases has proven helpful in taking all demands and requirements of the different phases of a dialogue process into account and preparing them adequately.

Overview: The four phases of Stakeholder Dialogues

Phase 1	***Exploring and engaging***	Understanding the context, understanding stakeholders' different viewpoints, engaging them into preparatory conversations, raising energy for action, building the case for change
Phase 2	***Building and formalizing***	Clarifying goals and commitment, establishing resources, creating formal agreements, planning process and joint implementation
Phase 3	***Implementing and evaluating***	Implementing agreed-upon or recommended activities, creating showcases for change, evaluating progress and outcomes
Phase 4	***Developing further, replicating or institutionalizing***	Bringing the dialogue to the next level, expanding or replicating dialogue activities, creating long-lasting structures for change

[6] developed in 2006 by the Collective Leadership Institute

THE DIALOGIC CHANGE MODEL: Implementing Stakeholder Dialogues in a result-oriented way

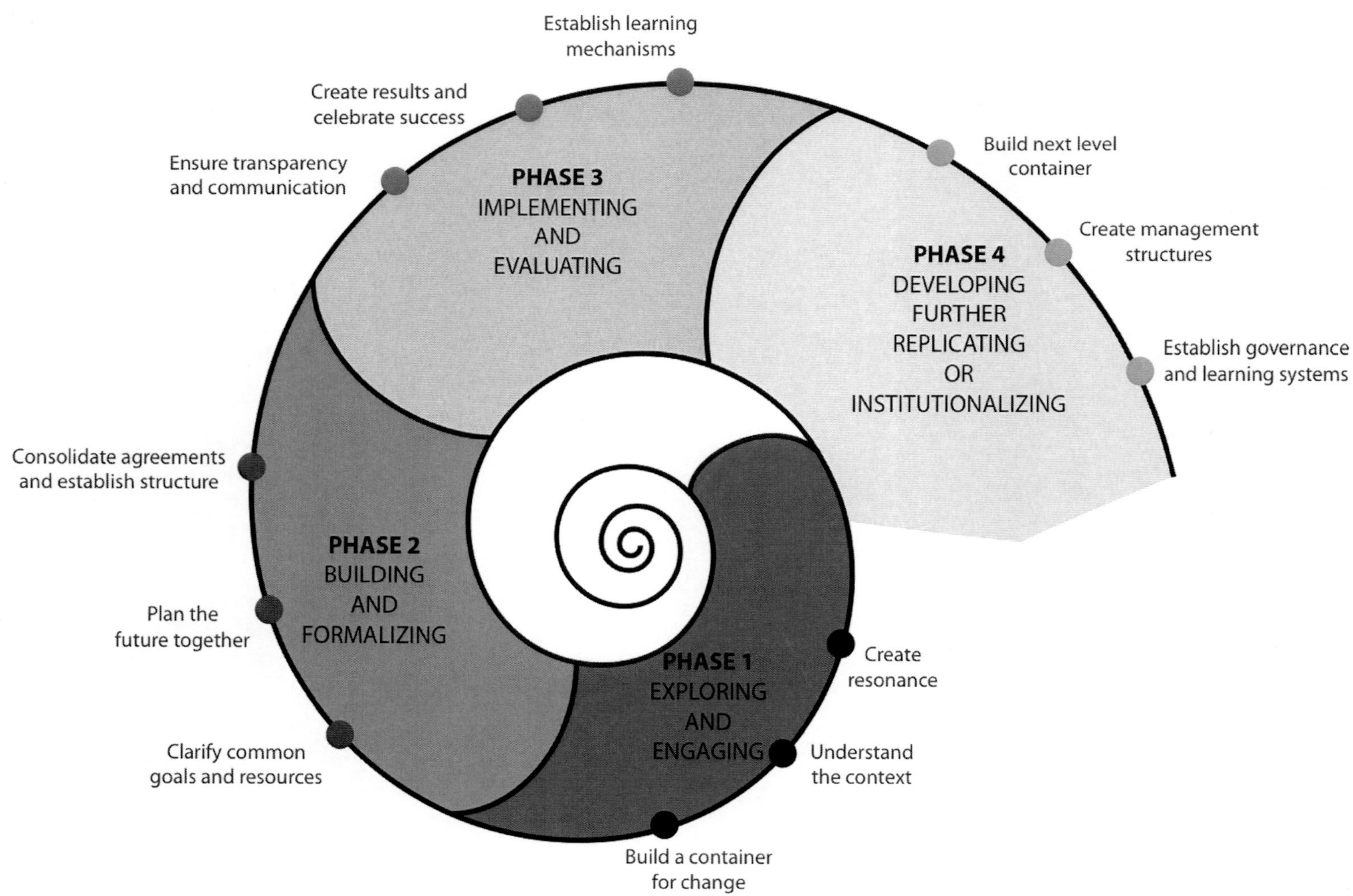

2.2 The different phases in Stakeholder Dialogues

The **Dialogic Change Model** is based on the ancient human knowledge of dialogue. It has taken the idea of creating space for collective intelligence through structured dialogue into the modern sphere of stakeholder engagement. Beneath the surface of the four phases in Stakeholder Dialogues is a wealth of knowledge about transformative communication processes. The model explains what needs to be taken into account to foster dialogic exchange and result-orientation at the same time. Because the success of Stakeholder Dialogues hinges on the design and implementation of result-oriented dialogic processes, it offers an integrated approach by combining change methodology, dialogic skill and reflection. The guiding principles are based on the dialogic practices of ***voice, listen, respect and suspend.***

➲ *Chapter 3: 3.1 Accessing the field of dialogue, page 80,*
➲ *Chapter 5 : Resources, 5.6. Enhancing dialogue : the art of thinking together, page 123, 5.7. Stakeholder Dialogues and the emergence of collective intelligence, page 128, 5.8.2. Dialogic practices, page 137*

The **Dialogic Change Model** also offers outcome-focused, well-structured planning and attention to important details that can make such a process succeed or fail. It recommends the areas of attention in the four phases and suggests key questions for reflection.

2.2.1 Phase 1: Exploring and engaging

Phase 1 is essentially about raising the energy for change and dialogue. In this phase, stakeholders explore the Stakeholder Dialogue's context, taking other existing initiatives and the people involved into account. This requires understanding the external context, the factors that will influence the dialogue, and the dynamics of the complex system in which the Stakeholder Dialogue will take place. Talking to selected but relevant stakeholders and opinion-leaders informally in this phase can help to understand the prospects and potential obstacles for dialogue and change. A small cross-sector team of engaged people, called the Core Group (*Container*), can meet at various opportunities, exchange ideas and receive inputs from interested and knowledgeable people in this phase.

➲ *Chapter 6: Tools, 6.5. Checklist for the Dialogic Change Model, page 176*

GETTING ACTIVE

"Only dedicated circles can give birth to something new".
Saying by a circle of African wise women

➲ **The Core Group as a '*Container*'**

The term '*Container*' refers to the function and relational quality of an initiating team or core group of interested actors in Stakeholder Dialogues. A good *container* exists if these actors are dedicated to the change envisaged, emotionally engaged with future possibilities and if they are committed to initiating and implementing the intended change jointly. Ideally, this group of people already represents – to some extent, at least – the diversity of stakeholders so that it can embody the range of interests in the change initiative. It is composed of people who are willing to respect each other and who are committed to the goal. In this way, the core group, in its function as a '*Container*', creates a holding space for the planned change, an emotional home for the joint initiative and an initial pattern of the envisaged dialogue or cooperation. This core group requires attention: the more this group is able to provide coherent collective leadership, the more likely the Stakeholder Dialogue will be set on a route to success. Core groups that are "good" *Containers* help to bring about change by establishing ever broader *containers* for change. Such *Containers* can develop and sustain the kind of legitimacy that comes not from hierarchy but from the fact that core groups as *Containers* act in the interests of the whole, consistently.

➲ *Chapter 5: Resources, 5.5. Stakeholder Dialogues as a pathway to collective leadership, page 120*

Informal dialogue is a melting pot for screening possibilities. As people are asked to shape the idea, they begin to commit. Central to Phase 1 is building trust, creating resonance and building the case for dialogue and change. So, the quality of an engagement process is the key element in Phase 1. Good relationship management and a broader understanding of the context are crucial. It is important to anchor the potential goal in as many minds as possible, particularly in the minds of people who are relevant for the success of such an initiative and need to be actively engaged. Formal structures for the Stakeholder Dialogue, agreements, or defined procedures are not a priority at this point. Creating structures too early can prevent the idea from taking root because structures often develop their own dynamic. This absorbs creativity; and actors who have not been involved from the beginning can perceive these structures as imposed.

➲ *Chapter 5: Resources, 5.9. Engaging stakeholders: building a container for change, page 143, 5.10 Pitfalls in engagement processes, page 146,*

The quality of trust and relationship building in Phase 1 is an important prerequisite for formalizing and implementing the Stakeholder Dialogue in Phase 2. Success in the long run depends immensely on the flexible but careful design of Phase 1. Building a core group as a stable '*Container*' in this phase is essential: a team of dedicated people that ideally contains important stakeholders and helps to move the Stakeholder Dialogue forward (see a good **container for change** above). Phase 1 of a Stakeholder Dialogue can last from two months to over a year. This depends on how much time and effort is needed for the engagement process and consulting with all relevant stakeholders in a complex system.

➲ In order to understand the importance of a good container, it helps to review one's experiences of change processes. Very often, if a good container for change was missing, change did not happen, failed or was difficult to achieve.

Phase 1: Exploring and engaging

	Understanding the context, the different viewpoints of stakeholders, engaging them into preparatory conversations, raising energy for action, building the case for change	
Duration	From minimum two months for singular Stakeholder Dialogue events to over a year for Stakeholder Dialogues focusing on collaboration for implementation	
Expected results	• Trust among key stakeholders • Explicit resonance for the dialogic initiative or change process • Credibility for implementation • Participating stakeholders identified • Context and external influencing factors explored	
Areas of attention	***Create resonance***	
	Understand the context	
	Build a 'good' Container for change	
Most common difficulties or mistakes	• Lack of ownership of key stakeholders due to lack of involvement in project/initiative design • Insufficient context analysis • Neglecting important other actors in the field of operation • Hurrying into agreements without real commitment of stakeholder partners (lip-service commitment) • Actors and participating institutions do not understand the requirements/cultures and decision-making structures of the different stakeholder groups well enough • Insufficient *Container* building (absence of committed core group to carry the process)	
Readiness check: Phase 1	Have we identified relevant key stakeholders?	✔
	Have we created resonance among key stakeholders?	✔
	Are we aware of the factors influencing the endeavor?	✔
	Have we understood the context well enough?	✔
	Have we researched best practices that we can adopt or learn from?	✔
	Have we assessed potential threats to the initiative?	✔
	Have we assessed the resources required?	✔
	Is our *Container* strong enough?	✔

Area of attention: Create resonance

In the context of both formal and informal exchanges, the initiators of a Stakeholder Dialogue clarify the interest, commitment and participation of the actors in a specific area of activity during Phase 1. During this exchange process, the idea or the planned course of action becomes clearer. In informal bilateral conversations, the initiators can help to clarify the different possibilities for change and test for resonance with the relevant actors. This way, the common goal becomes clearer and is further developed with the help of stakeholder feedback.

The most important task at the beginning is establishing trusting relationships with potential partners. As much as possible, these actors should be involved in a joint thought process towards a mutual goal, as well as in a brainstorming about its implementation. The more actors are involved in the development of an idea, the more interest and readiness to take responsibility for the dialogue process will develop.

One of the biggest challenges can be bringing together different institutions and actors for one common goal. It must be clear whether there is a case for change and action, and how a stakeholder approach will help to achieve a goal most effectively. A central requirement for the future success of dialogue and collaboration is the development of a network of actors who are truly interested in change. It is especially important to win the support of stakeholders who are central to the success of a common goal when testing for resonance.

➲ Guiding questions for creating resonance

- Who shares the common goal?
- Which important stakeholders can support our cause?
- What makes our cause attractive for the different actors?
- Where is there already energy/willingness for change?
- With whom do we need to speak?
- Who can help to clarify goals and possible implementations?

Area of attention: Understand the context

➲ *Chapter 6: Tools, 6.3. Stakeholder analysis, page 168*

In Phase 1, it is important to understand the initiative's context. A timely stakeholder analysis, conflict mapping and situation analysis is recommended. The objective of analyzing the field in this way is to understand formal and informal structures that have led to the current situation and to examine which structures and behaviors are currently impeding the change process.

Context analysis may include benchmarking; for example, evaluating similar experiences in other sectors, countries or subject areas. In some cases, technical studies or thematic situational analyses may be meaningful, the results of which can flow into the ongoing process. To insure that all stakeholders participate professionally on an equal basis, publications and/or information events can be planned. Such kinds of *capacity development* can be integrated into a Stakeholder Dialogue at any time.

If, as a result of the stakeholder analysis, it is discovered that certain stakeholders are insufficiently organized, it must be discussed how these stakeholder groups can be further strengthened. It is also relevant to the chosen strategy how familiar stakeholders are with the stakeholder approach. It may be necessary to reinforce stakeholders' knowledge of cooperation, dialogue and process by holding *capacity-development* workshops on how to engage in Stakeholder Dialogues.

It is important to discover which political or high-level support the Stakeholder Dialogue requires, and to gain this support actively. This requires knowing how the Stakeholder Dialogue can be integrated into existing processes and structures in the corresponding field of action. This is particularly relevant for Stakeholder Dialogues that the public sector initiates.

> ➲ **High-level sponsorship**
>
> High-level sponsorship is the lifeblood of high-stakes change initiatives like Stakeholder Dialogues. It is critical to obtain the support of high-ranking people from one or more of the stakeholder groups, or, in some cases, to ensure that there is patronage for the intended change. High-level sponsors need to support Stakeholder Dialogues, but may not need to be directly involved in them. But it is important that the people who are critical to this change endeavor can take a stand on its behalf.

It is necessary to re-analyze the situation in which change is to take place continually throughout the entire process. For this reason, in more complex processes, Phase 1 is never really complete: complex Stakeholder Dialogues cannot be planned in a linear way because they are mutual learning processes that need room to develop and change.

> ➲ **Guiding questions for understanding the context**
>
> - Which stakeholders do we need to involve?
> - What do we need to know about the current situation and about future events?
> - Which partners do we need to ensure the success of our cause?
> - Who has influence in the outcome of our initiative, and how can we influence them?
> - Are there existing best practices that we can adopt?
> - Do we have to do any research on the issue?
> - Who do we have to talk to in order to complete our understanding of the overall system?
> - What do we know about experiences in similar situations?
> - What are the potential difficulties?

Area of attention: Build a good *Container* for change

Stakeholder Dialogues need people who see collaboration and dialogue as an important resource and who are capable of implementing it. Building a good *Container* for change consists of creating a small core group (between two and six people) made up of a few dedicated stakeholders. Its role is to organize the collaboration and dialogue of all participating stakeholders reliably and to keep the dialogue process on track. It is beneficial if the core group is able to work together informally, and it is important for its members to build mutual trust and to create understanding of the needs and demands of the institutions they represent. Many stakeholder involvement processes fail or have little impact because there is no solid *Container* of people who feel collectively responsible for fostering and holding the process from beginning (planning the participation) to end (taking action on the basis of the results of participation).

➲ *see above, page 56: the core group as "Container"*

GETTING ACTIVE

Since Stakeholder Dialogues can be a strenuous exercise, it is of crucial importance that people in influential positions not only approve of the process, but get actively involved or stay supportive. Developing a broader *Container* for change is the primary task for initiators, conveners and process facilitators: this means to extend the actively engaged group of supporters of the Stakeholder Dialogue beyond the core group.

➲ *Chapter 5: Resources, 5.9. Engaging stakeholders: building a container for change, page 143*

Ideally, the core group acts as a source of energy for progress toward a common goal. This works best when it consists of highly motivated people whom the other stakeholders trust. The core group ensures that the common goal is kept on track but also makes allowance for the complexity of the specific political arena and considers possible points of conflict. It is also responsible for assuring a sustainable process design and for keeping this process as open as required to ensure authentic participation. This group provides a frame and a structure for the common goal – in other words, an informal 'home' for it. A core group as a stable *Container* will pave the way for the broader stakeholder *Container*. This can be seen as a microcosm of stakeholders from the various stakeholder groups that represent the macrocosm of the system in which change is to take place. Not all stakeholders are always equally interested in or committed to the common goal. Without being over-inclusive, it is nonetheless important initially to let all the relevant stakeholders participate in the dialogic change process. Personal engagement is key, one should therefore avoid creating a system composed only of delegates who may or may not be fully committed to a cause.

➲ Guiding questions for building a *Container* for change

- Which actors do we need at the beginning of the dialogue?
- Who are the people who can drive change?
- Which actors represent the larger system?
- What setting for the first meeting will enhance stakeholders' commitment and process ownership?
- What needs to be discussed during the first meeting?
- What could compel the actors to support the Stakeholder Dialogue's cause?

● Case examples: The Common Code for the Coffee Community (4C)

4C is a basic quality standard for sustainability in green coffee production for the mainstream coffee sector. It was developed by an international group of stakeholders, including coffee producers from most important coffee-producing countries, coffee roasters, and coffee traders, as well as international NGOs. They combined forces to develop a common standard and to lay out the conditions needed for its application.

➲ Phase 1: Exploring and engaging

When people met repeatedly to discuss similar issues and specific topics around coffee and sustainability, the idea of developing a long-term mainstream standard slowly began to take root. Representatives of the coffee industry recognized the increasing need to begin a shift toward a more sustainable form of coffee production. Through intensive conversations, the idea was born to develop a basic sustainability standard for mainstream green coffee market. In Phase 1, informal talks helped to map out the general contextual issues, analyze the actors involved, and identify stakeholders with a particular interest. Regular consultation with the stakeholders shed light on potential points of conflict and helped to identify the major challenges in the coffee sector. This phase concentrated on creating constructive relationships, identifying future opportunities for cooperation and building a solid initial *Container*, which could take responsibility for advancing the project. Premature formal structures or obligations would have created false expectations and criticism. This would have hindered the phase's exploration process. At this time, it was far more important to engender a sense of ownership in those closely involved in the project – for both the process and the driving force behind it.

2.2.2 Phase 2: Building and formalizing

Whereas Phase 1 deals with the task of building trusting relationships and positive resonance between stakeholders, Phase 2 is geared more toward consolidating the system of stakeholder collaboration and formalizing stakeholders' commitment to change. The objective of Phase 2 is to find an appropriate formal structure for moving an initiative forward and to build a stable collaborative system for implementation. Goals are agreed upon jointly, and roles and resources are defined. Initial structures can be developed, project teams defined and regular meetings planned. This usually leads to agreements – the signing of a contract, a Memorandum of Understanding (MoU), a project plan or a public address in the interest of the change endeavor. The initiative shifts to a formalized process. In more complex Stakeholder Dialogues, there may also be issues of division of tasks, decision-making, resource allocation or internal and external communication strategies. Often, there is a need for an official launching ritual for a Stakeholder Dialogue. Phase 2 is, therefore, characterized by events, workshops or conferences. With an official event, and an agreed–upon, written document, the Stakeholder Dialogue officially comes to life. It is communicated publicly and the idea is promoted more formally.

➲ ***Chapter 5: Resources, 5.13. Principles of successful process designs for Stakeholder Dialogue events, page 152***

GETTING ACTIVE

The structure for the Stakeholder Dialogue needs to build confidence: contribution, roles and allocation of work as well as communication and process designs need to be agreed upon jointly. The plan for the way forward needs to offer a sufficient degree of 'process safety' in an otherwise unpredictable and complex environment. Phase 2 is more likely to be successful if Phase 1 has been done thoroughly and the potential partners have a common understanding of the collaborative or dialogic approach.

The work of stakeholders in the initial *Container* (the core group of initiators holding the intention for change) needs to be strengthened, commitment needs to be built beyond the initiators and complemented by a more formalized structure for implementation. This protects the Stakeholder Dialogue from being too vulnerable to unavoidable change of personnel. It also strengthens individuals' ability to promote the intention of the Stakeholder Dialogue within their respective institutions. It enhances the learning and communication capacity, and thus the ability to solve difficulties.

Phase 2: Building and formalizing

	Clarifying goals and commitment, establishing resources, creating formal agreements, planning process and joint implementation	
Duration	From one day (workshop) to several months (sequence of workshops), characterized by meetings/workshops/conferences with all stakeholders	
Expected results	Depending on the form and purpose of the Stakeholder Dialogue, anything that shows commitment and gives structure to move forward, e.g.: • Recommendation and clarity on the use of Stakeholder Dialogues • Agreements to collaborate • Project or activity plans • Agreements on implementation procedures • Formal structures to steer the process (e.g. committees, expert working groups, etc.)	
Areas of attention	***Clarify goals and resources***	
	Plan future together	
	Consolidate agreements and establish structures	
Most common difficulties or mistakes	• Rushing into signed agreements and road maps without proven operational commitment of stakeholder partners • Absence of joint problem- or situational diagnosis as a basis for joint process planning • Process design not jointly agreed on but determined by one party • Too much focus on technical/legal/structural issues instead of on building collaboration and dialogue (process management, relationship management, trust-building) • Insufficient taking into account of existing rules, regulations and procedures	
Readiness check Phase 2	Do all stakeholders have a common understanding of the goals?	✔
	Have we sufficiently considered the different viewpoints of stakeholders?	✔
	Have we jointly analyzed the current situation with all stakeholders?	✔
	Have we created a setting for the stakeholder meeting (context, program, space) that enhances commitment and ownership?	✔
	Have we generated and maintained sufficient high-level support?	✔
	Have we consolidated the results in an appropriate form of agreement?	✔
	Have we agreed on roles and responsibilities for further implementation?	✔
	Have we developed a realistic implementation plan and follow-up meetings?	✔
	Have we transparently documented results, agreements and planning?	✔

Area of attention: Clarify goals and resources

The interest and commitment of stakeholders that has been built up informally during Phase 1 is formalized in Phase 2. Here, the goal is to strengthen the core group's role, to clarify which stakeholders are willing to participate actively in collaboration and dialogue, and to determine who will contribute (and how) to reaching the common goals. The purpose and goals of a Stakeholder Dialogue that were held mainly by a small group of stakeholders (the *Container*) at the beginning in Phase 1 now need to be discussed, agreed upon, and, finally, held by a larger number of stakeholders. This may require modifying or adjusting purpose and goals so that all stakeholders can identify with the way forward.

It is important to create a climate for shaping the Stakeholder Dialogue goal and – in the case of stakeholder initiatives or partnerships – to agree officially on the different contributions by stakeholders. This usually requires a series of workshops with important representatives from the different stakeholder groups present. In such meetings, all participants gain a clear understanding about individual and overall objectives, and about how the common goal can also enhance the different stakeholders' institutional goals. It is important to stress that not only financial contributions are valid. Resources can be employed in many different ways: networks, in-kind contribution, working time, office space, expertise, access to funding, etc.

➲ *Chapter 6: Tools, 6.4. Resource mapping page 173*

It makes sense to ensure transparent documentation of meeting results and to consider the concerns, suggestions and expectations of different partners. Ideally, this generates a sense of affiliation and commitment of stakeholders to the purpose of the Stakeholder Dialogue. A preliminary plan for further dialogue and collaboration should be agreed upon and the distribution of tasks may be agreed in writing.

Here, it is important to be aware of the different sub-objectives and interests. Real commitment only comes about with actual involvement and the perception that it is possible to make a difference. Nonetheless, doubt and occasional mistrust by different stakeholder groups cannot always be avoided: this is a normal part of a complex endeavors. Most important for the success of a Stakeholder Dialogue is how the core group keeps common goals alive.

➲ Guiding questions for clarifying goals and resources

- Which actors represent the larger system and need to be included in the dialogue?
- How can it be guaranteed that stakeholders feel their views are being taken seriously?
- How can stakeholders be encouraged to develop ownership of an initiative?
- What will make the actors feel they are receiving competent guidance?
- What do we want to achieve with the dialogue?
- What resources can each actor bring in?

Area of attention: Plan future together

In Phase 2, the Stakeholder Dialogue becomes visible from the outside – sometimes in the form of large public, events, in which all significant stakeholders participate. It is important to plan the events so that visible results can be reached within one or two days. This requires a communication structure adapted to creating tangible results.

To develop ownership among all participating stakeholders, it is crucial to discuss both the analysis of the current situation and the planned changes together with all stakeholders. It can be helpful to bring in external assessments of the situation at stake. However, the most powerful base for collective change is a joint diagnosis of the situation. Only then will the case for change become rooted among all participating stakeholders.

Stakeholder Dialogues become successful if people engage emotionally: with the possible future, with the form of dialogue and collaboration, and with each other. The design of meetings, events or conferences needs to take this into account. It may also be useful to integrate expert input on individual topics to keep all participants equally informed. It can be useful bringing results of context analysis, benchmarking or research from Phase 1 into the stakeholder events. This may be also useful in mobilizing more stakeholders for future change. Content *capacity-development* as well as methodological know-how about Stakeholder Dialogues should be integrated into the process design for Phase 2.

➲ ***Chapter 6: Tools, 6.6 Seating orders for Stakeholder Dialogue events, page 182***

In Phase 2, a common vision for the future needs to be embedded in the participating stakeholder groups. Quite often, the dialogue process can lead to changes in the way forward, and already-planned procedures may need to be re-modeled. The core group is responsible for collecting ideas and translating them into feasible proposals. This group must also make sure all stakeholders are equally heard.

➲ Guiding questions for planning the future together

- Have we taken enough time for Phase 1?
- Are enough stakeholders prepared to shape the future together?
- Have we gathered all necessary perspectives and expertise to shape the future together?
- Which type of processes would assist the actors in jointly shaping the future?
- How can we design stakeholder events that enhance commitment?

Area of attention: Consolidate agreements and establish structure

Consolidating agreements is of utmost importance: while the structure of dialogue and collaboration in Phase 1 is more formal and loose, it is crucial that this finds a more formal expression in Phase 2. The form of agreements can be different according to the form and purpose of the Stakeholder Dialogues, e.g. setting milestones for collaborative work or clarifying the roles of certain stakeholders in the dialogue process or implementation.

➲ ***Chapter 6: Tools, 6.7 Agreements in Stakeholder Dialogues , page 186, 6.8. Steering and implementation structures, page 189***

It is important that the participating stakeholders reach a transparent agreement that is perceived as trustworthy and dependable. The form and regularity of internal communication between the participating stakeholders and with the public can also be laid out at this point.

The signing of a *Memorandum of Understanding* is only one possibility of formalizing a Stakeholder Dialogue. In other cases, it may be jointly created project or implementation plans that bring a certain formal structure into a dialogue process. In more conflict-prone situations, the agreement may just be that another meeting will take place.

➲ *Chapter 3: Ensuring dialogue – communication in Stakeholder Dialogues, page 78*

In Phase 2, it may be meaningful to formalize the core group and to equip the members with a mandate by all stakeholders. In more complex Stakeholder Dialogues, more elaborate organizational structures are often needed. These may consist of a steering committee, a task-force and regular stakeholder meetings or expert working groups to discuss specific thematic issues. It is crucial to transparently document all agreements, results and decisions made during Phase 2 and to distribute this documentation to all participating stakeholders.

➲ **Guiding questions for reaching joint agreements**

- What support do the participating stakeholders have for the road ahead?
- Which type of agreement is suitable for a specific process? (Agreements, Memorandums of Understanding, project plans, pictures, joint project- or implementation plans)
- Which type of agreement will guarantee the ongoing trustworthiness and dependability of the collaboration process?
- How can a plan of action be developed, so that all participants are inclined to support it?
- What milestones are still ahead?
- Are roles and responsibilities for the implementation of the initiative clear?
- Is there an agreed-upon internal and external communication strategy?
- Is clear planning and documentation available to all stakeholders?
- Have follow-up meetings been planned, guaranteeing process dependability?

● Case example: Common Code for the Coffee Community (4C)

➲ Phase 2: Building and formalizing

The joint initiative to create an international sustainability standard for the mainstream green coffee market took concrete form in 2003 with a kick-off Stakeholder Dialogue event. The purpose was to test and consolidate the commitment of the stakeholders involved at that point. In a follow-up event the collaboration became more formalized, clear working and communication structures were established, and a project secretariat was mandated to support the management of the initiative. The latter took on the role of a neutral stakeholder broker, and was responsible for coordinating and supporting communication, consensus-building and decision-making.

The steering committee eventually took over responsibility for decision-making. Initially, there were about 20 steering-committee members, but this number grew to approximately 45 stakeholders, representing the entire supply chain.

The actual development of the standard took place in working groups, which consisted of representatives from the public and private sectors as well as from civil society. Difficulties were numerous: obstructions, coalition-building and conflicts nearly caused the initiative to fail on several occasions. The sensible and service-minded actions taken by the project secretariat, in close collaboration with an external consultancy, made a decisive contribution to helping the initiative get through these difficulties. Participants were thus able to refocus on common goals and start moving the project forward again. In 2004, it was possible to write up the first draft of a code of conduct.

2.2.3 Phase 3: Implementing and evaluating

The key to achieving tangible results towards a common goal through Stakeholder Dialogues is not only joint development and planning, but also the implementation and evaluation of results. This phase can be seen as the actual implementation of planned activities and includes the establishment of an internal Stakeholder Dialogue monitoring system to ensure results and learning. Its focus is on creating visible results in a reasonable timeframe so that all actors involved can see the success of the Stakeholder Dialogue. A decisive factor for a successful dialogue and collaboration in implementation is the degree of joint implementation (respectively sufficiently coordinated implementation) and the opportunity for joint review. If the implementation is complex, a secretariat or support team can be appointed to assist in the coordination of implementation and the monitoring of results.

If a Stakeholder Dialogue never moves past the stage of discussion and exchange of ideas, it may be a sign that the stakeholders can discuss the issue, but are not willing enough to implement actual change. However, for Stakeholder Dialogues to deliver, it is crucial that stakeholders perceive visible change during the dialogue process; otherwise they might lose interest in the dialogue and in implementing change. So, results orientation is a key factor for success. Visible results – even small ones – are the guarantee that stakeholders will stay involved in the process and will solve conflicts and problems constructively. It helps – particularly at the beginning – to concentrate on easily achievable results. The goal of a well-structured Phase 3 is to show that change is possible.

During the implementation, there must be opportunity to regularly reflect on the original initiative as well as on the ongoing process. Sometimes it becomes apparent during the implementation that certain contextual aspects were not adequately considered or that important stakeholders were not yet included in the process. At this point, it may therefore be helpful to take up the approach used in Phase 1 again to clarify the context fully, extend capacity building or integrate new stakeholders into the process. Phase 3 often shows how different stakeholders use decision-making. Much patience and consideration for differences among stakeholders is therefore required during this phase. The core group, or a dedicated project team, should be responsible for communication, keeping the common goal clear and driving the agreed upon action. Phase 3 can take months or years, and is concluded when the agreed-upon goals have been reached.

➲ *Chapter 3: Ensuring Dialogue – Communication in Stakeholder Dialogues, page 78, Chapter 5, resources: 5.12, The role of communication in the 4 phases of Stakeholder Dialogues, page 148*

The complexity of a process often becomes evident during this phase, sometimes in the form of a crisis. Crisis symptoms may include criticism from external parties, stakeholders voicing new, previously unspoken interests, negative press, counter initiatives, endless non-productive discussions, or a group of actors threatening to back out of the dialogue process. Political interests can often hold up an initiative's development or complicate consensus-building. The more stability and trusting relationships have been created in Phase 1 and 2, the better such phases of instability can be overcome.

Phase 3: Implementing and evaluating

	Implementing agreed-upon or recommended activities, creating showcases for change, evaluating progress and outcomes	
Duration	From several months to years, depending on the issue, characterized by regular review meetings with all relevant stakeholders	
Expected results	Depending on the form and purpose of the Stakeholder Dialogue and area of implementation: • Showcases of success • Achieved milestones • Project implementation reports • Public communication and media coverage • Established monitoring systems	
Areas of attention	***Ensure transparency and communication***	
	Create results and celebrate successes	
	Establish learning mechanisms	
Most common difficulties or mistakes	• Uncoordinated implementation (lack of proper process management) • Insufficient communication between partners or implementing stakeholders • Implementation plans that are too ambitious, instead of focusing on small, achievable successes • Lack of transparency in the communication and decision-making process • Too little focus on maintaining the core group's commitment • Loss of motivation of participating partners	
Readiness check Phase 3	Have we identified areas in which success stories are more likely?	✔
	Is the implementation plan in place and are we keeping up with it?	✔
	Have we agreed with all stakeholders on internal and external rules of communication?	✔
	Have we designed measures to foster relationship-management and trust further?	✔
	Can we show success, and have we found the appropriate way of celebrating success?	✔
	Do we have a system in place to monitor progress and the quality of the dialogue process?	✔
	Are we keeping up with capacity-building needs?	✔
	Have we included additional relevant stakeholders, if required?	✔
	Do we have a system of regular review meetings with all stakeholders in place?	✔

GETTING ACTIVE

Area of attention: Ensure transparency and communication

In Phase 3, Stakeholder Dialogues need sufficient structure and attention to value-base, relationship management and goal clarity. They can make use of project management tools, operational planning and workshop protocols familiar to most institutions. Frequent review meetings are equally crucial to keep stakeholders engaged. The frequency of such meetings depends on the situation and the type of Stakeholder Dialogue. More complex Stakeholder Dialogues often require secretarial support for organizational purposes. An office can be situated in a mutually trusted organization, chosen by representatives from the various stakeholder groups, or outsourced to an external organization.

➲ ***Chapter 3: Ensuring Dialogue – Communication in Stakeholder Dialogues, page 78, Chapter 5, resources: 5.12, The role of communication in the 4 phases of Stakeholder Dialogues, page 148***

Additionally, a continuous communication of progress is of utmost importance in Phase 3, making the process as transparent as possible for all stakeholders. This can take the form of a newsletter, regular meeting reports or progress updates to all stakeholders. Observing agreed-upon communication policies helps to keep or rebuild trust. Stakeholder Dialogues are fragile systems: transparent and reliable communication can act as the stabilizing factor.

Phase 3 is a big challenge for the core group or, in complex Stakeholder Dialogues, the project secretariat, responsible for moving an initiative forward. There is major pressure on this group to produce results. There is the danger that this group reacts negatively to 'disturbances', or for it to see criticism as 'corrective action'. The better the core group acts as a good *Container* and has learned to reflect on its role and its relationship to the system as a whole, the better it will cope with the increasing complexity. Constructive criticism can easily and transparently be integrated into the process, although temporary slowdowns can be expected if matters need to be clarified. In this phase, questions of inclusion and involvement of additional stakeholders may be raised again. For complex Stakeholder Dialogues it is helpful to agree on mechanisms of stakeholder inclusion.

> ● In Phase 3 of the development of the Common Code for the Coffee Community more and more actors in the coffee chain became interested in the initiative and requested to participate at the initiative's steering committee meetings. This, however, would have disabled the committee to function properly. The participating stakeholders therefore agreed on a transparent mechanism of how to include additional stakeholders. Each stakeholder group, in this case, civil society, industry and producers, defined criteria of representation that would regulate membership in the steering committee.

Clear process planning is central to Phase 3. This promotes real cooperation and transparent communication. During the implementation phase, Stakeholder Dialogues require a transparent process architecture, including a series of workshops, events, expert meetings, task forces, etc.

● The development of the **Common Code for the Coffee Community** required expert input and content work. At the end of every steering committee meeting the project secretariat suggested an activity for a few months ahead. It showed all activities, like e.g. the implementation of expert working groups, research or visits to producing countries for dissemination or consultation workshops. The stakeholder-composed steering committee could comment on the roadmap and amend it, if necessary. Between the steering committee meetings which took place 3 times per year, all participating stakeholders received a regular update on implementation of the activity plan.

➲ **Guiding questions for ensuring transparency and communication**

- How do we keep stakeholders regularly informed?
- Which aspects of the implementation need to be reliably transparent?
- What are indicators of good communication?
- How can we ensure continuity of trust?
- What additional support do we need to implement an initiative successfully?
- What measures can help to engender trust and strengthen working relationships?
- Are additional capacity-building measures required?
- Have guidelines been established for internal/external communication?

Area of attention: Create results and celebrate success

During Phase 3, it is essential to highlight the achievements of a Stakeholder Dialogue. 'Prototypes' – examples of future broader results – must be created, and they must be visible to stakeholders and non-participating actors alike. In a Stakeholder Dialogue, it often makes sense initially to focus on easy-to-reach results. But this does not necessarily mean that one should lose sight of larger, more important goals. Stakeholders stay engaged when they can readily relate to joint successes, and can thus overcome difficult situations together. Success should be celebrated in Phase 3, and, where possible or appropriate, with effective publicity. The more stakeholders involved can spread an initiative's philosophy and achievements, the more likely it will be to continue to support the implementation phase and future endeavors. It is important for stakeholders to agree formally on the form of communication to be used, e.g. with media, to avoid recurring mistrust and conflict within or between stakeholder groups. No confusing or misleading results should be communicated.

➲ **Guiding questions for creating results and celebrating success**

- In which areas can we achieve quick results more easily?
- How can we best convey the showcases to participating stakeholder and the public?
- How can we learn from positive results?
- Which wider audience do we need to keep informed about progress?

GETTING ACTIVE

Area of attention: Establish learning mechanisms

Similar to other change projects and initiatives, Stakeholder Dialogues require establishing some form of learning mechanisms, for example procedures for monitoring and evaluation. During the implementation phase, it is important jointly to spell out the form of such mechanisms. Nonetheless, it is equally important that all stakeholders understand and comprehend the learning mechanisms chosen. For example, different stakeholder groups often have different understandings of monitoring and evaluation. It is therefore recommended to invest time in agreeing on how results are to be tracked, how general stakeholder satisfaction (with results and with the stakeholder process) is measured, and how stakeholders can collectively learn to improve the impact of the dialogue process. This will help to avoid stakeholders from getting the impression that the process is controlled from the outside. Activity- and impact-monitoring are especially suited to the task of measuring results and effects. Process-monitoring instruments that focus on self-assessment are particularly appropriate for ensuring the quality of Stakeholder Dialogues. It is crucial that any learning or monitoring framework is designed as continuous. For example, it may be helpful for stakeholders to agree jointly on the monitoring or assessment criteria used in such a process.

➲ *Chapter 4: Getting reflective – creating a culture of learning in Stakeholder Dialogues, page 92*

➲ Guiding questions for establishing learning mechanisms

- How can we determine if we are on the right path?
- How can we integrate stakeholder feedback?
- How can we ensure that stakeholders feel their input is taken seriously?
- How can we ensure that we collectively learn from experience?
- What is the internal monitoring and evaluation system?
- How can progress best be measured?

● Case example: Common Code for the Coffee Community (4C):

➲ Phase 3: Implementing and evaluating

The main focus of Phase 3 was the practical implementation of the code of contact that had been jointly laid out in Phase 2. This required the creation of more formal work structures. Participants defined roles and responsibilities more closely, outlined rules of participation for the private sector and developed a verification system as well as a capacity-development program. This was decisive in ensuring that interested producers were respected, integrated and involved in the long term. Lack of trust and stereotypes still present at this stage also caused some degree of difficulty in negotiations. However, the stakeholders' overall engagement in the process kept the dialogue process on track. Once again, the project secretariat and the process-support team played an important role in keeping things in balance. A final goal in this phase was securing a sustainable exit strategy for the initiative by developing a self-financing system and a platform for capacity development on the implementation of the code of conduct.

2.2.4 Phase 4: Developing further, replicating or institutionalizing

Once a Stakeholder Dialogue has reached the agreed-upon results, the question remains whether an initiative should stop there, or if it should be further developed. If the desired goal has been achieved, success should be adequately celebrated: participation and contributions of individual stakeholder groups should be acknowledged and appreciated. Many Stakeholder Dialogues terminate successfully after Phase 3.

Some Stakeholder Dialogues may want to consolidate their outcomes into sustainable structures. This can mean taking the endeavor to the next level, replicating it at another location, integrating a new issue or further institutionalizing the dialogue on a more formal level. If taking the initiative or project to the next level seems to be a worthy option, Phase 4 needs to concentrate on building appropriate structures without losing sight of the crucial role of people and process. It is about creating the next-level *Container* by inviting and integrating new participants. This often requires building new structures and developing a governance system that represents the stakeholder groups. Sometimes, it can make sense to set up an institution with the appropriate management structure.

An important factor in the transition from a Stakeholder Dialogue to a more institutionalized structure is that in principle, the future setup stays faithful to the key features of the initiative. It needs to ensure that the major aspects of Stakeholder Dialogue – transparency, stakeholder representation, dialogue, ownership, consensus-building and outcome orientation – are also reflected in the institutionalization. Although the new structure will have its own dynamic and build a new identity around itself, its origins need to be recognizable, whether this is reflected in the governance structure, the openness towards continued dialogue and learning or the willingness to integrate stakeholder perspectives.

When a Stakeholder Dialogue is further developed, new stakeholders need to be integrated into the process, especially when the implementation of change is handed over to a third party. Previously uninvolved actors must quickly understand the urgency and importance of an initiative and be able to emotionally connect with the larger goal.

The process from the more loosely structured initiative to an institution is not necessarily an easy process. Replication or institutionalization often requires a professional management structure. Roles change and decision-making structures have to become more efficient. Existing management structures require additional legitimacy and credibility. Therefore, it is recommended that the original core group remains actively involved in Phase 4 of a Stakeholder Dialogue, progressively handing over their function to new actors and transferring the process step by step into its future structure.

A decisive factor for the success of Phase 4 lies in how many steps have been taken to integrate new actors over time and to allow them to participate in the initiative's success. Such actors are, by far, more interested in taking the idea further. The major challenge in Phase 4 is keeping the spirit of change alive.

Phase 4: Developing further, replicating or institutionalizing

	Bringing the dialogue to the next level, expanding or replicating dialogue activities, creating long-lasting structures for change	
Duration	Unlimited, depending on issues at stake, purpose and structure	
Expected results	Depending on the form and purpose of the Stakeholder Dialogue and area of implementation: • Extending the goal and stakeholder participation • Institutionalizing a successful dialogue form • Using the experience gathered in dialogue in another process	
Areas of attention	***Build next-level Container***	
	Create management structures	
	Establish governance and learning systems	
Most common difficulties or mistakes	• Insufficient *Container*-building for scaling up, replicating or institutionalizing • Insufficient engagement process for the integration of new stakeholders • Insufficient attention to the need for institutionalized and professional management structures • Insufficient investment into integrating the goal/content/objectives into stakeholder institutions • Fragmented success stories rather than system-wide solutions • Insufficient adjustment of strategies to a new situation	
Readiness check Phase 4	Have we thoroughly assessed the scaling-up and replication potential?	✔
	Have we sufficiently integrated new stakeholders for collaboration?	✔
	Have we found the appropriate structure for institutionalization?	✔
	Have we evaluated the new situation?	✔
	Have we evaluated and re-adjusted our strategies?	✔
	Have we created a new and emotionally engaged core group?	✔
	Do we keep up relationship management and trust building?	✔
	Have we designed an appropriate governance structure?	✔
	Have we designed a system for learning and evaluation?	✔

Area of attention: Build the next-level *Container*

When the time comes for broad-based dissemination of the result of a Stakeholder Dialogue, to replicating its success or to institutionalizing the form of collaboration between stakeholders, new challenges are bound to arise. It is not always possible for the core group or a project secretariat that successfully implemented a Stakeholder Dialogue to manage an initiative's long-term implementation as well. They may have done their best to take the initiative to this point; now other people need to take over and continue. In such cases where a politically consensual outcome has been achieved and publically portrayed as thus, interest in a particular topic may fade away. This may result from, for example, a lack of know-how or a lack of resources. This is why main actors in Stakeholder Dialogues who see the need to continue the dialogue in a different form need to communicate the prospects of such new tasks in a timely manner to all participating actors. If new stakeholders need to be engaged, it is helpful when the original core group, or the project secretariat can accompany this process. They can lobby for new supporters and participants, spread ideas, and promote change. It is important to establish a new network of interested and dedicated parties, to create a feeling of trust and to design the new process architecture accordingly. Taking a Stakeholder Dialogue to the next level requires building a new, next-level *Container* of dedicated people. To do this, it may be necessary to repeat some of the steps of Phase 1, 2 and 3.

➲ **Guiding questions for building the next-level *Container***

- Can we replicate the process at another location?
- Did we correctly assess the Stakeholder Dialogue's potential for formalization or institutionalization?
- Are there cooperation partners present who will promote the development, formalization or institutionalization of the Stakeholder Dialogue?
- Who are the new stakeholders that need to be integrated to increase the impact?
- What strategies need to be adapted or reviewed?
- How can we create a broader interest group that identify with the initiative?
- How can we help currently involved stakeholders to become messengers for the further development?
- What alliances need to be maintained?
- How can ownership, trust and commitment be sustained?

Area of attention: Create management structures

Some Stakeholder Dialogues have served their purpose after Phase 3 and do not need to be continued. However, others may warrant the further development of more formal structures, or institutionalization, due to the success of the dialogue. Some aspects from Phases 1 and 2 may need to be reinitiated at this point, such as:

- Further context analysis
- A new engagement process
- Adjustment of agreements
- Creation of management structures

The dialogue now needs a larger 'home', an institutionalized management and implementation structure, and, possibly, additional funding. In some cases, the sustainability of results requires creating an institution or a stakeholder-governed body. This means that an institution is created, or that formal or regulative processes are adopted from the forgoing Stakeholder Dialogue into existing institutional procedures. Such a transition is not always easy, and may lead to new problems or conflicts. Travelling this rough road can be difficult, but it can be made easier if there is a sufficient degree of continuity in the composition of the main supportive stakeholders, the core group or a project secretariat.

➲ **Guiding questions for creating management structures**

- What form of structure does developing the Stakeholder Dialogue further require?
- Do we need to create an institution or a legal body, or can we integrate the form of dialogue and collaboration into existing institutional procedures?
- What is the management structure that can sustain outcomes?
- How can we ensure the sustainability of results?
- What is an appropriate process architecture for continuation?
- Have we sufficiently attended to people in the creation of new structures?

Area of attention: Establish governance and learning systems

By institutionalizing or replicating the Stakeholder Dialogue, new challenges arise. Stakeholders or supporters expect increased results and impact. The public, or actors who are not directly involved with the dialogue, may question whether the dialogue is representative enough. Political supporters might demand stronger proof of results, which could make external evaluation necessary. The visibility of the Stakeholder Dialogue continues to increase, and with it the possibility for criticism. When Stakeholder Dialogues are developed further or institutionalized, they require new, adapted learning and management structures such as councils or steering committees, and executive committees that consist of equal numbers of representatives from each stakeholder group involved. Decision-making processes must become more formalized: *governance* structures must be created, the treatment of external criticism must be formalized in complaint mechanisms and results orientation must be regularly attested for.

Every institutionalization poses the risk of the initiative losing its forward drive, but too little structure can also put future implementation in danger. It is important to communicate the purpose and function of a Stakeholder Dialogue, as well as an enduring vision for the future, to find the right balance between ample room for creativity and sufficient structure and organization. For motivation to stay high, crises to be overcome and the original goal to be kept in the forefront, institutionalized management structures must also serve as reflection and learning structures

One of the biggest challenges in Phase 4 is the constant renewal of an initiative's spirit of change. It may be helpful at this point to recall the approach in Phase 1 as well as to adapt the processes for building confidence, trust and willingness for change.

➲ Guiding questions for building governance and learning structures

- What are the learning structures that the continuation of the Stakeholder Dialogue requires?
- What governance structure does a Stakeholder Dialogue require?
- What expertise is required for successful collaboration?
- How can we integrate further capacity-development measures?
- How can we measure the progress of success?
- Have we re-evaluated/adapted our strategies for Phase 4?
- Have we evaluated the lessons learned and integrated them into the next Phase?

● Case example: Common Code for the Coffee Community (4C):

➲ Phase 4: Developing further, replicating or institutionalizing

The definitive step for converting this initiative into an institution was completed in Phase 4 when the 4C Association was founded in 2006. A steering body was appointed, and a board of directors and a director were elected. In addition, a management structure was established to enable the enforcement of the code of conduct and to coordinate training aimed at coffee producers. The 4C Association was thus accessible for membership to the entire coffee sector.

The greatest challenges of this phase were to build a supporting structure for the institution while accepting equal involvement from all three sectors; to create a self-financing organization; and to apply, enforce, and develop capacity for the implementation of the code of conduct through a credible verification system.

ENSURING DIALOGUE – COMMUNICATION IN STAKEHOLDER DIALOGUES

CHAPTER 3

ENSURING DIALOGUE – COMMUNICATION IN STAKEHOLDER DIALOGUES

For Stakeholder Dialogues to be successful, it is important for participating stakeholders and their institutions to see the added value of engaging in them. This **engagement value** can be different for each participating institution, and is not always explicit. It can be transparent or opaque, outspoken or reserved. The engagement depends on a number of factors, such as perceived gains for a stakeholder group, risk of not participating, emotional connection to the larger goal, interest in collaborating with different stakeholders, or a genuine interest in change. If the engagement value drops, the continuation of the dialogue is endangered.

➲ *Chapter 5.: Resources, 5.9 Engaging Stakeholders, page 143, 5.10 Pitfalls in engagement processes, page 146, 5.11 Understanding the need to engage different stakeholder groups differently, page 147*

Sometimes, neither the engagement value nor the common goal is clear at the outset. Both develop over time, but not necessarily by themselves: they both need continuous attention. Vested interests, power imbalances and one-sided attempts to influence the process are as common to Stakeholder Dialogues, as they are to conflicts and crises. Stakeholder Dialogues are fragile processes that often depend on the ability of initiators, conveners, or facilitators to hold them together.

Once a participant in a Stakeholder Dialogue has moved from the role of the critical observer to the role of the engaged implementer, they have a genuine interest in success. Only then does it become more important to reach agreements, despite the presence of world-views that are sometimes contradictory. The clarification of the goal is not a once-off planning step but a continuous process. Reinforcing the strength of the vision is crucial for the alignment of a diverse group.

**THE CORE OF STAKEHOLDER ENGAGEMENT:
A visible common goal**

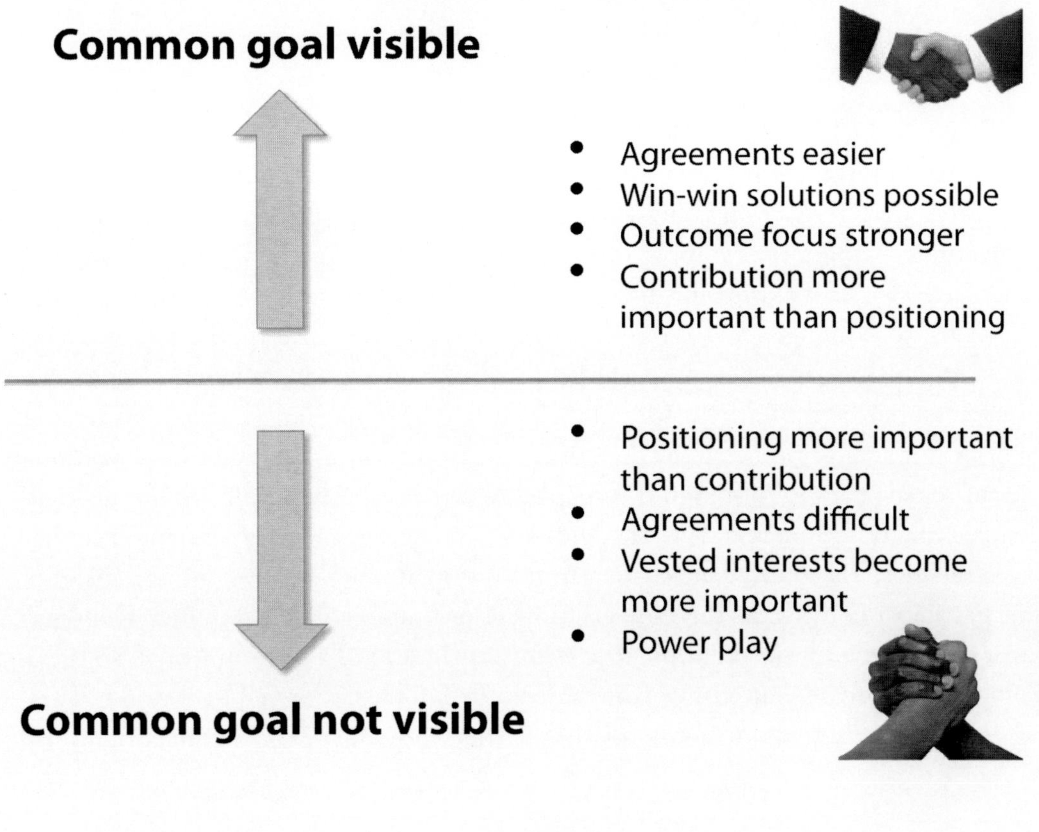

ENSURING DIALOGUE

It is only through getting to know each other more personally that patience and the understanding of different points of view can develop. Once participants know each other on a more personal level, they can accept the differences between their decision-making logic and the ways in which they act more easily as part of their political and organizational cultures and their history. Gradually, the participating stakeholders' world view changes: what seems to be rigidly defensible in the beginning begins to look different the more the participants are prepared to expose themselves to the complexity of multiple perspectives.

➲ *Chapter 5.: Resources, 5.3 Stakeholder Dialogues and theories of change, page 115, 5.4 Stakeholder Dialogues and different dimensions of change, page 117*

Here exactly lies the potential for reconciling differing interests: the world suddenly becomes more whole. People realize that their previous ways of thinking were fragmented. This is the fertile ground for collective responsibility. With more understanding of the complexity, but also coherence of the whole, it is easier to suspend inflexible positions and to take care of the common good. A pragmatic consensus is easier to reach. A dynamic Stakeholder Dialogue creates a network of interested and committed people. Building good relationships establishes the safety net that carries the process through ups and downs, crises and resolutions, challenges and successes. Particularly in collaborative Stakeholder Dialogues, this network of relationships also serves as an energy pattern that draws more and more people into the initiative.

In mature Stakeholder Dialogues:

- participating stakeholders are willing to take collective responsibility for global or local change;
- all actors involved are willing to communicate and cooperate across the boundaries of mental and political world views;
- all stakeholders are connected and committed to a larger goal (the contribution to the collective good) that lies beyond the interests of any one particular stakeholder group; and
- change is led collectively.

3.1 Accessing the field of dialogue

"Human beings dwell in the house of language [...] we speak to each other and in so doing bring forth the world for each other [...] it matters what words we use and what our listening is. That is, what worlds we call forth. In words we carry the world with us."

Connelli, 1986, p. 79

The way in which we 'do dialogue' has developed throughout the history of humankind's communication. For hundreds of years, around the globe, we have communicated in different ways, all of which have, essentially, the same setting: people in meetings – traditionally, most often set in a circle – expressing their views in a structured way. This expression has always been held by goodwill and by the belief that collective intelligence can only emerge from diversity and difference, and that it is the right thing to do because the truth will always arise from being receptive to differences. In recent times, the idea of dialogue has been taken up and made available for communication processes in the corporate world[7], in a variety of organizations and for social change. Although it is helpful to remember the origins of the dialogic setting – the traditional circle – Stakeholder Dialogues can be implemented in different settings. They derive their strength from the diversity of opinions and insights that participants bring to the conversation. The number of Stakeholder Dialogue participants depends on the topic, the event, or the size of the community, so these dialogues can involve anything from a few participants to several hundred. They can last for anything from hours to weeks. They can consist of one meeting, or of

[7] *Isaacs, 1999; Wheatley, 1999; Bohm, 1996*

a sequence of meetings. But their aim is always to come to a decision that is in line with the collective good and in the collective interest. Key for success is an inner orientation towards tolerance and respect for each other. Leaders in Stakeholder Dialogues must lead by example, by developing awareness about themselves and the space around them and by acknowledging the value of diversity.

➲ Dialogue is a stance

It is a different way of bringing oneself into the world. At the core of it is the quality of presence, a way of being in the world that helps others to bring out their best. As practice among a group of people, it is also the cornerstone for an approach to significant systems change. The purpose of negotiation is to reach a compromise between parties who differ; the intention of dialogue, however, is to reach a new level of understanding and, in doing so, to form a new basis from which to think and act collectively. Dialogue, therefore, is the basis of collective leadership for a more sustainable world.

➲ ***Chapter 5: Resources, 5.5 Stakeholder Dialogues as a pathway to Collective Leadership, page 120, 5.6 Enhancing dialogue : the art of thinking together, page 123, 5.8 Developing dialogic competence, page 129***

Dialogue is as old as the human race. It is an art of talking together that enables a flow of meaning among people. It is, then, the 'art of thinking together'[8] in a way that leads to progress through understanding differences and enacting respect. People who have experienced dialogue often feel that they have rediscovered something that seemed lost in their ordinary day-to-day conversations, something absent from most of our conversations during meetings, conferences and workshops. Ideally, **dialogue** enables people to bring out differences and to make sense of them. It does this by fostering a way of thinking and reflecting together that allows inquiry in a setting in which tension and conflict can be explored.

➲ What is required for dialogue?

Since dialogue implies that no position is final, and that new and unthought-of possibilities or solutions might arise from a conversation, it requires us to suspend our habitual ways of talking with each other. It requires the capacity to listen to the already-existing wholeness, to respect the integrity of another person in reaching out to understand, to observe and suspend one's own assumptions and to speak with an authentic voice.

Dialogue requires awareness about underlying paradigms and models of the world and how it works. It requires the capacity to notice when these paradigms and models are at odds with each other in a group, team, organization or community, and the capacity to explore the tension arising from difference rather than advocating a stance.

It requires awareness about oneself, one's own habitual way of bringing one's personality into a conversation, and an observation of the pitfalls arising from that. It invites the person engaged in it to develop a stronger balance within herself or himself, a balance that allows one to explore the common good or shared meaning.

[8] *See also Isaacs, 1999*

3.2 The role of Stakeholder Dialogue facilitators

The dialogic approach to change is built on the premise that connection, cooperation and communication are essential elements in creating a sustainable future. The invitation to integrate multiple perspectives is seen as a cornerstone for jointly enacting reality to benefit the collective good. The core task of a Stakeholder Dialogue facilitator is therefore leadership, albeit in a different form than traditionally perceived in organizations. This form of leadership is far removed from a model of heroic or hierarchical leadership. Stakeholder Dialogue facilitators initiate and sustain change for the better, in a context that goes beyond the limitations of their own organizations.

What is a Stakeholder Dialogue facilitator?

A Stakeholder Dialogue facilitator is a person who – in conjunction with others – initiates, coordinates, convenes, facilitates and/or implements Stakeholder Dialogues.
Important abilities of Stakeholder Dialogue facilitators
• The ability to facilitate the exchange of different viewpoints and to look at things from different perspectives. • The ability to act in very complex processes without familiar structures. • The ability to handle conflicts, crises, protest and obstacles in a productive way. • The ability to organize and facilitate structured dialogue processes and settings. • The readiness to take risk and to stay flexible. • The ability to engage stakeholders to support one common goal. • The ability to celebrate success as a joint achievement.

Stakeholder Dialogue facilitators are people who engage with different stakeholders in a constructive and outcome-oriented communication and collaboration. They can belong to one stakeholder group or to the lead agency that brings the Stakeholder Dialogue forward. So, they do not need to be neutral about a goal: they can have 'stakes' in an issue. But they must be willing to be open to different stakeholder perspectives, and, if need be, to mediate between the different interests and to ensure that different viewpoints are heard and integrated.

Facilitating Stakeholder Dialogues supports a collective intervention into a complex system, and those who do this act as guardians of change. Such facilitation can contribute tremendously to a collectively held vision and, subsequently, to joint implementation. This requires awareness and regular adjustment, excellent communication and a high degree of self-reflection. Stakeholder Dialogue facilitators foster communication, tap into people's creativity and cultivate relationships. They do this with an inner attitude of service and an orientation towards performance. This is an art of leading that maintains perspective in the face of crisis, uses conflict productively to access collective wisdom, and aims at bringing forth new possibilities. Ideally, this can unblock blocked energy among different players, create a healing atmosphere, and allow people to engage in meaningful conversations and collective endeavors. Stakeholder Dialogues can become a cornerstone for large systems change. Stakeholder Dialogue facilitators know that all change begins within: that is why they cultivate their minds, build their own capacities to integrate difference and stay open to learning.

Developmental pathways for Stakeholder Dialogue facilitators

The development of awareness	This includes self-awareness and awareness of systems: personal, interpersonal, organizational and systems dynamics. Awareness increases choice and flexibility, cultivates humility and helps people to act more purposefully and effectively way.
The cultivation of relationships	Empathy, trust in others and the ability to share shortcomings create an atmosphere of respect that can become a supporting element in achieving the collective purpose.
The 'commitment to something larger than oneself'	The insight that there is more to change than achieving objectives. It is the attention to the larger story that unfolds through Stakeholder Dialogues. Contributing to the lives of others is valued highly.
The commitment to connection, communication and respecting diversity	A model of change in which a sustainable future needs collective commitment, and in which only diversity (of views, experiences, competencies, interests, etc.) reflects life's way of staying in balance dialogically. Only multiple perspectives can create an understanding of the whole.

The ability to facilitate dialogue is an important capacity for sustainable development efforts. It helps people in projects, teams and stakeholder meetings to achieve joint goals. It also allows people to maintain perspectives in the face of crisis, to use conflict productively, to know what to ask or do when things don't move, to access collective intelligence, and to invent new possibilities that bring out the best in people.

➲ ***Chapter 5: Resources, 5.3 Stakeholder Dialogues and theories of change, page 115, 5.4 Stakeholder Dialogues and different dimensions of change, page 117***

Stakeholder Dialogue facilitators know that change in action is always preceded by change in thinking. They learn to tune into the complex system of actors by acknowledging differences and developing an art of communication that furthers thinking together. They know when people speak their truth, and when relationships receive enough attention that changes in thinking are more easily achieved, understanding between different stakeholders grows and so does tolerance. They know that vision, values and direction can take on deeper meaning, if held in a collective space. One of the most important facilitation tasks is, therefore, the creation of 'space' for people to communicate well together while creating new realities.

The success of Stakeholder Dialogues often depends on the initiatives of particular individuals. In this way, Stakeholder Dialogue facilitators 'broker' between different perspectives and viewpoints. This requires a new leadership competence, one that is outside the framework of traditional hierarchical or heroic management models.

Stakeholder Dialogue facilitators

- **create new possibilities for development**, which would otherwise be neglected. They take on a leadership role in complex systems, which can only then come to innovative solutions when traditional, factual and mental barriers can be collectively overcome.
- **are visionaries** because they are prepared to take risks and dare to enter unknown terrain. They search continually for new solutions and take the path less travelled. They can convince not only their colleagues but also the other stakeholders to engage. With the knowledge that people can only begin to find creative and innovative solutions when they respect and overcome differences, they play a supporting role in consensus-building and in the integration of stakeholder perspectives. They know that complex problem-solving requires a wide range of perspectives, and that only respect for differences can lead to pragmatic collaboration for a larger goal.
- **are innovative** because they push ideas forward – ideas that others sometimes consider to be unrealistic. They typically have a high level of endurance because they believe that in time, collective intelligence will prevail. They have an inner conviction that dialogue is the best way to finding a solution to a complex problem, and that it is worth successfully overcoming crises. Stakeholder Dialogue facilitators have an eye on the future, because they constantly consider the big picture and keep alternatives close at hand. This allows them to take on a challenge, crisis, or conflict situation with a certain degree of calmness.
- **ensure that all relevant stakeholders stay on board,** that goals are constantly re-examined and jointly agreed upon, or that the stakeholder partnership is regularly evaluated. They are persistently capable of building networks, are masters of both formal and informal communication and are able to keep the entire process in perspective.
- **always consider different points of view,** constructively deal with resistance and are capable of de-escalating difficult situations. They organize structured dialogue and motivate participants to achieve the higher goal.

Stakeholder Dialogue facilitators play a leading role in initiatives that specifically target social or global changes by helping a group of diverse stakeholders to develop a sense of collective leadership through increased collective responsibility. They guarantee that the different actors participating in a change endeavor stay committed to the common goal and they help to establish the coherence that is necessary within a group to find new solutions.

They are aware that there will always be a certain degree of mistrust, indifference and side-taking when stakeholders are not accustomed to working in a diverse and complex environment of collaborative change endeavor. This makes Stakeholder Dialogue facilitators an essential requirement for establishing and maintaining a culture of authentic consultation and collaboration. Their role is to ensure that the engagement value remains high enough for all involved stakeholders.

Process facilitation skills are a core competence for people initiating, coordinating and implementing Stakeholder Dialogues. Stakeholder Dialogue facilitators need to develop their conceptual skills and communicative competence in supporting change in complex systems. But not every Stakeholder Dialogue facilitator also needs to be a professional workshop facilitator. People who bring forward Stakeholder Dialogues may want to make use of professional workshop facilitators when it comes to preparing and implementing larger Stakeholder Dialogue Events in particular.

➲ **How can you recognize good facilitation skills?**

➲ **Good facilitation is the ability to make things happen through and with others in a way that ensures an ongoing dialogic conversation between people.** It is the ability to help a group through difficulties, to move to a certain end point or to reach a new level of thinking together. It is the skill that enables effective participation in Stakeholder Dialogue meetings. Dialogic facilitation ensures that:

- participants' different perspectives or viewpoints are considered, especially in complex situations when this is particularly important;
- the voices of all relevant participants or stakeholders are heard and listened to;
- meetings are held more efficiently and effectively;
- the quality of decisions is improved and problem-solving is enhanced; and
- more participation, energy and enthusiasm is encouraged during implementation of decisions.

What do Stakeholder Dialogue facilitators do?

Promote the idea of the Stakeholder Dialogue to all relevant participants:	• They need to be able to understand the interests and the different internal logic of the different stakeholders and participants to engage them • They need to be able to inspire participation by understanding different needs
Communicate the common goal, or developing it together with the group:	• They need to know and communicate the benefits of the Stakeholder Dialogue for each participant • They need to support participants in the development of a common goal
Create a climate of trust among participants:	• They need to embody the engagement they seek from others • They need to develop trusting relationships with all participants • They need to be as impartial as possible, without disengaging from the common goal • They need to be as transparent as possible about process, procedures and outcomes • They need to ensure that people can voice their views, that people are listened to and respected
Network among existing and potential participants:	• They have an important function as nodes in a network and as facilitators of the exchange between stakeholders

ENSURING DIALOGUE

To enhance one's own dialogic competence as a Stakeholder Dialogue facilitator, it helps to become aware of people's conversation patterns, as well as those of stakeholders and institutions. These patterns sometimes play out in stakeholder meetings, group conversations and workshops related to the Stakeholder Dialogue, where they can lead to ineffectiveness. Awareness starts with observation. The more the Stakeholder Dialogue facilitator begins to notice subtle patterns, the better he or she will be able to diagnose what steps are required to facilitate successful communication and integration.

➲ *Chapter 5: Resources, 5.8.1 The four action modes, page 130, 5.8.2 Dialogic practices, page 137*

3.3 Understanding levels of communication in Stakeholder Dialogues

Attending to the quality of communication is a crucial factor for success in Stakeholder Dialogues. This includes communication among participating stakeholders as well as with external actors. Communication processes in Stakeholder Dialogues may differ, depending on whether they are for internal or external purposes.

➲ **Internal communication** refers to communication between actors or institutions that are directly involved in the Stakeholder Dialogue.

➲ **External communication** refers to communication with the general public or with other stakeholders, who are relevant but not directly involved in the process.

Each of these levels of communication has a direct influence on the course of a Stakeholder Dialogue and, therefore, also on its results. Regular and authentic communication is indispensable for building trust. Mistrust leads to delays, and, in some cases, can undermine the stakeholder consultation or cooperation all together. Quality communication is the 'oil' for creating cohesion among the otherwise diverse, and at times conflicting or mutually distrustful, stakeholders. It can overcome difficult situations and contribute to a sense of belonging in an otherwise complex endeavor. For the core group in its function as a good Container, dialogic competence is crucial for finding an appropriate and efficient form of internal communication that engenders trust and a sense of collective leadership, and permits an uncomplicated, informal collaboration. Similarly, the core group needs to create good communication with other stakeholders and ensure that the stakeholders all agree on the form of external communication.

➲ *Chapter 5: Resources, 5.9 Engaging stakeholders: building a container for change, page 143*

The following paragraphs highlight important aspects of communication in Stakeholder Dialogues.

Area of attention: Internal communication

Communication within the core group

It is an enormous asset for the success of a Stakeholder Dialogue if the core group (the small group of initiating Stakeholder Dialogue facilitators) becomes more than an official committee or a task force: the more informal the style of communication between members of the core group is, the more it becomes a good Container for change, the better the chance that the members can reflect together, quickly discuss and address challenges, or adjust strategies. An atmosphere of mutual trust and support is crucial. This is greatly enhanced by acknowledging diversity in the core group as a cross-sector team that brings the dialogue process further. An investment in team-building can pay off. Relationship-building is key.

Communication with participating stakeholders

In addition to communication within the core group, communication between the core group and other stakeholders who participate directly in the Stakeholder Dialogue is important. This is particularly true in the Phases 2 and 3 of the Stakeholder Dialogue process. It is important that all participating stakeholders feel well informed and well looked after. The more open and transparent the form of communication, the more constructively feedback and criticism can be handled. It is helpful to agree on the form and sequence of internal communication among all participating stakeholders.

Communication between participating stakeholders and their institutions

Stakeholders directly involved in a Stakeholder Dialogue represent participating institutions. Examples are company employees, public servants, association members or representatives of civil society organizations. This implies that they are not necessarily representing their own personal beliefs, but rather, and primarily, the interests and perspectives of their employers. However, people engage in Stakeholder Dialogues as people: they develop a sense of understanding for the complexity of the situation and for other points of view. But these individuals do not always have the required decision-making power in their organizations to be able to agree on a course of action on behalf of their organizations. Some concessions may first need to be approved by their superiors. This process can prove difficult and tenacious in many Stakeholder Dialogues. So, all stakeholders should be made fully aware of this eventuality and approach it with sufficient understanding. Members of the core group can support communication between participating stakeholders and their institutions. Thus, the need for information about, and confidence in, the Stakeholder Dialogue by other actors within participating stakeholder institutions needs to be considered. Interest, trust and confidence can be built by information consisting of recent results and achievements or simply of an update on the state of affairs. This aspect should be carefully considered during each of the four phases to keep silent supporters on board and to prevent active critics from becoming obstructers.

Communication to maintain high-level support

To ensure the continued backing of high-level supporters of a Stakeholder Dialogue process – politicians, for example – it is essential to keep them informed. This can take different forms and depends on the relationship between members of the core

THE STAKEHOLDER SYSTEM

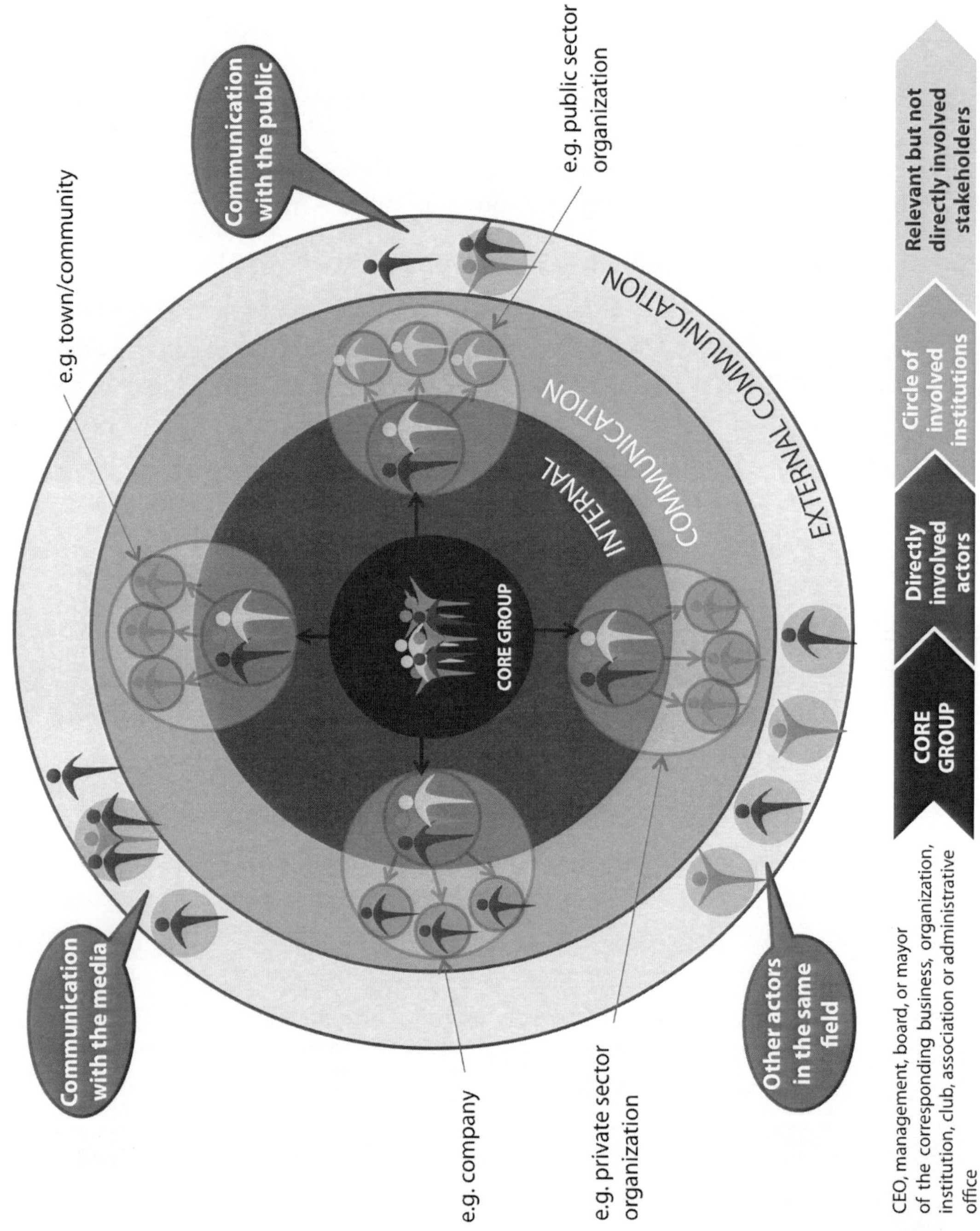

group and the supporting hierarchy or patronage. Key to success is to ensure that any progress or success in the Stakeholder Dialogue also becomes the success of the high-level supporters.

Communication with critical participating stakeholders

It is equally important to plan and maintain steady communication with potential critics of the initiative carefully, as well as with important individuals within the specific field.

Area of attention: External communication

External communication consists of all communication between the Stakeholder Dialogue system and its environment regarding goals, courses of action and results. This may include communication with non-participating but observing actors, the general public and the media. External communication is often one-dimensional, meaning that information mostly flows in one direction, e.g. information about the course of the Stakeholder Dialogue. The form and content of information that should go to non-participating stakeholder always needs to be agreed upon among the participating stakeholders.

Communication with non-participating actors

Non-participating actors often observe Stakeholder Dialogues closely. These observers may be actors who have not yet decided to participate in the dialogue; individuals who are only indirectly interested in the topic; people who doubt the dialogue's chances of success or the initiative's validity; or people who have been consciously or unconsciously excluded. The degree of observation depends on the topic and on the political importance of the Stakeholder Dialogue. In Stakeholder Dialogues that have a more political dimension, and where progress can, or should, have an effect beyond participating stakeholders, attention to the need for appropriate external communication is key. Criticism from non-participating actors can have a negative effect on the Stakeholder Dialogue, bring the fragile system into discredit, and endanger the Stakeholder Dialogue process as a whole. Such communication should be strategically planned. This may involve withholding certain information, on one hand, if communicating it to the outside world would mean a loss of trust within the group of stakeholders directly involved. On the other hand, it may be in the interest of the Stakeholder Dialogue to make certain information public, if it will have a positive effect on the process and advance it further. At the end of Phase 2, or in Phase 3, it is often important that stakeholders agree on the form of communication that should take place with the public or non-participating stakeholders.

Communication with the media

In some Stakeholder Dialogues, especially in political processes, observation by the press plays an important role. In other cases, Stakeholder Dialogues receive relatively little media attention – but an upbeat portrayal of achievements by the press could facilitate the implementation of goals. In general, the media should not be informed of a Stakeholder Dialogue process too early, unless this is unavoidable for political reasons. Generally, the media should be informed after initial successes result from the Stakeholder Dialogue. These successes are often more tangible in Phase 3.

⊃ *Chapter 5: Resources, 5.12 The role of communication in the four phases of a Stakeholder Dialogue, page 148*

Levels of communication in Stakeholder Dialogues: Internal communication

Internal communication refers to communication between stakeholders or with institutions that are directly involved in the Stakeholder Dialogue, individuals and the institutions they represent

Recommendations for	***Purpose***
Communication within the core group Ensure that members of the **core group** are fully informed about all relevant issues Plan Stakeholder Dialogue jointly Conduct regular formal or informal meetings (or conference calls) Emphasize team-building/relationship-building Cultivate informal communication Ensure joint reflection	• Build trust • Keep **core group** engaged • Show reliability • Create confidence • Build the core group into a good Container for change
Communication between core group and participating stakeholders Ensure that all relevant stakeholders can track and see progress Ensure that changes in the process are communicated and justified appropriately Keep stakeholders regularly informed (progress reports, newsletters, meeting documentation, etc.) Create appropriate settings for face-to-face meetings or telephone conferences Attend to relationship-building during meetings Agree on the form and sequence of communication and information among participating stakeholders	• Enhance credibility through transparency • Build trust • Show openness to feedback • Keep stakeholders on track and engaged • Show reliability • Create confidence
Communication between participating stakeholders and their institutions Consider the different information needs of different stakeholder groups Provide information in different forms (e.g. short and crisp for private sector, reports for public sector, background information for civil society) If required and permitted, let the **core group** support by presenting progress reports or important content to stakeholder institutions	• Build the support-base in the management of participating stakeholder institutions • Enhance credibility of the Stakeholder Dialogues • Build confidence that participants' time is time well spent
Communication between core group and high-level support Keep high-level supporters up to date with results Keep them engaged and consider an important role for them in stakeholder meetings	• Ensure support

Levels of communication in Stakeholder Dialogues: External communication

External communication refers to communication with the general public or with other relevant stakeholders who are not directly involved in the process.

Recommendations for	*Purpose*
Communication between Stakeholder Dialogue participants and observing, non-participating actors Decide among participating stakeholder how to communicate with non-participating actors Keep interested but non-participating actors regularly informed Develop mechanisms of bringing external feedback into the Stakeholder Dialogues Withhold information from the outside if this would mean losing trust among participating stakeholders	• Build trust in the course of action • Keep external actors sufficiently informed • Show progress • Create confidence
Communication between Stakeholder Dialogue participants and the media Avoid involving the media at an early stage, before results have been produced Agree on media involvement among all stakeholders Focus on success stories when involving media	• Enhance credibility • Make results known • Broaden support • Pave the way for the engagement of additional stakeholders

GETTING REFLECTIVE – CREATING A CULTURE OF LEARNING

GETTING REFLECTIVE – CREATING A CULTURE OF LEARNING

CHAPTER 4

Stakeholder Dialogues require patience and persistence, but, when managed well, they can build the cross-sector stability we need to address global challenges. But any attempt to initiate, implement or facilitate Stakeholder Dialogues is an intervention into a fragile and often controversial system of actors. So, it requires careful attention to the quality of process, the quality of relationships and interaction among stakeholders, as well as to the quality of the formal and informal structures that are created to make the Stakeholder Dialogue work. They are based on principles and can be implemented by following a recommended methodology, but there is no single blueprint for a successful Stakeholder Dialogue. A complex or controversial system of actors is too unpredictable to be addressed by the contents of a simple toolbox. After all, people's passion counts in this process.

"We are here in a global learning process. We must accept that we learn as we go."
(Participant of the Stakeholder Dialogue leading to the Common Code for the Coffee Community)

However, understanding methodology and instruments can offer just the degree of orientation that key actors need. Learning in time and adjustment of process designs is an important faculty to develop. A key to learning is structured reflection: certainly by key actors, and by the core group, but ideally by a wider group of people involved in a Stakeholder Dialogue. Reflection can be a challenge, because most highly engaged actors will be overworked and not used to spending time for reflection. Hence, developing a culture of learning requires attention right from the start. If a core group as a good Container has established a pattern of regular reflection on process and progress, and sees the task in front of them as a learning space, this culture will more easily be reflected also in the collaboration with a wider group of stakeholders.

➲ *Chapter 2: The core group as container, page 56*

4.1 Understanding key factors for successful Stakeholder Dialogues

Stakeholder Dialogues may be influenced by external factors that the initiators have little power to change, such as political instability or economic crises. But most factors crucial for the success of Stakeholder Dialogues can actually be influenced to a certain degree. These factors – in combination – can determine the quality of a Stakeholder Dialogue and, eventually, its success. Paying attention to them helps to maintain the dynamic, to keep stakeholders sufficiently involved and finally to achieve tangible outcomes or successful implementation.

The key factors for successful Stakeholder Dialogues may differ depending on the form of the dialogue, its purpose, or the stakeholders involved in it. However, a network of factors seems to be strong contributors to success throughout the different forms of Stakeholder Dialogues. They are based on the experiences of a large number of practitioners, and are summarized here in a form that should give guidance to other practitioners.

The factors are interrelated and mutually supportive. They can be seen as lenses through which a group of initiators or conveners can look at the quality of their Stakeholder Dialogue process and review which areas require attention. None of the factors is entirely distinct from another – they influence each other, but they all are leverage points for the improvement of process quality and, subsequently, leverage points for the effect that a Stakeholder Dialogue can have. How much emphasis needs to be placed on each of the factors depends on the form and purpose of the Stakeholder Dialogue.

The 8 key factors for successful Stakeholder Dialogues: Overview

Leadership and high level sponsorship	Stakeholder Dialogues are change initiatives and need to be strongly led: not by one person, but usually by a group of initiators or conveners. Because there is no disciplinary hierarchy between stakeholders, leadership is a capacity that a core group of stakeholders in its function as good Container needs to develop jointly. High-level support is essential for impact.
Cohesion and relationship-management	An often undervalued factor is creating a sense of belonging. This involves making sure stakeholders feel that they are part of something larger. Relationships require attention throughout Stakeholder Dialogues. Protocol, boundaries and territories must be respected.
Goals and process clarity	People engage when they see the bigger picture and understand how they can contribute to positive change. Stakeholder Dialogues may look unpredictable, so stakeholders want to know what to expect, when. Keeping the goal high helps stakeholders to connect emotionally; clarity on process planning provides the minimum level of certainty that people require to stay engaged.
Knowledge and competence	Most Stakeholder Dialogues take place around content issues. Expertise and information need to be provided in a way that helps stakeholders to see the issue's full picture. Capacity-building, particularly for weaker stakeholder groups, helps to strengthen their voices and improves the quality of their contribution.
Credibility	Credibility is composed of different aspects: the reputation and position of the initiators or conveners of Stakeholder Dialogues; the transparency in communication among participating stakeholders and the public; the reliability with which recommendations or inputs from different stakeholders are taken into account; and the degree of representation of stakeholders involved.
Inclusivity	Stakeholder Dialogues that exclude important stakeholders will lose credibility, cause distrust among non-participating stakeholders, or have reduced impact. Integrating the concerned or affected, but weaker, stakeholder groups ensures that outcomes are based on a broader picture.
Ownership	People implement what they have helped to create. Ownership develops when the goal of the Stakeholder Dialogue is relevant to all stakeholders and when they perceive that their contribution counts. Keeping people engaged is an important road to success. Authentic participation, in the way contributions are handled, workshops are run and communication takes place, ensures ownership.
Delivery and outcome-orientation	Focus on outcomes is a prerequisite for commitment. In Stakeholder Dialogue process planning, it is important that tangible results are always visibly achieved: this can range from a basic agreement to meet again, to documented recommendations, or from agreed-upon action plans, to progress reporting on implementation.

Key factor 1: Leadership and high-level sponsorship

Leadership in Stakeholder Dialogues is different from leadership within organizations. Although hierarchical differences and differences in influence and power play an important role in Stakeholder Dialogues, there is no disciplinary hierarchy between stakeholders, no leader who has the final say in what needs to happen. Leadership is, therefore, a capacity that stakeholders need to develop jointly. Stakeholder Dialogues thrive on a combination of passionate drivers and a spirit of collective responsibility for change. But they also need to take influential actors into account: obtaining their support can be a crucial success factor.

➲ *Chapter 2: Phase 1, Exploring and engaging, page 55*

● **The Common Code for the Coffee Community (4C)** is a basic quality standard for sustainability in green coffee production for the mainstream coffee sector. It was developed by an international group of stakeholders, including coffee producers from most important coffee-producing countries, coffee roasters, and coffee traders, as well as international NGOs. They combined forces to develop a common standard and to lay out the conditions needed for its application.

The European Coffee Federation, two German ministries, as well as Dutch, Belgian and eventually Swiss public sector institutions supported the stakeholder initiative. Such high-level and cooperative support gave the initiative the reputation it required to push forward an international Stakeholder Dialogue.

Key factor 2: Cohesion and relationship-management

An often undervalued factor is creating a sense of belonging to an effort geared at the common good. Stakeholders commit when they feel that they are part of something larger. Stakeholder Dialogues are more than the collaboration between different actors – they develop a life of their own, and become a Stakeholder Dialogue system with its own internal rules. The degree of cohesion is an important contributor to success. If participating stakeholders do not identify strongly with the dialogue and cooperation process, its effect will remain low. If this is the case, stakeholders will rarely implement results developed during the dialogue; they will refrain from taking results back to their institutions; and external influences will easily jeopardize the process. So, relationships require attention throughout Stakeholder Dialogues. Protocol, boundaries and territories must be respected. As shown in Chapter 3, the oil in Stakeholder Dialogues, and a cornerstone for the appropriate level of cohesion, is trust – if participating stakeholders learn to trust the process despite differences in opinion and waves of occasional mistrust (which will always be a feature), the Stakeholder Dialogue has a chance to succeed.

➲ *Chapter 2: Phase 1, Exploring and engaging, page 55*

GETTING REFLECTIVE

● The purpose of the **"African Cashew initiative"(ACi),** which is funded by the Bill & Melinda Gates Foundation, is to strengthen the global competitiveness of the African cashew production and particularly enhance the production and processing capacity in five pilot countries (Mozambique, Ghana, Burkina Faso, Côte d'Ivoire and Benin). This result-oriented stakeholder initiative is implemented by German development cooperation, a US-based not-for-profit organization, a not-for-profit foundation based in the Netherlands; and the "African Cashew Alliance" (ACA), a supranational stakeholder platform of private and public partners involved in the cashew value chain. Further implementing partners are: farmer cooperatives, traders, local processors and a number of large global private sector companies, who all contribute to the project and allocate resources.

The initiative has a strong focus on delivery of targets, however requires optimal coordination in a very complex implementation structure. All partners need to fully understand the goals, and find an effective complementary approach to delivering results. At the beginning of the implementation phase this required to invest time in fostering alignment and a spirit of collaboration.

Key factor 3: Goal and process clarity

People engage when they see the bigger picture and understand how they can contribute to positive change. Clarity about goals and about process are Siamese twins in Stakeholder Dialogues. Although the purpose of bringing stakeholders together is often clear to the core group, this does not necessarily mean that the goal is understood or even agreed upon between all invited stakeholders. Often – particularly in stakeholder consultation, for example – the goal remains vague, and participating stakeholders feel more like observers than engaged participants. But even when the goal seems to be clear, it needs to be developed further, adjusted, or reshaped by all main stakeholders involved. Developing an agreed-upon goal and pushing the Stakeholder Dialogue towards outcomes requires a solid process architecture. Stakeholder Dialogues may look unpredictable, so stakeholders want to know what to expect, and when: keeping the goal high helps stakeholders to connect emotionally, and clarity on process planning provides the minimum level of certainty that people require to stay engaged. Goal and process clarity support each other: the less developed, more changeable and more distant the goal, the more reliability the process needs to offer.

➲ *Chapter 2: Phase 2, Building and formalizing, page 61*
Phase 3, Implementing and evaluating, page 68

● **Land management, land allocation and land distribution are pressing issues in Cambodia** that can determine the social stability of the country. The adequate management of natural resources as well as the improvement of poor people's income through better land allocation and management require the formulation and implementation of a state of the art land policy. Jointly supported by the German development cooperation and the Worldbank the Cambodian Ministry of Land aims at developing a White Paper on land. This was preceded by the development of a land policy declaration. An inter-ministerial technical working group had collaboratively worked on reframing the country's vision on land policy, and the main areas for its implementation. This process took approximately four months and was designed as a sequence of government-internal dialogue events. Although the process was steered by the Ministry of Land, goal and process design had been openly discussed and agreed upon by all members of the inter-ministerial working group.

Key factor 4: Knowledge and competence

Most Stakeholder Dialogues focus on content issues. Expertise and information need to be provided in a way that helps stakeholders to see the issue's entire picture. Capacity-building, particularly for weaker stakeholder groups, helps to strengthen stakeholders' voices and improves the quality of their contribution. Stakeholder Dialogues build on the emergence of collective intelligence and the assumption that integrating different interests and competence leads to joint progress. Both aspects require expertise, experience and knowledge in the understanding of content, as well as the capability to collaborate constructively. If Stakeholder Dialogues lack knowledge and competence, the consultation, decision-making or implementation process they intend to deliver will be inadequate for the achievement of the goal.

➲ *Chapter 2:*
Phase 2, Building and formalizing, page 61
Phase 3, Implementing and evaluating, page 68

● The **Cambodian land policy** declaration was not exclusively developed by experts on land management but rather by an inter-ministerial technical working group in order to foster a sense of ownership. This created the need for a basic capacity building in state-of-the-art land management in order to ensure that informed decisions were made. In addition, the process design included capacity building in the methodology of Stakeholder Dialogues. This ensured the high level of collaboration between representatives from the different ministries. Both capacity building measures were integrated into the dialogue events.

Key factor 5: Credibility

Stakeholder Dialogues need credibility to be effective. Credibility involves a number of factors, such as:

- the reputation, neutrality and credibility of the initiator, convener or facilitator;
- an adequate representation of stakeholder groups in the dialogue process;
- the transparency of decision-making procedures;
- the transparency in communication among participating stakeholders and the public;
- the reliability with which recommendations or inputs from different stakeholders are taken into account;
- how well the stakeholders are represented;
- the significance of participating in the dialogue for its participants, as well as the significance of the issue that the Stakeholder Dialogue aims to address; and
- how embedded the Stakeholder Dialogue is in relevant societal processes.

The more credible a Stakeholder Dialogue is, the more likely participants will be to identify with the goal and the process and to justify their participation in the Stakeholder Dialogue to their constituencies, organizations, superiors, etc.

➲ *Chapter 2:*
Phase 2, Building and formalizing, page 61
Phase 3, implementing and evaluating, page 68,
Chapter 3: Ensuring dalogue – communication in Stakeholder Dialogues, page 78,
Chapter 5: Resources, 5.12. The role of communication in the 4 phases of Stakeholder Dialogues, page 148

● As the **Common Code for the Coffee Community** is a stakeholder initiative with strong representation of European private sector and much supported by European development organizations, a number of indirectly involved stakeholders were extremely critical towards the initiative. The project secretariat made a deliberate and successful effort to involve more representatives from producing countries than from industry and also ensured that large international NGOs became part of the initiative. Regarding the role the basic standard would play in future, the stakeholder group was always aware that the standard needed to be implemented in a way that would not only keep small scale coffee growers in the market, but enhance their contribution to and income from the coffee market.

Key factor 6: Inclusivity

Stakeholder Dialogues that exclude important stakeholders will lose credibility and will cause mistrust among non-participating stakeholders. They will also be less effective, because stakeholders who are important for implementing or supporting results are absent from the dialogue process. Integrating stakeholder groups with weaker voices, such as small or informal businesses, communities, women's groups, small NGOs, and so on, is important to ensure that participants can base their decisions on a broader picture. Inclusivity, however, does not mean including everybody: the art is to find out, in Phase 1, which stakeholders can help to create the change in thinking and acting that the Stakeholder Dialogue requires.

➲ *Chapter 2: Phase 1, Exploring and engageing, page 61*

● After all participating stakeholders had agreed upon the first draft of basic sustainability standard, the **Common Code for the Coffee Community**, the initiative began to focus more on issues of implementation. Although key actors kept close communicative relationships with the International Coffee Organization (ICO) where all coffee producing countries were represented, there was still skepticism towards the possible impact of the initiative on coffee producing countries. Some of these countries, led by Brazil as one of the most important coffee producing countries, joined together and drafted an open declaration that strongly attacked the initiative. As a consequence the project secretariat had to deal with unexpected uncertainty in the continuation of the initiative. They not only discussed the impact of the declaration with various stakeholders, but reflected on what might have been missing in the engagement strategy of the initiative. The consequence was a delay in implementation, but also an improvement in process design. The initiative more actively informed key stakeholders in the skeptical countries about the goal and principles of the initiative and spurred an engagement process. As a result, not only more producer representatives, but also the Brazilian coffee industry became members of the steering committee.

Key factor 7: Ownership

People implement what they have helped to create. Ownership develops when the goal of the Stakeholder Dialogue is relevant to all stakeholders and when they perceive that their contribution counts. Keeping people engaged is an important road to success. If participants in a dialogue process have the impression that their time is being used to deliver recommendations whose implementation is unclear, if their concerns are not heard, their perspectives not integrated, or if the implementation of decisions and plans is not transparently linked to the agreements achieved during the Stakeholder Dialogue, they will withdraw, reduce their engagement, fail to implement decisions, or just observe the dialogue without much engagement. Authentic participation in the way contributions are handled, workshops are run and communication takes place, ensures ownership.

● In the framework of a development program to **promote the competitiveness of Senegalese small and medium sized enterprises (SMEs)**, a wide group of key actors in SME development from public and private sectors had been invited to a capacity building in the implementation of Stakeholder Dialogues and collaborative change. For the participants this was seen as a good opportunity to critically exchange ideas on approaches to SME development in Senegal. Despite lingering territorial sensitivities in the support for small businesses, the participating stakeholders unanimously agreed to establish a national round table on SME development that would enable them to continue dialogue and collaboration.

➲ ***Getting active – Making Stakeholder Dialogues work, Phase 1, page 61, Phase 2, page 68, Chapter 6: Tools, 6.9 Managing difficulties in Stakeholder Dialogues, page 191, 6.6 Saeting orders in Stakeholder Dialogue events, page 182***

Key factor 8: Delivery and outcome-orientation

Focus on outcomes is a prerequisite for commitment. When planning and implementing Stakeholder Dialogues, it is important to make sure that tangible results are always visibly achieved. If stakeholders get the impression that a dialogue process is not meant to deliver, or that the use of their inputs is not transparent, they will most likely withhold their engagement. Not every Stakeholder Dialogue can have the same level of outcome and delivery. However, it is important to keep in mind that the focus on outcomes is a prerequisite for commitment. In the planning Stakeholder Dialogues, it is, therefore, extremely important to ensure that outcomes become visible, no matter how small they are. These small outcomes can range from an agreement to meet again, to agreements on action plans, and small success stories in progress-reporting on implementation. It is helpful to assess the delivery capacity of a Stakeholder Dialogue system in Phase 1, and to keep track of this throughout all subsequent phases.

➲ ***Chapter 6: Tools, 6.7 Agreements in Stakeholder Dialogues, page 186, Chapter 5: resources 5.13 The role of communication in the 4 phases of Stakeholder Dialogues, page 148, Chapter 6: Tools, 6.8 Steering and implementation structures, page 189***

● As a time-bound implementation project, the **"African Cashew initiative" (ACi),** has a detailed implementation plan with milestones to be achieved by each implementing partner over a period of four years. The funders of the initiative, the Bill & Melinda Gates Foundation, the German Federal Ministry for Economic Cooperation and Development and a number of private sector companies each require progress reports to justify their further engagement in the initiative. Although implementation may be slow and complex in the five pilot countries, which vastly differ and require different approaches, there is a need to regularly report results in an aggregated way to keep the funders engaged.

KEY FACTORS FOR SUCCESSFUL STAKEHOLDER DIALOGUES

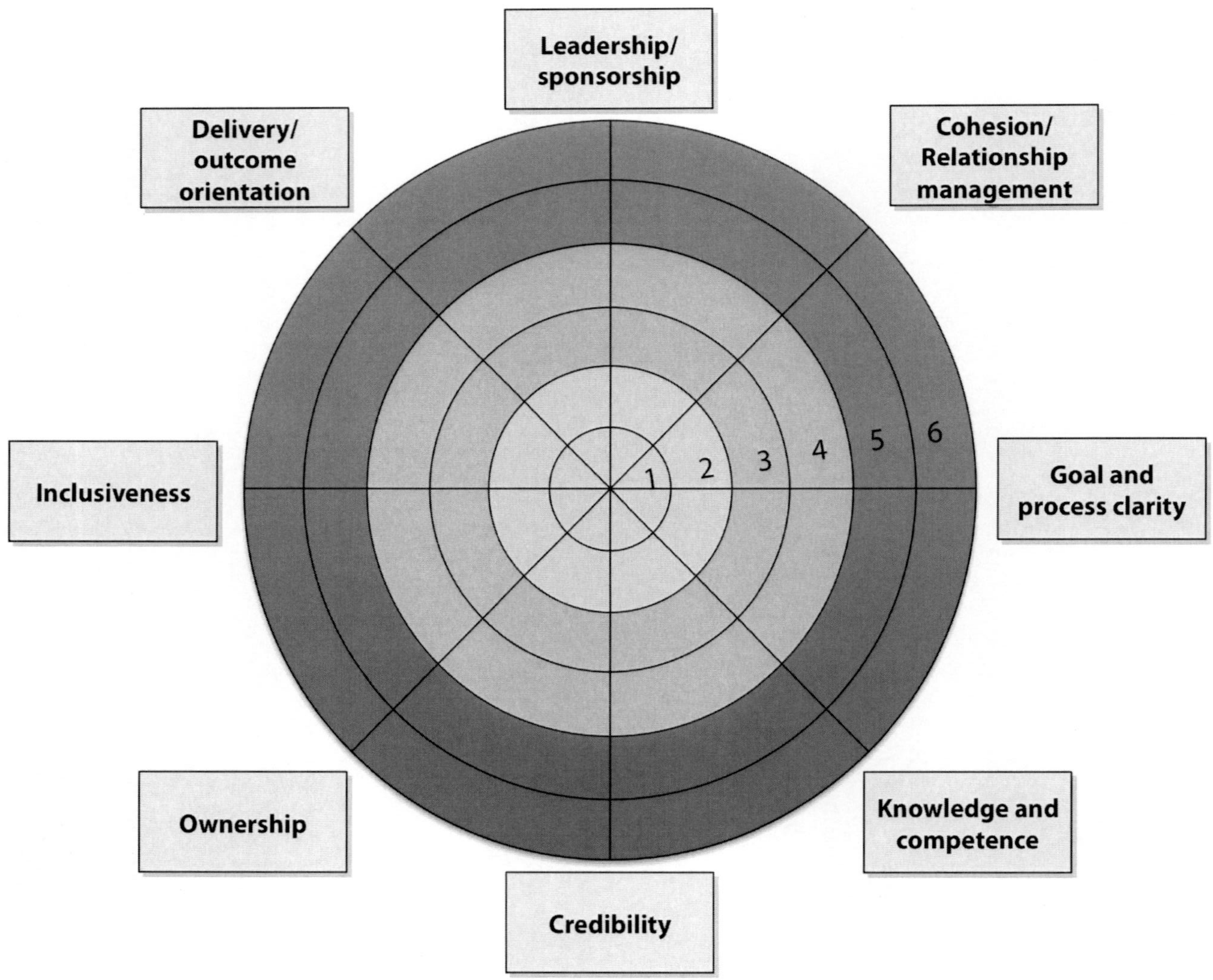

How to attend to the key factors for successful Stakeholder Dialogue

Key factor	Focus of attention
Leadership and high-level sponsorship	**Build a strong Container**[18] A committed core group as a good Container of actors represents the larger system of stakeholders. This core group is ideally composed of different stakeholders. Initially, it can be a small team consisting of the Stakeholder Dialogue initiators who are prepared to hold the process, reflect continuously and learn. They need to be prepared to go a long way towards achieving the goal, and to be willing to act as brokers between the Stakeholder Dialogue and the management of their institutions. In complex, well-structured Stakeholder Dialogue systems, this core group needs to be complemented by an agreed-upon, stakeholder-composed steering structure, such as a steering committee.
	Solicit high-level support In many Stakeholder Dialogues, particularly those that enter the political arena, high-level sponsorship is an important contributor to success. People with influence, but who do not take part in the actual dialogue themselves, need to have a positive – and, ideally, supportive – attitude towards content, goal and approach. In government-led Stakeholder Dialogues, high-level sponsorship often means a supportive high-level government official (such as a minister or secretary of state). In private-sector-led Stakeholder Dialogues, this sponsor could be the CEO of the initiating company (or companies) or the top management of a business association. And in multi-stakeholder initiatives or stakeholder partnerships, it could be high-level management of the participating institutions.
	Engage and commit main actors beyond the core group Not all stakeholders in a dialogue will be equally committed to process and the desired outcome. But if main actors are either indifferent to, or reserved about, the goal and the agreed-upon process, the likelihood of the Stakeholder Dialogue living up to its potential is low. Identifying influential key actors, engaging them and soliciting their support is crucial. Stakeholder Dialogues require participants who are willing to take intention and results back into their institutions and to ensure implementation. This also means that decision-makers in participating institutions need to support the Stakeholder Dialogue.
Cohesion and relationship-management	**Apply conscious relationship-management** Success in Stakeholder Dialogues, or the delivery of outcomes, thrives on good relationships. Give stakeholders the chance to meet people as people, by allowing informal settings before or during Stakeholder Dialogue events, ensuring respectful communication, and ensuring that all voices are heard.
	Ensure transparent communication Transparency is one of the main contributors to the development of trust. In most Stakeholder Dialogues, rules for communication need to be developed. While in the beginning it may be extremely important that a core group can easily communicate informally with each other, in Phase 2 and 3 of the Stakeholder Dialogue it becomes equally important to develop agreed-upon procedures on how to communicate with each other, how to communicate progress, and how to communicate with the larger public that is not participating in the Stakeholder Dialogue.
➲ *Chapter 2: The core group as container, page 56*	**Manage relationships with stakeholder institutions** It is important to take care of the relationship between the Stakeholder Dialogue and the management of the participating institutions: a good rapport is the road to success. The purpose and goal of the Stakeholder Dialogue must be relevant to the participating stakeholder groups and institutions. Keeping the goal clear is an important task for the core group and the representatives from stakeholder groups.

How to attend to the key factors for successful Stakeholder Dialogue

Key factor	Focus of attention
Goals and process clarity	**Keep the relevance of the Stakeholder Dialogue clear to all involved** When people are aware of the relevance of the Stakeholder Dialogue for them and their institutions, and of what their specific contribution is, they stay engaged. Awareness and interest is best generated in Phase 1 with bilateral conversations or small meetings. This preparatory phase also helps to shape the goal. In Phases 2 and 3, goal and process clarity is greatly supported by good communication and transparent facilitation of events.
	Attend to the alignment behind the goal Stakeholder Dialogues are based on consensual processes. The road to consensus, however, is most often bumpy. Stakeholder interests are not always put out openly on the table; backstage 'diplomacy' and more informal bilateral consultations might be required to keep participants on board. If people stay emotionally connected to the larger goal, it is easier to overcome dissent.
	Create reliable process architecture with authentic participation Since people help to implement what they can shape, they must feel that their participation counts. Reliable process and participation means sticking with agreed-upon plans, ensuring that participation is authentic, and achieving consensus on planning and process design. Particularly in fragile stakeholder systems, reliability of process is the glue that can prevent conflicts by binding a diverse group of stakeholders together behind a task.
Knowledge and competence	**Bring in content capacity-building and input of information** This can broaden the views of stakeholders: it can be benchmarking information, best-practice information, baseline studies, research results, training in content issues, exposure, etc., presented in a way in which stakeholders are not taught, but can reflect the inputs and adjust them to their particular case.
	Support involved actors in understanding the methodology of Stakeholder Dialogues: Stakeholders need to learn what it means to dialogue and collaborate in a non-hierarchical setting across institutions with participants coming from very different organizational or geographical cultures. Bringing in knowledge and capacity building for the implementation of Stakeholder Dialogues helps.
	Ensure adequate level of resources Stakeholder Dialogues require adequate funding for meetings, research, process facilitation and communication. Particularly if less resourceful stakeholder groups, such as NGOs, farmers, small business associations, women's groups and community organizations, are part of the dialogue, neutral funding is needed to ensure sufficient representation of stakeholders in the dialogue.

How to attend to the key factors for successful Stakeholder Dialogue

Key factor	Focus of attention
Credibility	**Attend to the reputation, neutrality and service orientation of initiators and process-management teams** Stakeholder initiators need to have a mandate to invite to a dialogue, or need to gain this mandate by convincing stakeholders that their effort is of service to them. Bringing in high-level support can be as important here as a transparent orientation towards the goal, the capability of initiators to listen to the concerns of the different stakeholders and their ability to build trust in a complex stakeholder system.
	Ensure participation of an adequate level of hierarchy Stakeholder representatives should have an adequate degree of decision-making power, or at least, hold a position in their organization that enables them to influence the course of action. If participating institutions only send representatives at a lower level of hierarchy, they may not see the relevance. A revived engagement process may be necessary.
	Ensure transparent decision-making procedures Stakeholders gain trust in the process when they are clear on how decisions are achieved in stakeholder partnerships or initiatives, or, in the case of stakeholder consultations, how recommendations are worked with and integrated into future plans. The more reliable planning and communication is, the more initiators or supporting process-management teams agree upon decision-making procedures, and the more participants acknowledge results. This is particularly important in Phase 3.
Inclusivity	**Integrate affected but often weaker stakeholder groups** This is not always easy. Some stakeholder groups do not have an 'organized voice', or they may not have the capacity to participate equally in a dialogue process. In some cases, weaker stakeholder groups may need organizational support first, capacity–building, or separate dialogues whose results are than brought into the larger dialogue. What is required to integrate weaker stakeholder groups should be part of understanding the context in Phase 1; how this can be done should be part of process designs in Phases 2 and 3.
	Integrate critical voices Stakeholder Dialogues, particularly on contentious topics, will always receive criticism – towards the goal, the process, the capability of the initiators, the political impact, etc. A credible dialogue process will be able to handle criticism. However, it may be helpful at the beginning to think about the most critical voices and how best to integrate them into the dialogue process. This is an important task in Phase 1, but will remain important throughout all phases. Some Stakeholder Dialogues agree in Phase 3 on a complaint mechanism: this ensures that criticism can be dealt with in a structured way.
	Ensure representivity A careful selection of participants following a stakeholder analysis and a context analysis can ensure that the Stakeholder Dialogue system can function as a microcosm representing the larger system of stakeholders. Concerned and affected stakeholders, specifically those crucial for the implementation of change, need to be adequately represented. One needs to take into account that only people with decision-making power can influence future behavior of their organization. At times stakeholders speak on behalf of others, often weaker stakeholder groups: here it is important to assess how far this is legitimate and the extent to which it really represents the interests of the weaker stakeholder group.

How to attend to the key factors for successful Stakeholder Dialogue

Key factor	Focus of attention
Ownership	**Assess the relevance of the goal for participating stakeholders** People engage when they feel that an outcome is relevant to their constituencies' lives and organizations, or that a significant change would affect them. Finding out about the relevance, the concerns and the expectation is an important task in Phase 1 and requires attention throughout all other phases.
	Guarantee the adequate say of the participating stakeholders in the outcomes of the dialogue Not every Stakeholder Dialogue can delegate decision-making power to the participants, as this depends on the form and purpose of the Stakeholder Dialogue. For consultative Stakeholder Dialogues, it is important to make clear how recommendations are dealt with, the way, sequence and form in which they will be integrated into decision-making processes. For cooperative Stakeholder Dialogues such as stakeholder initiatives and stakeholder implementation partnerships, it is important that rules for joint decision-making are agreed upon and adhered to (see Phase 2).
	Acknowledge contributions Stakeholders who make the effort of working towards a common goal in a Stakeholder Dialogue need to be taken seriously for their contribution of time and resources. If their expertise and experiences are acknowledged and they notice that their contribution counts, they will develop a strong sense of ownership.
Delivery and outcome-orientation	**Focus on achievable results and task orientation during stakeholder meetings** Stakeholder Dialogues in the implementation phase need to build 'prototypes' quickly, demonstrating that outcomes are achievable. Stakeholder meetings (see Phases 2 and 3) should always end with a short review of progress made, decisions taken or information about the use of contribution, time planning etc. It is also helpful when stakeholders work during meetings on actual tasks collaboratively: tasks such as joint comments on expert inputs, an assessment of the current situation, a paper to be agreed upon, priorities in action plans, joint recommendation to the political level, and so on. The experience of having created results together is an enormously important building block for collaborative commitment and ownership.
	Keep roles and structure clear Particularly in Phase 2 and 3, it is important to ensure that roles of different stakeholders in the dialogue process and implementation are clearly agreed upon. In government-led Stakeholder Dialogues, it is equally important to respect and take into consideration existing protocols, structures and procedures. If a Stakeholder Dialogue agrees to set up support or steering structures such as process management teams, steering committees, task forces or expert working groups, it is important that these structures are equipped with competent personnel and adequate resources as well as clear terms of references.
	Regularly review progress Results can be measured, plans can be reviewed, and the purpose of regular Stakeholder Dialogue meetings is to achieve visible progress. Progress reviews in the form of progress or monitoring reports are a cornerstone of outcome orientation. But even when Stakeholder Dialogue focus more on consultation it is important to inform all stakeholders involved regularly what the impact of the Stakeholder Dialogue had been (e.g. integration of certain recommendations into public policy processes or company policies, etc.)

4.2 Process-monitoring in Stakeholder Dialogues

Monitoring and evaluation procedures are familiar to most stakeholders in initiatives for sustainable development. In development cooperation, but also in private sector corporations, civil society projects and public sector services, some kind of monitoring and evaluation systems are known and applied. The form, focus and application might differ from sector to sector or organization to organization, but the main feature remains the same: the need to find agreed-upon instruments to track implementation and ensure learning.

> ➲ **Monitoring and evaluation[9]:**
>
> The OECD (2002a) defines monitoring and evaluation as follows: Monitoring is a continuous function that uses the systematic collection of data on specified indicators to provide management and the main stakeholders of an ongoing development intervention with indications of the extent of progress and achievement of objectives and progress in the use of allocated funds (p. 27). Evaluation is the systematic and objective assessment of an ongoing or completed project, program, or policy, including its design, implementation, and results. The aim is to determine the relevance and fulfillment of objectives, development efficiency, effectiveness, impact, and sustainability. An evaluation should provide information that is credible and useful, enabling the incorporation of lessons learned into the decision-making process of both recipients and donors (p. 21).

One can broadly distinguish between three different aspects of monitoring in Stakeholder Dialogues:

Activity and result-monitoring in Stakeholder Dialogues:

The purpose of this is to keep track of the activities agreed upon and to assess the results achieved. Guiding questions are:

- Did we do what we agreed to do in the implementation or action plan of the Stakeholder Dialogue?
- Is what we agreed to do leading to the agreed-upon outcomes?

Here, most of the known instruments of monitoring and evaluation can be used. It is important to keep track of activities agreed upon, agreements signed, road maps, and operational and implementation plans. Often, a designated process- or project-management team or secretariat, and/or a steering committee, is tasked with keeping track of activities and results. At the beginning of each larger stakeholder meeting or steering committee meeting, the process- or project-management team/secretariat usually provides an overview of the progress made. Activity-monitoring can start in Phase 1 already for the core group, and needs to be agreed upon between stakeholders as an essential element in Phase 2.

[9] *Kusek & Rist, 2004: page 12, OECD, 2002*

GETTING REFLECTIVE

Impact-monitoring for Stakeholder Dialogues[10]:

The purpose of this is to look beyond activities and results, and to assess if a Stakeholder Dialogue had the effect it was expected to have. Guiding questions are:

- What effect did Stakeholder Dialogues have on:
  - the participating institutions?
  - the beneficiaries?
  - a wider community?
- In what way has the Stakeholder Dialogue contributed to the goal that the stakeholders set out at the beginning of the dialogue process and agreed upon?
- Has the Stakeholder Dialogue approach served its purpose?

Impact-monitoring enables stakeholders to observe desired or undesired changes. It creates a foundation for discussions around such changes, and, subsequently, a basis for adjusting, planning and implementation, for reviewing approaches, or for creating the basis for continuous learning. As Stakeholder Dialogues are fragile and complex systems, impact-monitoring can only start when:

- the stakeholder collaboration system is stable enough and stakeholders trust each other sufficiently; and
- the Stakeholder Dialogue has shown its first results.

Impact-monitoring can build on participatory instruments available. It is best started during or at the end of Phase 3. Results can be integrated into Stakeholder Dialogue meetings.

Process-monitoring in Stakeholder Dialogues:

The purpose of this is to keep track of the quality of the process design and key factors for success. It helps to check if the Stakeholder Dialogue is leading towards the expected outcome – a commitment to progress.

Guiding questions are:

- What is the quality of process design and management of the Stakeholder Dialogue?
- Does the process we have designed lead to the expected result and effect?

Process-monitoring enables:

- the core group to keep track of the best possible process, and to learn from its experiences; and
- the stakeholders to understand the conditions of success of a Stakeholder Dialogue.

Process-monitoring is best done in the form of a self-assessment and can be based on the **key factors for successful Stakeholder Dialogues**. It needs always to be done in combination with result-monitoring and impact–monitoring. However, it has a specific role, and can provide key actors and wider stakeholder groups with a better sense of what it requires to make Stakeholder Dialogues a success. Process-monitoring can start early in a Stakeholder Dialogue (in Phase 1) if the core group decides to review the process design and its progress in relation to key factors regularly. In

[10] *see also Vahlhaus, Kuby, 2001*

this way, process-monitoring can continue throughout the Stakeholder Dialogue at different stages. It can also be introduced as a reflective tool to a wider group of stakeholders as a basis for a reflective dialogue on progress (in Phase 3). This, however, requires that the Stakeholder Dialogue system has reached a sufficient degree of stability and that people have begun to trust the approach. Process-monitoring can then be an innovative basis for learning together, and can increase the commitment to participation and implementation. It is important to see process-monitoring as a set of tools in the Stakeholder Dialogue that is used to improve outcomes and to adjust the steering or management of the process.

➲ **Process-monitoring**, as with all other forms of monitoring, is based on the continuous observation of objective and subjective data on specific indicators. It can tell key actors facilitating or coordinating the Stakeholder Dialogue how they are progressing. It can be combined with other forms of monitoring, such as activity- and result-monitoring based on implementation plans, or impact-monitoring based on the participatory involvement of stakeholders and beneficiaries.

Introducing monitoring procedures and self-assessment systems into Stakeholder Dialogues is a challenge. It is, by far, more complicated than doing this for one particular organization. Different participating stakeholder groups will have different approaches to monitoring. Different actors in Stakeholder Dialogues will have different assumptions about how change can happen. Stakeholder Dialogues are, particularly in the beginning, fragile and loose systems that depend on consensual agreements. Introducing monitoring systems too early can therefore endanger the process if the systems are imposed by one stakeholder group or by donor organizations. If trust is low, or if stakeholders are ambivalent towards the dialogue approach, a proposal to introduce monitoring systems can further endanger the process, as some stakeholders might perceive this as pressure to perform, an attempt to manipulate, or an exertion of undue power of influence. However, as with all change processes, Stakeholder Dialogues require monitoring. The benefits of introducing monitoring tools are as follows:

- **The initiators and the main actors need process learning**: it is important to track progress and systematically to learn from experiences, ensuring that success factors are noted and that early-warning systems function to avoid conflicts and difficulties.
- **Stakeholders can see progress**: this, in turn, increases their commitment to participate more.
- **Stakeholders become more aware of critical success factors for Stakeholder Dialogues**: as their understanding of the potential of Stakeholder Dialogues increases, they become more capable of participating and contributing.
- **Funders or external supporters build trust**: the building of confidence in the delivery capacity of Stakeholder Dialogues is an important issue in sourcing and maintaining the finances and resources required for implementation. It also keeps high-level sponsors on board.

➲ *Chapter 6, Tools: 6.10 Process-monitoring in Stakeholder Dialogues, page 195*

➲ *Links and literature: Monitoring page 210*

Monitoring in Stakeholder Dialogues

Type of monitoring	Purpose	Tools	Guiding questions
Activity- and result-monitoring	***Keeps track of activities agreed upon and assesses results achieved***	Any known and applicable monitoring system can be used and should refer to agreed-upon plans	• Did we do what we agreed to do in the implementation or action plan of the Stakeholder Dialogue? • Is what we agreed to do leading to the agreed-upon outcomes?

Impact-monitoring	***Looks beyond activities and results and assesses if a Stakeholder Dialogue had the effect it was expected to have***	If jointly agreed upon, this can also be done as an external assessment using methods known and understandable to the different stakeholders (as e.g. Rapid Appraisal, participatory impact monitoring, etc.)	• What effect did the Stakeholder Dialogue have on:
			  • the participating institutions?
			  • the beneficiaries?
			  • a wider community?
			• How has the Stakeholder Dialogue contributed to the goal set out at the beginning of the dialogue process and agreed upon between the different stakeholders?
			• Did the Stakeholder Dialogue serve its purpose?

Process-monitoring	***Keeps track of the quality of the process design and key factors for success, checks if it is leading towards the expected outcome – a commitment to progress***	Use the Dialogic Change Model, a self-assessment as described in this chapter, or an assessment or self-assessment among stakeholders with agreed-upon monitoring criteria	• What is the quality of process design and management of the Stakeholder Dialogue? • Does the process we have designed lead to the expected result and effect?

Ground rules for introducing monitoring in Stakeholder Dialogues

Do not introduce monitoring too early	As long as stakeholder facilitators are busy building trust and relationships, the introduction of a monitoring tool would probably endanger the process, unless it is done in a small and committed Container. At a later stage, once the Stakeholder Dialogue is running smoothly, monitoring can actually enhance trust and stabilize the system as people see that progress and monitoring supports the reliability of the approach.
Jointly agree on the form of monitoring	The introduction of a monitoring tool requires the commitment of at least the key stakeholders, but ideally of all participants of the Stakeholder Dialogue. This also reduces the fear of outside control.
Introduce self-assessment tools rather than external assessment	Unless jointly agreed upon by all stakeholders, it is much more helpful to progress if monitoring tools are based on a self-assessment approach.
Use instruments that everyone can understand clearly	Stakeholder Dialogues are already complex enough, so it is advisable to avoid any complicated tools.
Respect that all participating institutions will have their own monitoring and evaluation systems	There will always be stakeholder-specific approaches to monitoring. So, do not overload the Stakeholder Dialogue with more than that is absolutely necessary regarding monitoring. Make sure the monitoring does not conflict with any of the participating institutions' monitoring systems.

RESOURCES

RESOURCES

These resources provide background knowledge about concepts and approaches that have proved helpful for initiating and implementing Stakeholder Dialogues. They can be seen as the kind of background music that sets the tone for a successful change process. Each section in this chapter focuses on a particular aspect of change with relevance to implementing Stakeholder Dialogues, as described in Chapter 2.

Note that this chapter is not a substitute for change-management tools: there is ample literature available on this subject, and there are many different schools of thought on organizational and social change. Rather, these resources focus on a particular aspect that is neglected in conceptual thought on leadership and change management: the practical process steps of engaging a variety of actors in a successful dialogue and change process.

5.1 Stakeholder Dialogues as a step towards (global) learning societies

Stakeholder Dialogues are an approach to change in a complex environment where different actors need to work towards a common goal and collaborate across political, cultural or organizational differences. They can be seen as a pathway to a (global) 'learning society', a term adopted from the concept of 'learning organizations'[11].

Learning societies require:

- **respect for difference** – monocultures are not sustainable;
- **iterative learning** – only systems that integrate feedback will contribute to sustainability;
- **continuous innovation** – sustainability requires new forms of inventiveness;
- **dialogic competence** – a balance between difference in interest requires dialogue
- **a new conception of freedom** as a collective responsibility to ensure access to sustainable livelihood for all;
- **a new level of attention** – we need to be more aware of the effects of our actions; and
- **the development of a new level of consciousness** – only the increasing conception of the world as a whole will change behavior.

The Stakeholder Dialogue approach can be looked at from different perspectives:

The perspective of science on the evolution of consciousness	Stakeholder Dialogues are collective learning spaces. Sustainable development needs this balance at the edge of chaos; it needs innovative capacity, fast learning, cooperation and creativity.
The perspective of (economic) development	Stakeholder Dialogues acknowledge a cross-sector approach, ensuring that different expertise in societal development is brought together; they also hold the potential to alleviate economic imbalances and to balance differing economic interests.
The perspective of social and political science	Stakeholder Dialogues exemplify what is reality anyway: economy, environment and social structure are interrelated – any change in one area affects the others.
The perspective of change management	Stakeholder Dialogues are an answer to modern global and local complexity. Social advancement requires the participation and contribution of all relevant actors to ensure the progress of the system as a whole.

11 Senge 2000

5.2 Stakeholder Dialogues as an approach to dealing with the complexity of modern societies

Stakeholder Dialogues are an effective way of handling the complexity of modern societies. In our globalized world, dealing with complex situations is a decisive factor when searching for answers to modern global challenges. The table below shows the different types of complexity that any change endeavor in modern societies needs to take into account.[12]

[12] *Scharmer 2000*

Different types of complexity relevant for Stakeholder Dialogues

	Dynamic complexity[13]	*Generative complexity*	*Value-orientated complexity*	*Social complexity*
Characteristics	Cause and effect are separated in time and space	Patterns of the past cannot be transferred to the future	Civil, organizational and personal values are dissociated	World views and interests of stakeholders are different
New approach to change (relevant for Stakeholder Dialogues)	Integrated and systemic change, iterative planning, qualitative and quantitative monitoring	Innovation through dialogue: 'sensing' the future and 'presencing', changing through learning panels, openness to 'emerging solutions', cultivating contemplation	Value-based leadership and meaningful engagement, bringing to the surface the humanity in each person, fostering an authentic culture of contribution	Engage various views in structured conversations, ensure different voices are heard, develop cross-sector collaboration
Old approach to change	Linear planning, one part after the other, quantitative monitoring	Reference to existing experience, applying existing solutions	Norm and value setting, normative interventions, moral appeals	Separate tasks and keep boundaries between stakeholder groups neatly defined, defend territories, delegate tasks to experts, rely on authority

[13] *inspired by Scharmer, 2000*

Individual theory of change

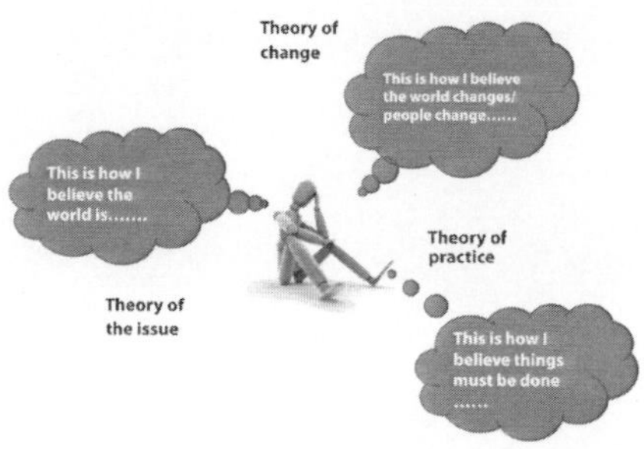

Most people build their action for change on an implicit model of change: often, a not entirely conscious belief in how and when change comes about and how people can best be influenced to change. This is built on the assumption that there is a causal process through which change comes about as a result of an intervention. Most initiatives, strategies and actions follow such an implicit or explicit 'theory of change': a way in which practitioners believe that individual, intergroup, and social/ systemic change will happen and how a specific action or intervention will produce positive results.

> ➲ **Implicit theories of change**
>
> We all distil our life experience in a certain way. We use this distillation to draw conclusions from our experience about how the world works, how it would be best to go about things, and which would be the best structure to work in. Most often, we unconsciously assume that what we are most used to or what we find most comfortable must be the best way of operating for everybody. Based on how we see the world and what we want to change or achieve (our implicit **theory of the thing**), we develop our implicit **theory of change**, and finally develop our **theory of practice.**

Example of a more linear implicit theory of change

Depending on where we have chosen to find our mental 'home', depending on the stakeholder group we operate in, our theories of change and theories of practices may differ enormously. This, not surprisingly, is a serious obstacle to Stakeholder Dialogues that are designed to lead to concrete change. Understanding one's own theories of change, therefore, helps one to notice the different paradigms among stakeholders, to respect them, and to address them accordingly as facilitator. Reflecting about one's own implicit theories of change helps not only to clarify one's own preferences, but also to accept that other stakeholders may have very different implicit theories of change. The following table suggests questions that can help a group of stakeholders, such as the core group, to reflect on their implicit theories of change.

Example of a more non linear implicit theory of change

RESOURCES

Reflective questions for a Stakeholder Dialogue Core Group on implicit theories of change

Theory of the 'thing'	• What is the situation that needs to change? • How did the current situation come about? • What are we trying to achieve? • What do we believe about how the intended change will manifest? • What then is our 'theory of the thing'?
Theory of change	• How do we believe change comes about? • How do we believe people change? • How do we change ourself? • How are we trying to influence reality? • What then is our 'theory of change'?
Theory of practice	• How do we usually do things? • What do we believe works best? • Which approach do we normally feel comfortable with? • What then is our 'theory of practice'?
Intention	• Why are we trying to do this? • What is our larger purpose for it? • How does our intention fit into a larger picture? • What larger story is our intention to change something a part of?
Attention to the system	• Who is involved? • Who or what are we trying to influence? • How do others see the issue? • Which theory of the thing do they hold? • Which theories of change do others have? • Which theories of practice do they have?
Attention to the self: one's own profile	• Who am I? • How does my internal world influence what I see, what I am trying to do and how I do it? • What is my own theory of change?

5.4 Stakeholder Dialogues and different dimensions of change

Often, there is a difference in how the individual believes change happens, and the underlying model of change of a particular professional intervention strategy, such as a project, initiative, or program. For example, somebody may firmly believe that change happens on the very personal level of insight, but is engaged in a project that is designed to change structures and regulations.

The model below helps you to become aware of the different dimensions of change that need to be taken into account for Stakeholder Dialogues as an approach to social or global change. Based on our implicit 'theories of change', we tend to focus on one or two particular dimension of change: where we think change most likely begins, or how we think people can best be brought to change[14]. We assume that others would think alike; if they do not, we try to convince them that our preferred dimension of change is the most important one.

However, all four quadrants of the dimensions of change in the model below offer complementary, rather than contradictory, perspectives. The right sides of the quadrants focus more on empirical observation, while the left sides of the quadrants consider subjective interpretation. The upper quadrants target more individual change, the lower quadrants collective change. Each by itself offers only a partial view of reality, and all of the four perspectives are equally valid at all levels of existence.

It is important to realize that people involved in a Stakeholder Dialogue may have preference for very different dimensions of change. Subsequently, they may focus their attention on one, or at least not all, of the quadrants. Stakeholder Dialogue facilitators, however, need to know their own preferences, but also need to learn to respect the differences. They can act from their area of strength, but still need to build Stakeholder Dialogues as change initiatives in a way that integrates all four dimensions of change.

[14] *Inspired by Ken Wilber's Integral Theory, see Wilber, 2003*

The four dimensions of change in Stakeholder Dialogues

	SUBJECTIVE	OBJECTIVE
INDIVIDUAL	***Transforming individual consciousness***	***Changing behavior patterns***
	• Self-awareness, personal and spiritual growth • Reflection and contemplation • Individual education • Transformation of mental models and belief systems • Broaden knowledge and competence • Individual skills-development • Individual value-orientation	• Broad education • Influencing through information • Influencing through requirements • Setting conditions • Offering incentives • Developing and making available new technologies • Influencing behavior through technology
	Underlying assumption: 'People change by themselves ... consciousness determines the being ...'	**Underlying assumption: 'People need to be influenced to change habitual patterns of behavior ...'**
COLLECTIVE	***Transforming culture and relationships***	***Changing structures and systems***
	• Changing dysfunctional collective patterns of thought and action • Collective reflection • Changing or reviving collective value systems • Promoting reconciliation, inclusion and participation • Interpersonal communication • Awareness of interdependence • Respect and recognition	• Reforming regulations • Creating bodies, organizations, institutions • Creating laws • Changing organizational structures • Institutional restructuring • Changing policies • Re-allocating resources • Developing systems to measure change
	Underlying assumption: ' ... only as a result of a transformation of collective patterns of thought and respectful dialogue people will act in a different way ...'	**Underlying assumption: '... structure determines consciousness ... and behavior ...'**

The model above can be used by Stakeholder Dialogue facilitators in the following way:

Self-awareness

Reflect on your preference, identify the dimension of change that you are convinced is the starting point for change. Also reflect in which area you are particularly strong, and which dimension of change you tend to leave to other people. Consider widening your scope of abilities so that you can work in all of the quadrants comfortably.

Systems awareness

Notice and observe different actors' implicit theories of change, and the dimensions of change that certain stakeholder groups may want to focus on. Respect and acknowledge the differences, and explore, if possible, the underlying assumption. Try to create an understanding for the integration of all quadrants.

Process competence

Learn to become more aware of which dimension of change is important at what time to bring into a Stakeholder Dialogue. Become attentive to what makes a Stakeholder Dialogue successful, and try to integrate the different dimensions of change. Include the different dimensions of change into the process design.

Example for integrating the four dimensions of change into process designs for Stakeholder Dialogue events:

➲ **Transforming individual consciousness:**

- Stay aware of the importance of personal encounter in Stakeholder Dialogues as a pre-requisite for change of attitudes and the willingness to collaborate. Hence, try to create possibilities for personal encounter during Stakeholder Dialogue events between different actors who might not know each other or may have conflicting interests. This could be informal-pre-meetings, small table discussions, informal gatherings or content work in task forces composed of different stakeholders.

➲ **Changing behavior patterns:**

- Identify the significance of information for the success of Stakeholder Dialogues. Include content-capacity building, if required. Develop communication strategies that ensure all stakeholders involved understand technical of scientific aspects of a required change.

➲ **Changing structure and systems:**

- Be courageous about meeting set-ups, and stay aware of the influence that physical structure has on results. For Stakeholder Dialogue events, create a space in which people can talk **with** each other, and do not become passive listeners or observers. Stick to programs, announcements and process plans, as they create a reliable structure that helps participants in a Stakeholder Dialogue to handle complexity.

➲ **Transforming culture and relationships:**

- Ensure that the more powerless stakeholders are listened to and that they have the opportunity to "tell their story". Design elements of exposure of participating actors to each other' world-views and experience.

5.5 Stakeholder Dialogues as a pathway to collective leadership

In a Stakeholder Dialogue, the development of a vision, or a future to be enacted, is a co-creative conversational process that often begins with a core group in its function as a good initial *Container* and is extended to a wider group of stakeholders. Stakeholder Dialogue facilitators need to learn when it is important to let differences emerge and when it is important to build consensus. Ideally, their engagement accesses the leadership aspiration of every other individual involved, and invites them to share leadership roles by supporting them to engage in collective co-creation towards a larger goal.

Change initiatives like Stakeholder Dialogues suggest new leadership concepts that take into account the diversity of stakeholders and create acceptable solutions for all. The notion of sustainability calls for a leadership paradigm that acknowledges the role of collective contributions to decision-making. Old paradigm leadership concepts are often based on the charismatic leadership of one individual. This implies that leadership capabilities are based on inherent characteristics or that leadership competence is acquired through technical, social and conceptual skills development.

The new paradigm of collective leadership breaks with the dichotomy of leaders and followers. It does this by embracing the human ability to collaborate across cultural, political, technical or disciplinary boundaries. Collective leadership does not undervalue the wealth and power of individual capabilities, ideas and vision, or the commitment and sustenance it requires to bring these to life. However, it adds a significant insight to the individual leadership endeavor: leaders know that their vision and contribution is important, but that it is never entirely manifested and held by one person or one stakeholder group alone. By the time it is expressed, it has undergone a process of its own emergence predicated on encounters and dialogues with many people. When leaders and change agents accept that the future is constantly emerging as a result of encounters between people, they become more aware of the quality of communication and the quality of relationships. The more this quality is built on dialogue and humanity, the more likely it will lead to sustainable co-creation.

➲ Collective leadership for sustainability

Collective leadership for sustainability is the capacity of a group of leaders to deliver their contribution to a more sustainable future through assuming joint and flexible leadership in service of the common good. At the core of collective leadership is the human capacity to dialogue and transform differences into progress. It enables the transcendence of self-centered views, a prerequisite for successfully addressing the challenges of globalization and sustainability.

Leadership challenges in Stakeholder Dialogues

Creating a case for change	Collective leadership emerges when, in addition to mutual benefit, people connect emotionally with the possibility of collectively making a difference.
Leading change in a non-hierarchical environment	In most Stakeholder Dialogues, there are differences in power and influence between stakeholders, but there is no clear hierarchy, particularly between different stakeholder groups.
Being open to new leadership roles	New leadership roles emerge: facilitating dialogue and brokering the commitment within participating organizations is required.
Developing one's communicative competence	Leadership action is often invisible, hardly structured, most often informal. It requires high flexibility in communicative competence and the willingness to learn the 'language' of different stakeholders.
Holding processes	Leadership in Stakeholder Dialogues needs the ability to hold a collective process together in the midst of conflicts and through phases of doubt and mistrust. It helps to develop the capacity to listen and to suspend judgment.
Being open to the unknown	Leadership in Stakeholder Dialogues invites experimentation: being willing to venture into the unknown is a prerequisite for success.
Embracing complexity	Stakeholder Dialogues take place in complex environments where different approaches and perspectives will always prevail.
Servicing a larger goal	Leadership in Stakeholder Dialogues requires servant leadership: the willingness to lead in favor of a common goal and consensus. This may require maintaining and exemplifying principles and values rather than positions.

RESOURCES

Collective leaders create pathways for collaboratively finding innovative solutions to the challenges of sustainability and for implementing them in a spirit of collective responsibility. This includes collaborative action and collective input into the creation of a future that many can own. They know that this requires personal maturity as much as the capacity to lead structural change.

Collective leadership is therefore held in an inner space of responsiveness and contribution to the common good. Collective leaders for sustainability cultivate the capacity to see future possibilities, and they facilitate innovation, inventiveness and collective learning. Their strength lies in their mindfulness because they have taken steps to access the whole of humanity through their own humanity. As a result, they become caring, compassionate and more concerned about the collective good.

For me, ***collective responsibility is responsibility shared****. I don't deny hierarchy, there could be hierarchy, but it is more … that whatever position you have you share the entire concern of the endeavor and then from that vantage point you are committed to complete your contribution.*

Manager of a multinational company

Is ***collective leadership*** *possible? You know, it is out there and has always been … it keeps the world in balance, barely, but still … It is enormously powerful and if one pays attention to that, that aspect of oneself, then suddenly one sees and hears how many others there are and how powerful it is, for me it is like a big stream, a river of interconnectedness … of people who have a similar sense of responsibility and a similar focus.*

Director of an NGO

I do believe ***collective leadership*** *is possible, I think it is probably the only viable option for the future. There might be times when command and control are needed. But I think collective leadership is not only possible but healthy. I* ***think of it as the way nature operates … as much complexity as needed and as much simplicity as needed, an adaptive system.***

Public sector representative

Collective leadership sets the pace for collective responsibility, commitment, and willingness to find a common solution to global and local challenges. Including stakeholders in consultation, collaboration, or decision-making processes builds trust and enables a creative and constructive exchange between participants. Motivated by a common purpose, people start to build relationships with each other that are respectful enough to create a base for result-oriented collaboration.

5.6 Enhancing dialogue: The art of thinking together[15]

Communication in Stakeholder Dialogues takes place in two different types of structures. The first kind is the visible, more concrete structure, such as the physical space of a room, an agenda, a program, and so on. The second kind of structure is one that is felt subjectively, but not necessarily apparent to everybody. These could be atmosphere, moods, un-discussables, memories, injuries, mistrust or trust, or hidden agendas.

These visible or underlying structures have a greater effect on the course of a meeting, its content and its results then we would like to believe. Sometimes, facilitators try to change structures by changing agendas, allowing the space, moving chairs or tables, or shifting between large-group and small-group conversations. But often it is not the visible structure that makes a difference in a conversation. The underlying mental models, mental frames or belief systems determine much more of what is said, what is unsaid, and how things are said. Conversation can only really change if these underlying structures are accessed. Stakeholder Dialogues are more likely to be successful when participants can overcome underlying, repetitive patterns of thought. Only then they can find new and innovative solutions for challenges, or reach agreements about implementation quickly. The goal is to bring people into direct dialogue: this increases the chance of hardened positions in a Stakeholder Dialogue being softened in favor of greater engagement and increased creativity, so that participants begin to feel like part of the solution.

Dialogic conversations are conscious designs of communication processes that allow people to voice their reality and create an atmosphere of respect and inclusion. Creating and maintaining a space in which people can express themselves, contained through respectful structure, is an important task for facilitators. Becoming aware of structure – the formally agreed structure as well as the subtle structures that people have not formally agreed upon –can be helpful for Stakeholder Dialogue facilitators who intend to enact the wisdom of the whole through communication. Patterns of behavior, as a kind of invisible order, are a result of the ways in which people communicate with and relate to each other, as well as to the task, the Stakeholder Dialogue and the change endeavor.

The basic principle of every good dialogue is creating an atmosphere of 'thinking together'. This raises the energy for acting collectively. Stakeholder events or meetings with a predominantly 'thinking-alone' mindset often only achieve a low level of collective intelligence. More important actors often dominate communication and most participants do not feel their contribution made a difference to the results. This can impede real commitment on the side of the participating stakeholders and prevents them from taking a collective approach to solving a challenge. This is most obvious when stakeholder events are characterized by long official speeches, in which little or no room for exchange is given, or when one stakeholder group's communication dominates another's so much that the latter group cannot express its members' opinions. The goal of a well-structured Stakeholder Dialogue should, then, be, as far as is formally possible, to replace rigid forms of communication with a more interactive event model.

On the path to a form of communication that enables this, the following typical patterns of communication are observable in large groups: the order in which the table below presents them reflects the development of 'thinking–alone' patterns to 'thinking–collectively' patterns.

[15] *The deliberations are inspired by the work of William Isaacs, 1999*

Communication patterns

<table>
<tr><th>Communication patterns</th><th>Typical characteristics</th><td rowspan="6">Everyone thinks for themselves

Individual intelligence at the forefront and individuals compete with one another

An atmosphere of thinking together emerges

Collective intelligence is possible</td></tr>
<tr><td>Serial monologue</td><td>• Statements made
• Little reference made to other contributions
• No questioning of background</td></tr>
<tr><td>Discussion and debate</td><td>• Winner/loser situation
• No questioning of background
• Attempts to control results
• Attempts to convince others</td></tr>
<tr><td>Facilitated discussions</td><td>• Steered discussions
• Structured questioning of background
• Equal participation</td></tr>
<tr><td>Reflective dialogue</td><td>• Integration of different approaches
• Clarification of underlying assumptions, and decisions made
• Search for deeper concerns</td></tr>
<tr><td>Generative dialogue</td><td>• Transforms tactical thinking
• Allows the emergence of collective intelligence
• Leads to insight and identification
• Promotes innovation and respects differences</td></tr>
</table>

Communication pattern: serial monologues

Many meetings in institutions follow a design that lacks consciousness. One person alone speaks, or the meeting takes the form of serial monologues. Participants give their views one by one, without really making reference to the preceding speaker's contribution. This pattern can be worsened if the meeting has a speaker list. Although it is important that statements can be made in a sequential way, this structure evokes a series of individual statements but does not always lead to a productive discussion. Sometimes, such meetings have to be cut short, before all the speakers have expressed their views. The flow of the series of statements does not help the group to become more intelligent as a group. Instead of building on each other's thoughts, participants often compete with each other and attempt to convince others of their own position.

> ➲ This pattern of communication is not uncommon for Stakeholder Dialogues in international organizations, where political positions and protocol play a central role. Some speakers only show up when it is their turn to speak and often haven't heard the others' contributions to the discussion. But even at 'round table' discussions, where a u-shaped table arrangement with microphones is usually used, a similar situation can easily occur where individuals adamantly state their own point of view without constructively contributing to the overall result. Such patterns of communication may at times be unavoidable, but Stakeholder Dialogue facilitators should shift these patterns towards an atmosphere of communication in which participants reference each other and build on each others' contributions.

Communication pattern: discussion or debate

When the topic and the structure of a meeting allow for a real discussion, and where tension is allowed to surface, participants start to reference each other more, even though such a discussion can get stuck at two people or factions' opposing views. Often, a winner/loser situation emerges, with the stronger party, or those who have stronger arguments, ending up determining the direction of the discussion. Such discussions do not always lead to conflict, but the inherent tendency is always there. The more the conversation gets stuck in opposites, the more time is wasted: themes get repeated, and sometimes the discussion needs to be stopped by force and the topic changed. These conversations sometimes lead people to conclude that they need an outside facilitator.

➲ This pattern of communication is typical of parliamentary discussions. The goal is to expand one's position and convince others of one's opinion through discourse. This pattern also exists in Stakeholder Dialogues. A controversial argument can provide an important insight into the different aspects of a situation. But if this type of discussion persists, no solution can come of it. Even when one stakeholder group might believe it has convinced the other side, it may just be that the other side may have silently given up the fight. This is not a productive situation for continued constructive collaboration. It is, therefore, important for Stakeholder Dialogue facilitators to scout out the different positions and opinions before a stakeholder event kicks off. They can then structure the dialogue event to allow all positions to be heard. When two contradicting positions are at odds, informal bilateral preparatory conversations are important, as is creating an opportunity for people to get to know each other personally. This can be vital to the success of the Stakeholder Dialogue.

Communication pattern: Facilitated discussions

Facilitated discussions allow people to become aware of structures and patterns through the help of the facilitator. Particularly in cases where very different schools of thought or even world views are juxtaposed, the facilitator can create a suitable setting in which result-oriented and structured dialogue can take place with mutual respect. In such conversations, the facilitator helps people to generate a collective view of reality and to go beyond their limited individual perspectives. Communication acquires a new quality that can be felt in the room.

➲ This communication pattern has become typical for meetings in private-sector and civil-society organizations, but is used less often in the public sector. Good facilitation is a key to success in Stakeholder Dialogues. It is important to keep in mind that the facilitation team is not solely responsible for the quality of the communication: this can occur when participants lose sight of their dialogic competence. This is why the facilitators should give participants in a Stakeholder Dialogue ample opportunity to work in small groups without the assistance of a facilitator. At larger stakeholder events, this can be achieved by using round tables at which specific topics can be discussed throughout the event. The facilitators' role is to create an appropriate formal structure for the event so that the results of these smaller working groups can be presented to the plenary. Further discussion or decisions can be based on the results that the smaller working groups present.

Communication pattern: Reflective dialogue

Stakeholder Dialogues that intend to overcome rigid positioning require different forms of reflection. Reflection is collective (and individual) thinking about what went well and what did not go well, what took place, which invisible structure played out and what outcomes occurred or did not occur as a result of it. It leads people to start thinking about the process, about themselves in it, and, finally, it enables them to ask questions that lead to new levels of insight.

The step into **reflective dialogue** happens when people start thinking together, questioning assumptions and revisiting beliefs. Now the underlying structures of the thinking, as they come to the surface, can be changed. Participants develop a new quality of openness for each others' presence and history. Indicators for the emergence of reflective dialogue are: willingness for inquiry into difference; new insights that had not been there before; new themes coming up; or a deeper understanding of opposing positions.

Ideally, this process includes reflection on the overall quality of the communication: how satisfied/dissatisfied are we with our communication? To achieve this, Stakeholder Dialogue facilitators can integrate a feedback process, jointly carry out a strength/weakness analysis, or put a process-monitoring system in place. The more anchored a reflection process becomes in a group, the more easily those involved in the Stakeholder Dialogue will be able to handle difficulties and conflict. Once people have learned to talk about how they interact with each other, they can easily put conflicts aside. This can enable participants eventually to induce the process of reflection without the help of a facilitator. Indicators for a reflective dialogue are: individuals' openness to new opinions; new insights derived from conversations; new topics coming up; a deeper understanding of divergent positions; and questioning how to access the real topics that need to be discussed to take the dialogue forward.

> ➲ Joint reflection – especially concerning communication – is not common in more formal environments. But herein lies an enormous potential for improving communication, and also for promoting a result-oriented approach in Stakeholder Dialogue. Establishing a culture of reflection within a Stakeholder Dialogue is indispensible. This can start in the core group meetings by including a reflection on the progress and on internal communication. During Stakeholder Dialogue events, the first step can be to evaluate the event itself in smaller groups, looking back and reflecting on progress and internal communication, and then finally presenting these thoughts to the plenary.

Communication pattern: Generative dialogue

People who get used to communication in a dialogic context often experience conversations in which the participants genuinely listen, and are not only constructive, but also contribute to the discovery of new, innovative solutions. Those involved build on each other's contributions, and are mutually and genuinely interested in finding a common solution.

Establishing generative dialogue has practical advantages: it saves time and cost, decisions improve, solutions are found more quickly, and all involved are dedicated to the implementation. It becomes less and less important to defend one's own position; instead each participant is more interested in finding the optimal solution by tapping into the collective wisdom.

➲ Not all participants in a Stakeholder Dialogue may have developed their dialogic competence to the point that they can participate in a generative dialogue from the very beginning. Nevertheless, a good stakeholder process can assist stakeholders in developing this competence more rapidly. A milestone along this path is the internal communication culture that develops within the core group, if it has become a good *Container*. Along with the dialogic competence that the core group exhibits in its members' interaction with other stakeholders, this culture can enhance the quality of communication. At stakeholder events, it is important to leave room for internal exchange in the context of smaller working groups: this helps the individuals' respect for each other to develop more rapidly, which, in turn, improves their capacity to deal with differences. When smaller groups work with a focus on results, a feeling of having achieved something significant develops within the group, thus increasing the group members' willingness to deal with conflict constructively.

Generative dialogue is as old as the history of the human race. Every one of us has, at one moment or another, has experienced this kind of communication (even if it was with ourselves), and felt it as being positive, satisfying and even inspiring. Nonetheless, this ease of dialogue in our everyday life has become lost in the organizational and social structures that don't encourage this kind of exchange. However, it is possible to re-learn (or rediscover) the art of dialogue – but not in the prescribed manner of rules of behavior, specific instruments, or negotiation techniques.

On the way to developing one's own dialogic competence, it is also helpful to understand one's own capacity to listen and judge the quality of communication. By understanding what encourages or discourages a culture of 'thinking together', we discover the key to doing it differently. Our way of thinking actually shapes reality in a much more profound fashion than we might be prepared or able to admit, so a culture of 'thinking together' precedes a culture of collective action.

➲ ***Chapter 5, Resourcs, 5.8.2 Dialogic practices, page 137***

➲ In Stakeholder Dialogues that are not well designed, serial monologues often stand at the forefront: individual stakeholders give statements, without ever entering into a constructive dialogue with each other. However, it is much more important to facilitate authentic exchanges between stakeholders. When planning a Stakeholder Dialogue, it is of utmost importance to allow for a structured exchange of different opinions and to make sure all opinions are equally heard. Well-facilitated dialogues are a key success factor for stakeholder processes. The more the members of a stakeholder system grow together and develop feelings of mutual respect, the sooner it can reach the stage of reflective or generative dialogue.

5.7 Stakeholder Dialogues and the emergence of collective intelligence

If people think of dialogue, they often imagine the original form of dialogue where participants sit in a circle and open up to a meaningful conversation with each other. The purpose of such format often is to slow down communication, so that words and their meaning can be listened to, but also the space between the words gets attention. People who have experienced open dialogue sometimes report an impactful experience: new insights occur, their positions shifted, their judgments about other people changed, or they saw new paths opening during the conversation. It is important to keep the original purpose of dialogue in mind: enhancing people's ability to see the larger picture of a situation, so to say 'the whole', more easily as a result of genuine interest in each other's thought process.

> *"It is clear if we are to live in harmony with ourselves and with nature we need to be able to communicate freely in a creative movement in which no one permanently holds to or otherwise defends his own ideas … When we come together to talk, or otherwise to act in common, can each of us be aware of the subtle fears and pleasure sensations that block his ability to listen freely? Without this awareness, the injunction to listen to the whole of what is said will have little meaning. But if each one of us can give full attention to what is actually blocking communication while he is also attending properly to the content of what is communicated, then we may be able to create something new between us, something of very great significance for bringing to an end the at present insoluble problems of the individual and society."* [16]
>
> *David Bohm, 1996*

Stakeholder Dialogues will rarely be conducted as circles of freely flowing conversations. Most often, they require a more structured setting, a protocol determined by the participating stakeholder groups, and time pressure to achieve results. But they are based on the same premises as all ancient forms of dialogue: **the assumption that creative evolutionary processes require a continuous exchange of views, ideas and possible ways forward.** Only this leads to the emergence of collective intelligence.

> *"I don't know if you have ever examined how you listen, it doesn't matter to what, whether to a bird, to the wind in the leaves, to the rushing waters, or how you listen in a dialogue with yourself, to your conversation in various relationships with your intimate friends, your wife or husband … If we try to listen we find it extraordinarily difficult, because we are always projecting our opinions and ideas, our prejudices, our background, our inclinations, our impulses: when they dominate we hardly listen at all to what is being said … In that state there is no value at all. One listens and therefore learns, only in a state of attention, a state of silence, in which this whole background is in abeyance, is quiet; then, it seems to me, it is possible to communicate … real communication can only take place where there is silence."*
>
> *Krishnamurti*

16 Bohm, 1996: 4-5

5.8 Developing dialogic competence

In a dialogic approach, intervention is a very consciously designed communicative action designed to produce positive change in a stakeholder system. Every intervention, even the smallest, reflects on the functionality of the system. Entering into Stakeholder Dialogues is a challenge to the setup of existing organizational and inter-organizational systems with their relational and communicative structures. It is often, at times, a challenge for participating actors: they expose themselves to communicating with people whom they may under normal circumstances never meet. In changing stuck communicative structures lies the chance to change the nature of the system as a whole, ideally to improve its function. From this point of view, Stakeholder Dialogues are an attempt to create new communicative (and delivery) structures that can help to correct malfunctioning structures for the common good. Stakeholder Dialogue facilitators can perform their task better when they understand and explore helpful and unhelpful communicative structures before and during a Stakeholder Dialogue.

Stakeholder Dialogues bring actors with different perspectives and diverging interests together. In addition, communication in Stakeholder Dialogues usually takes place in a non-hierarchical context. Power differences do exist in such dialogues, but there is, most often, no line of authority between different stakeholder groups. Agreements and achievements must be reached through consensus and collaboration. This makes developing the core group's dialogic competencies paramount, so that its members learn to understand which communication patterns can move a dialogue forward and which ones can hinder it. This will allow them to use communication constructively, create lasting trust, avoid or overcome crises, and maintain a shared orientation between all stakeholders.

The dialogic approach is the foundation for consensus-oriented communication structures: it helps to improve collaboration, to make implementation of agreements more effective, and to achieve visible results.

The following models can help Stakeholder Dialogue facilitators to both develop their own dialogic competence and encourage a constructive communication between stakeholders.

The **four action modes** describe observable communicative behavior. The **four dialogic practices**[17] describe an underlying dialogic capacity – a mix between inner stance and communicative competence – which determines one's ability to contribute constructively to effective communication.

Stakeholder Dialogue facilitators need to develop their dialogic competence when they want to have a significant effect on the success of a Stakeholder Dialogue. They need to:

➲ *Introduction, see page 17*

- recognize their strengths and weaknesses in the dialogue and expand their competence to enact all modes and practices;
- determine which of the four action modes and the four dialogic practices are present or missing in the Stakeholder Dialogue (and possibly need special attention); and
- learn how they can help to bring in all aspects of constructive stakeholder communication (modes and practices) to strengthen result-orientation.

In the following section, both concepts – the four action modes and the four dialogic practices – are presented with reference to **self-awareness**, **systems awareness** and **process competence**.

[17] The models are based on the Action Positions of David Kantor, ➲ www.davidkantortheory.com, and the dialogic practices developed by William Isaacs (1999)

5.8.1 The four action modes

The action modes are based on decades of interpersonal communication research. This research has shown that communication is most effective when all four action modes are present in communication in a dynamic balance.[18]

The action mode **'move'** has as its underlying intention the setting of **direction**: it makes proposals, initiates, suggests, and pushes things forward. If one party lacks this movement, other parties might dominate it. If one party is constantly in move mode, the Stakeholder Dialogue system might become unbalanced, because direction will mainly be set by one actor. In dealing with dominating moves it is important to help the protagonists understand other actors' points of view.

The action mode '**oppose'** has as its underlying intention **correction**, and shows a different way of seeing things. Unheard or ignored, it can turn into opposition. If continuously ignored, this may turn into violent opposition. In Stakeholder Dialogues, this movement in its mild form is reflected in any action that seeks to counteract positions, suggests different routes to take, blocks the process, or threatens to exit the Stakeholder Dialogue. A continual pattern of move/oppose in a Stakeholder Dialogues blocks progress, and will finally lead to failure. In dealing with opposition it is important to inquire into the underlying intention of correction.

The action mode '**follow'** has as its underlying intention **completion**: it aims at consensus, integration, and is most often shown through confirming addition or agreement. Without some kind of following movement, Stakeholder Dialogues cannot succeed, as consensual agreements are the cornerstone of success. However, if a continuous pattern of move/follow develops, this might be as detrimental to the Stakeholder Dialogue in the long run as constant move/oppose patterns would be. Move/follow patterns seem to be effective and fast in the short term, but they usually lack the different perspectives and corrective views necessary for quality decision-making. In dealing with premature consensus or completion it is important to deliberately ask for differences.

The action mode '**bystand'** has as its underlying intention the bringing in of a different perspective. It is more than just observation, but an active search for **perspective** and collective wisdom, often as an attempt to inquire into the situation and into the interests of participating actors, or to describe observations that can take the conversation forward. When this action mode is missing, participants in a Stakeholder Dialogue lack the ability to look from a distance and assess their joint progress. But if is well-developed, regular reflection becomes part of the process.

If any of these four movements are missing or out of balance, a Stakeholder Dialogue will similarly become imbalanced. Dissatisfaction will arise, results will not be achieved, crises will become more common, and mistrust will spread.

All four action modes are necessary to move the dialogue along. Stakeholders enact the action modes temporarily as the conversation progresses. The person who opposed in one instance may make a constructive suggestion (move) in another, or inquire into a problem (bystand) later on. Without a **move**, there is no direction. Without the f**ollow** there is no completion. Without the **opposition**, there is no critical thinking and correction, and without the **bystanding**, there is no perspective, and no breakthrough to new solutions or a deeper understanding.

[18] *Adopted from: Kantor 1997: 45*

Stakeholder Dialogues require the skillful presence of the four action modes and their underlying dialogic practices. This can ensure a balance between **inquiry** – seeking to understand oneself, a situation and other points of view – and **advocacy** – arguing for a certain aspect at stake and making oneself understood.

The following tables summarize the characteristics of each action mode and elaborate how their presence or absence will manifest in Stakeholder Dialogues.

THE FOUR ACTION MODES

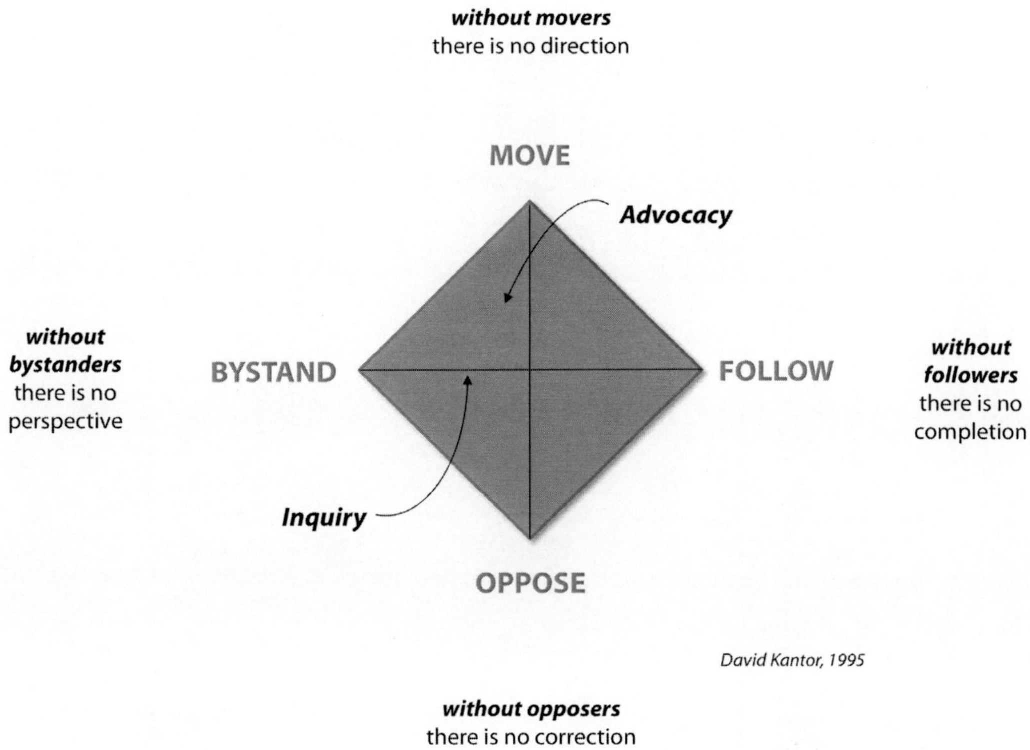

David Kantor, 1995

Table: The four action modes – aspects to consider for Stakeholder Dialogue facilitators

Action movement	*Characteristics and underlying intention*	*Aspects to consider for Stakeholder Dialogue facilitators*	
		Self-awareness	***Hints for systems awareness/process competence***
MOVE	The basic characteristic of 'move' is the need to push things forward. The underlying intention is to give direction and ensure progress and achievements.	Individuals who are strong in making things move often give direction, make suggestions, or initiate action. The absence of this movement means a lack of focus, determination and result-orientation.	If stakeholders are passive and do not bring the process forward: • If a stakeholder group appears to be lacking in this movement, it may be because the group has difficulties expressing itself or is badly organized. It could also be that despite its widespread influence, a stakeholder group has little or no interest in change. If stakeholders try to determine outcomes: • If a stakeholder group is constantly trying to influence the course, this can create an imbalance in the stakeholder system. Other participants will feel threatened, or gain the impression of having little influence on the agenda that the other stakeholder group is pushing. There is the danger that the dominated group may withdraw from the dialogue process.
	Important questions		
		• Am I moving change forward? • Am I considering other points of view? • Am I leaving sufficient room for innovation?	• Is the Stakeholder Dialogue result-oriented? • Are we getting things done? • Are all stakeholders as engaged as they should be? • Can they express themselves adequately?

Table: The four action modes – aspects to consider for Stakeholder Dialogue facilitators

Action movement	***Characteristics and underlying intention***	***Aspects to consider for Stakeholder Dialogue facilitators***	
OPPOSE	The movement of 'oppose' is strongly characterized by its underlying intention to correct. This can be both positive and negative. On the positive side, this movement challenges that which already exists, asks critical questions from another point of view, or indicates oversights. On the negative side, things may be brought into question simply out of principle.	***Self-awareness***	***Hints for systems awareness/process competence***
		Individuals with a well-developed movement of 'oppose' are critical and easily find faults – but they also make sure that all aspects of a situation are taken into account. Individuals with an underdeveloped 'oppose' movement tend to lack a critical eye. An overdeveloped 'oppose' mode risks permanently counteracting positions and making antagonism a routine practice.	Communication can become compromised in a Stakeholder Dialogue if too little understanding is shown for others' opinions. This can result in threats of breaking off the dialogue, public attacks on the dialogue's content, or a subtle undermining of the initiative's progress.
		Important questions	
		• Do I give constructive criticism? • Am I able to handle criticism well? • Am I oriented towards finding solutions?	• Are all stakeholders' points of view adequately acknowledged? • How can I assure that even critical points of view are brought to attention?

'Move' *and* **'oppose'** *are closely interlinked and often form a communication pattern which can take place between stakeholder groups – for example, between the private sector and civil society or between individual participants (when one individual makes a suggestion and another constantly challenges him or her). These patterns are quite common in Stakeholder Dialogues and can bring them to a standstill or even cause them to fail completely. Stakeholder Dialogue facilitators have the important function of guaranteeing that disagreement is sufficiently heard, that groups that want to move forward can develop an understanding for other points of view. They also need to ensure that all actors really support a decision made and that action follows commitment. It is important to understand what drives major criticism, to inquire into it, and to redirect it into more solution-oriented conduct.*

Table: The four action modes – aspects to consider for Stakeholder Dialogue facilitators

Action movement	*Characteristics and underlying intention*	*Aspects to consider for Stakeholder Dialogue facilitators*	
		Self-awareness	***Hints for systems awareness/ process competence***
FOLLOW	The movement of 'follow' is essentially an element of completion through confirming addition or agreement. Without some kind of following movement, Stakeholder Dialogues cannot succeed, as consensual agreements are the cornerstone of a successful dialogue.	Individuals with a well-developed movement of 'follow' are quick to agree and are often consensus-oriented. Underdeveloped, this movement can lead to endless discussions. An overdeveloped 'follow' lacks the ability to engage in critical discussions.	Some Stakeholder Dialogues easily achieve agreements without controversial discussion, However, if a continuous pattern of move/follow develops in a Stakeholder Dialogue without any concerns being brought forward, it must be asked whether all important aspects are truly being addressed. It may also be the case that one stakeholder group is imposing its agenda on the others. Move/follow patterns seem to be effective and fast in the short term, but may lack the difference of perspectives more sustainable solution require. On the other hand, if agreements cannot be reached, Stakeholder Dialogue facilitators must question if the interest in a common goal has been verified in the first place. Informal talks should be used to determine if criticism regarding certain issues has been withheld and if these issues need to be brought up again in the agenda.
	Important questions		
		• What can I agree with in good conscience to move the issue forward? • Can I support suggestions even when they are not my own?	• How can I determine whether support is sound and sincere? • How can I encourage consensus?

Table: The four action modes – aspects to consider for Stakeholder Dialogue facilitators

Action movement	*Characteristics and underlying intention*	*Aspects to consider for Stakeholder Dialogue facilitators*	
BYSTAND	The movement of 'bystand' is an active search for perspective and collective wisdom, often as an attempt to inquire into the situation, into the interests of participating actors, or to describe observations.	***Self-awareness***	***Systems awareness/Process competence***
		Individuals with a well-developed movement of 'bystand' have an inner desire to listen to different perspectives and to mediate between different standpoints. Often, facilitators seem to have a natural tendency to bystand actively. In Stakeholder Dialogues in which actors become confrontational (pattern: move/oppose), it helps if facilitators can see both sides of a situation and unearth the true reasons for discord. Stakeholder Dialogues need their participants to be able to reflect on and rethink their positions.	If a stakeholder group's tolerance for differences of opinion is low, or if it has little patience for dealing with different opinions or mindsets, it can be difficult to create an atmosphere of mutual respect. Stakeholder Dialogue facilitators can positively influence such a situation by demonstrating respect and tolerance and by assuring that all opinions are heard and respected. If too many stakeholders passively observe as bystanders and do not partake actively, the dialogue cannot be successful. Results will only be generated by selected stakeholders, and the focus will not be on achieving joint results.
	Important questions		
		• How can I distance myself from the situation and observe it from a bird's eye view? • Am I able to understand a point of view that I don't share?	• How can I assure that different points of view are respected? • How can I turn passive stakeholders into active and engaged participants? • How can I create a forum for different opinions?

THE DIALOGIC PRACTICES

How do I contribute to people speaking from the heart? How do I help people to take collective responsibility?

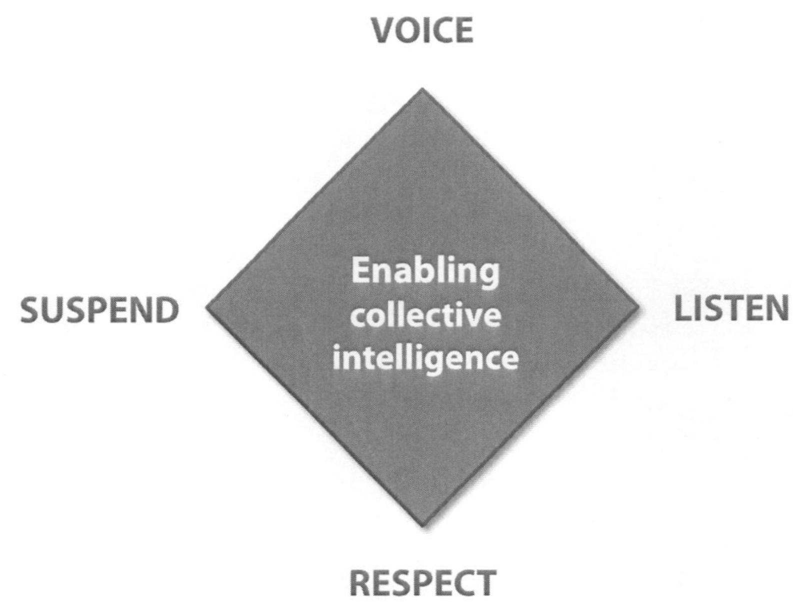

How do I help enabling an atmosphere of inquiry into the different points of view?

How do I contribute to a climate of tolerance and mutual understanding?

How do I help people see the larger issues and the common goal behind the difference on the surface?

5.8.2 The dialogic practices[19]

Dialogue is a dynamic process that requires a delicate balance of inquiry (seeking new understanding) and advocacy (seeking to be understood). Inquiry needs the skills of listening and the ability to suspend judgment: only then can one gain a deeper and newer understanding of an issue, a stakeholder position or a way forward. Advocacy requires the courage to speak one's voice or to speak on behalf of others; to convey a purpose and defend a course of action; and, at the same time, to underscore one's position or criticism of other positions while respecting difference. Balanced advocacy and inquiry is effective in helping participants of a Stakeholder Dialogue to see the whole picture and the best possible way forward. The more participants gain an (often intuitive) understanding of the dialogic practices of **voice, listen, respect and suspend**, the higher the likelihood that a Stakeholder Dialogue will move towards a communicative pattern of 'thinking together' – a generative dialogue. This type of dialogue stimulates collective intelligence, and, thus, the development of ideas; it facilitates efficient decision-making processes and encourages the taking of responsibility.

In this way, the four dialogic practices describe a quality of communicating and entering into conversation with others. They reflect an inner attitude as well as an outer ability to engender constructive, solution-oriented communication.

Successful Stakeholder Dialogues are often (most often unconsciously) built on the growing ability of all participants to exhibit their competence in enacting the quality of relating and communicating: be it in direct encounter with each other or in the way Stakeholder Dialogue events are designed. The presence of the dialogic practices changes the flow of the communication: consensus is easier to reach, but is built on the naming and respecting of different perspectives.

The following tables summarize the characteristics of each dialogic practices and elaborate how their presence or absence will impact on the flow of communication in Stakeholder Dialogues.

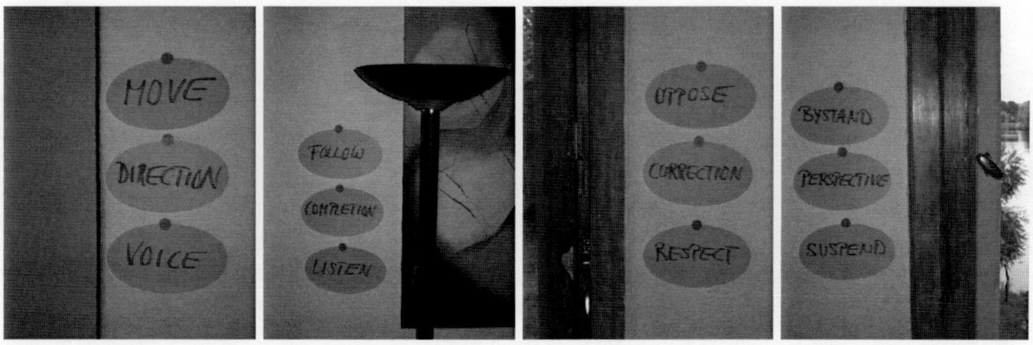

[19] The Collective Leadership Institute has adopted the model from DIAlogos, ➲ www.dialogos.com

Table: The dialogic practices – aspects to consider for Stakeholder Dialogue facilitators

Dialogic practice	*Characteristics*	*Aspects to consider for Stakeholder Dialogue facilitators*	
VOICING	Voicing means more than speaking something out loud. It is the ability to express one's concerns, ambitions, intentions or objectives with a voice from the heart, acknowledging that not everybody sees things in the same way. • It assumes that one's competence, intention and view can not only bring things forward, but also stall them. • It is built on the premise that every contribution, if authentically expressed, facilitates the emergence of collective intelligence. • It requires the ability to listen, because listening grants speaking. The way one speaks influences the way others listen and the way others listen influences the way we speak – if others are genuinely listening, a speaker can speak more freely, more authentically.	***Self-awareness***	***Hints for systems awareness and Process competence***
		It requires a degree of self-observation regarding the impact of one's voice (or voicelessness) on others, the situation, or the Stakeholder Dialogue.	It is important to ensure that all voices in the dialogue (different opinions, different stakeholder groups) are heard sufficiently. It is important to be aware of the dysfunctional side of voicing: e.g. domination by certain actors, fake talk, informal intrigues, non-transparent communication, etc.
		Reflective questions	
		• Can I make myself heard? • Do I get resonance? • In what way do I need to develop my voice? • Do I have access to my own voice, or is it that of others? • Do I dominate others with my voice? • What needs to be expressed now ? • Do I speak my authentic voice, with self-trust and confidence? • Can I authentically speak on behalf of the larger common goal?	
	Shadow	• When our voice is underdeveloped, we cannot bring out what we think in a way that lets us contribute our intention and gifts. • When it is over-inflated, we occupy enormous territory without listening to others.	

Table: The dialogic practices – aspects to consider for Stakeholder Dialogue facilitators

Dialogic practice	*Characteristics*	*Aspects to consider for Stakeholder Dialogue facilitators*	
LISTENING	Listening is the ability to create a space in which people can genuinely express themselves. This ability is at the heart of every dialogue process. Truly listening to someone means being able to recognize and accept another speaker's right to an opinion – even if this opinion diverges from one's own. Listening creates trust and contributes to resilience in Stakeholder Dialogues. • This requires not only listening to the different actors at stakeholder events, but also creating a space in which these individuals can genuinely listen to each other. • The more one learns to listen to and accord meaning to all points of view, the greater one's capacity becomes to see the whole picture. A culture of listening in a Stakeholder Dialogue allows for a faster, more effective and solution-oriented decision-making process. The quality of listening enhances the quality of talking.	***Self-awareness***	***Hints for systems awareness and Process competence***
		Good listening slows down thinking and enables us to suspend our judgments. Stakeholder Dialogue facilitators are quintessential listeners: this is the way they engage stakeholders – they listen to their concerns, ideas and aspirations.	It is important to observe in Stakeholder Dialogue events who expresses views and who is withdrawn. By gradually developing their listening skills, Stakeholder Dialogue facilitators can become more attentive to stakeholders' communication needs.
		Reflective questions	
		• Am I able to listen or do I tend to interrupt frequently? • Do I get impatient when others speak and do not express my opinion? • Am I able to listen to what is missing in a conversation? • Am I aware of my own patterns of thought? • Am I able to listen from the present moment, not from my memory? • Can I be still and listen to emerging thoughts? • Can I listen for the whole? • Do I listen for the emerging story?	
	Shadow	• When our listening is underdeveloped, we believe we are always right or more intelligent than others • When our listening is over-inflated, we lose our own stance and viewpoint.	

Table: The dialogic practices – aspects to consider for Stakeholder Dialogue facilitators

Dialogic practice	*Characteristics*	*Aspects to consider for Stakeholder Dialogue facilitators*	
RESPECTING	No Stakeholder Dialogue can be successful in the long run without genuine mutual respect. This means respecting others' opinions, even when one does not share their point of view. Further, it means looking for commonalities, even in the midst of a disagreement. If stakeholders truly wish to cooperate, respect – or the lack thereof – can mean the success or the failure of a Stakeholder Dialogue. It does not require acceptance and agreement at all stages, but the honoring of boundaries, the understanding of difference and the embracing of diversity. • At the root of the ability to respect is the ability to see others as legitimate in their being and acting differently. • Respect thrives on the willingness to acknowledge the integrity of another person and to reach out to understand their point of view. • If people are not treated with respect, they begin to treat others disrespectfully.	***Self-awareness*** An important task of Stakeholder Dialogue facilitators is to embody a culture of respect. It helps to accept that all differences are part of a whole.	***Hints for systems awareness and Process competence*** It helps facilitators, and subsequently the stakeholder system, to endure tensions without the dialogue process becoming endangered. If they spawn an atmosphere of respect, it will grow as an energetic element in the Stakeholder Dialogue.
		Reflective questions • Am I willing to look for coherence: why are things the way they are? • Can I embrace difference and diversity? • Can I respect difference without agreeing? • Do I honor the boundaries and integrity of another person? • Do I have self-respect? • Can I accept myself with my limitations, and yet strive to improve? • Am I prepared to take responsibility for a situation or do I blame others? • Am I able to hold tension and conflicts? • Can I stay equanimous when people challenge me?	
	Shadow	• An underdeveloped quality of respect leads to conversational violence, imposition of opinions, and attempts to manipulate others • Too much respect leads to shying away from expressing my opinion and a lack of personal boundaries	

Table: The dialogic practices – aspects to consider for Stakeholder Dialogue facilitators

Dialogic practice	*Characteristics*	*Aspects to consider for Stakeholder Dialogue facilitators*	
SUSPENDING	Suspending is the ability to withhold judgment of something – in other words, to shut off the tendency to come to conclusions too quickly. We all have the tendency to judge others constantly. As their capacity to suspend develops, Stakeholder Dialogue facilitators can acknowledge different opinions and uncomfortable experiences without identifying with them. • Suspending is the ability to distinguish consciously between listening, observing and judging. • The more participants in a Stakeholder Dialogue develop this ability, the better their chances of reaching a consensus, establishing constructive communication patterns and being able to concentrate on problem-solving. Suspending means developing the ability to question our own assumptions.	***Self-awareness*** Stakeholder Dialogue facilitators must live and demonstrate suspending as much as possible by showing the willingness to consider and integrate different opinions. It helps to develop the faculty of reflection in action: the ability to observe what is happening while it is happening.	***Systems awareness/Process competence*** Through good facilitation and a well-structured agenda, Stakeholder Dialogue facilitators can develop people's capacity to suspend. This can be done, for example, by having stakeholders present their opinions one after the other in a structured manner.
		Reflective questions • Can I hold what I think is certain lightly enough? • Do I want to be right? • Can I acknowledge different opinions without agreeing? • Am I learning to become more intuitively aware of what is going on in a communication? • If communication is blocked, am I willing to find out why? • Am I able to notice what is missing in a conversation? • What leads me to view things the way I do?	
	Shadow	• When the ability to suspend is underdeveloped, people display unshakable certainty, and have the desire to control the outcome of a conversation. • When the ability to suspend is over-inflated, people hold back their real opinions	

The four dialogic practices interact with each other: the conscious development of one aspect simultaneously supports the development of the other aspects.

That which is true for Stakeholder Dialogue facilitators is naturally also true for other participating stakeholders: the better developed one's communication skills, the more opportunity there is for reflecting together, the quicker a dynamic balance in communication can be developed, and the easier it will be to move forward in a solution-oriented Stakeholder Dialogue.

How to use the model

The level of self-reflection

It is important that Stakeholder Dialogue facilitators know their preferred action modes and underlying dialogic practices. Awareness of the consequences of these preferences helps them to accept their own limitations and supports them in knowing when and how they can bring people in who have different strengths. Considering different perspectives is one of the primary tasks of Stakeholder Dialogue facilitators – this can play a deciding role in a dialogue process. It can be useful to reflect on how to bring one's own action modes and dialogic practices into a dynamic balance by considering one's own strengths and the extent to which other aspects still need to be developed.

Evaluating the quality of communication in Stakeholder Dialogues

It is helpful to observe communication patterns in the stakeholder system, to notice opposing moves in their underlying intention of correction, and generally to be alert to patterns developing that, if sustained, could endanger the dialogue. The task of Stakeholder Dialogue facilitators is to discover what action modes or dialogic practices are missing, to ascertain who can bring in that which is needed, and to determine how to bring this in.

The level of understanding different actors

These models are useful for understanding differences among actors. In private companies, for example, there is a tendency to emphasize move/follow patterns. Civil society organizations are sometimes not only founded with the rationale of opposing movements (or letting the silent speak), but can also have a culture of internal dispute rather than quick agreements. The Stakeholder Dialogue facilitator's task is to become aware of the differences, acknowledge them when needed, and make them transparent, if this furthers mutual understanding. Finally, they help those involved in a dialogue to become more open to differences and to overcome patterns that hinder communication.

5.9 Engaging stakeholders: Building a *Container* for change

Stakeholders engage when they resonate with the content and goal of a Stakeholder Dialogue, regardless of whether it is a stakeholder consultation, a stakeholder platform, a broader initiative or a stakeholder partnership. Initiators of Stakeholder Dialogues often assume that other stakeholders must be interested in the same issue, and are, by default, willing to engage. However, this is probably the exception. The context of most change initiatives involving Stakeholder Dialogues is much more complex: there can be contradicting agendas of stakeholders, conflicting interests or actors who are overwhelmed by other commitments. Stakeholder Dialogue facilitators need to be aware that the intention and purpose they want to promote is, at the outset, one among many others on the agenda of most of the stakeholders. In addition to this, the importance of a Stakeholder Dialogue process, even if conceptually well-framed, may not necessarily be understood by stakeholders that should become involved.

At the outset of a Stakeholder Dialogue, initiators should talk about goal and content, and suggest, but do not over-emphasize, the methodology. Stakeholder Dialogues are not an end in themselves, but a methodology for achieving certain results. It helps always to place the result-orientation in the foreground.

Initial container

Engagement starts small, not big, and it requires a team of committed people. They form the **initial *Container*** and must become the driving force of a Stakeholder Dialogue. In that way, the engagement process starts with establishing and cultivating the initial *Container*.

➲ The Core Group as a '*Container*'

The term '*Container*' refers to the function and relational quality of an initiating team or core group of interested actors in Stakeholder Dialogues. A good container exists if these actors are dedicated to the change envisaged, emotionally engaged with future possibilities and if they are committed to initiating and implementing the intended change jointly. Ideally, this group of people already represents – to some extent, at least – the diversity of stakeholders so that it can embody the range of interests in the change initiative. It is composed of people who are willing to respect each other and who are committed to the goal. In this way, the core group, in its function as a '*Container*', creates a holding space for the planned change, an emotional home for the joint initiative and an initial pattern of the envisaged dialogue or cooperation. This core group requires attention: the more this group is able to provide coherent collective leadership, the more likely the Stakeholder Dialogue will be set on a route to success. Core groups that are "good" *Containers* help to bring about change by establishing ever broader containers for change. Such *Containers* can develop and sustain the kind of legitimacy that comes not from hierarchy but from the fact that core groups as *Containers* act in the interests of the whole, consistently.[20]

"Only dedicated circles can give birth to something new".

Saying by a circle of African wise women

[20] *In order to understand the importance of a good container, it helps to review one's experiences of change processes. Very often, if a good container for change was missing, change did not happen, failed or was difficult to achieve.*

The composition of a core group as an initial *Container* depends entirely on scope, context and purpose of the Stakeholder Dialogue. Most of the time, members of the core group will be on the operational level, but with sufficient decision-making power (or access to actors in decision-making position) to be able to take charge of the change initiative.

The broader container

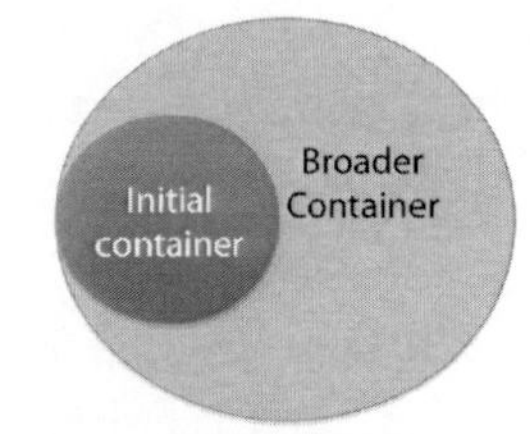

With a conscious process design in Phase 1 of a Stakeholder Dialogue, the core group in its function as a good *Container* gradually establishes a **broader *Container***. This broader *Container* is composed of people who are supportive of the Stakeholder Dialogue, may get involved in Stakeholder Dialogue meetings and take the dialogue process beyond those who form the initial *Container*. Hence, the members of the core group will engage high-level sponsors, decision-makers who are crucial to the success of the Stakeholder Dialogues, but also aim to get into conversations with selected key stakeholders, most often in a more informal way (e.g. in bilateral meetings or small focus-group meetings). Such conversations will always center on the content and the goal, but promote the Stakeholder Dialogue as an appropriate approach to achieve the envisaged results. It is crucial for the preparation of a Stakeholder Dialogue event that 'structurally significant' actors – decision-makers, people who can make things move – are sufficiently engaged. They must support the goal and form of the Stakeholder Dialogue and promote both within their respective stakeholder groups, institutions and constituencies. People engage when they get to experience meaningful conversations that tap into their desire to make a difference. Preparatory conversations with key stakeholders do not only serve to understand the stakeholder system better – they need to be conducted in a way that inspires potential participants to engage.

➲ ***Chapter 2, Getting active: Phase 1, page 55***

Engagement of the involved stakeholder system

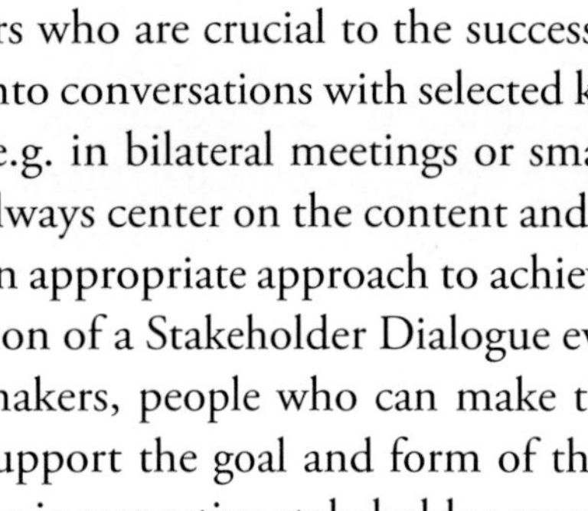

If the process design of Phase 1 has generated sufficient interest and resonance, it is time to prepare for the engagement of the **involved stakeholder system**. These are usually those actors who participate in one or several Stakeholder Dialogue events, such as consultation meetings, workshops, planning meetings, etc. Good preparation of such an event ensures that a sufficient number of participants have already been part of bilateral informal or formal conversations in Phase 1. The core group then knows already who is supportive, who is doubtful, who is opposed, or who is highly engaged. The structure and form of the event must support further *Container*-building. There must be room for respectful acknowledgement of difference, authentic listening to concerns, task-orientation in the meeting itself, transparency in planning the way forward, and result-orientation to ensure tangible outcomes.

Engaging stakeholders means gradually building larger and larger *Containers* for change. This is what makes the dialogic process successful. Stakeholder Dialogues that are geared towards collaboration and implementation benefit from the strong base of gradual *Container*-building. But even Stakeholder Dialogues with focus on consultation become more effective when participants feel engaged, acknowledged and taken seriously. Engagement does not necessarily mean consensus: critical stakeholders can play an important role in Stakeholder Dialogues. But only a well-built engagement process can ensure that they stay in the process, remain constructive with criticism and are willing to compromise if a successful outcome is at stake. Once the involved stakeholder system is willing to engage, the **wider system** of indirectly involved stakeholders will be affected. These can be people who know of the Stakeholder Dialogue, but do not participate directly, and people who are directly or indirectly affected by the outcomes of the Stakeholder Dialogue. When they perceive the existence of a diverse group of actors who (and not always in agreement) move an issue forward, they become attracted to engage, too.

Engagement of wider affected system

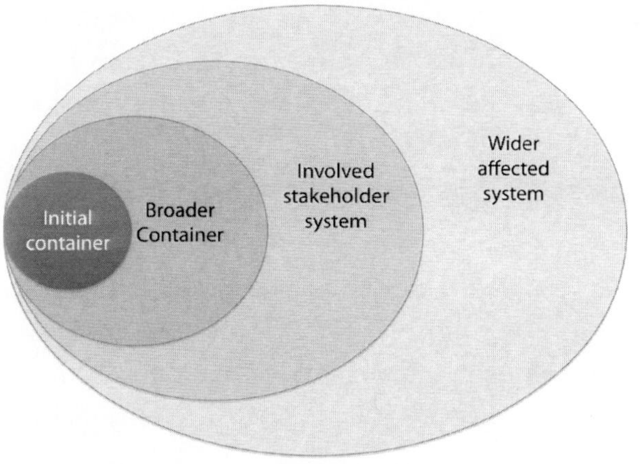

➲ ***Chapter 6, Tools, 6.3 Stakeholder analysis, page 168***

Good *Container*-building is the lifeblood of Stakeholder Dialogues as approaches to change. Thus, parallel to the development of the content of a Stakeholder Dialogue, initiators need to establish *Containers* of commitment in which people who are critical to achieving the goal can take a stand together on the dialogue's behalf. Core groups as good *Containers* often get their legitimacy not only from their official mandate but from the way they are able to engage the different stakeholders successfully. They recognize their success when they see people working together in Stakeholder Dialogues with others whom they have either ignored or consistently opposed in the past.

The container building process: the core of successful Stakeholder Dialogues

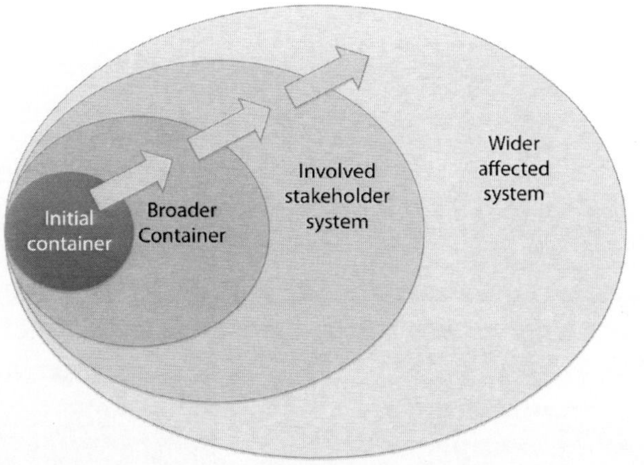

Many initiators of Stakeholder Dialogues do not take the engagement process in Phase 1 and 2 seriously. They sometimes skip it, or just pay lip service to it. Decision-makers may even put members of the core group under pressure to rush into stakeholder events without thorough preparation and engagement of stakeholders. It then helps to argue for the methodology and explain that the investment of thorough engagement will pay off both in consultative and cooperative Stakeholder Dialogues.

5.10 Pitfalls of engagement processes

Not all key actors will engage in the same way. Some stakeholders are more difficult to engage. In many organizations, people continually change position, send new people to meetings without briefing them or drop out of processes pressured by other commitments. 'Staff turnover' may lead the core group to include people who were not included before, or to deal with the loss of a key supporter who is suddenly called to a different task.

With some new participants (such as those in positions of authority or those who represent key constituents), everything may need to slow down or stop until they have been brought up to speed in their role as core group members, supporters or high-level sponsors. A Stakeholder Dialogue process cannot always be delayed, but it pays off to invest very consciously in *Container*-building when new people need to brought on board. In such a situation, relationship-building is key.

Sometimes, people do not understand the difference between a good *Container* for change and a formal committee or task force composed of representatives. Of course, any committee or task force can become a good container, but this will not happen automatically. The emotional commitment between people, as well as between people and the goal of the Stakeholder Dialogue, will only build up gradually, and only if the initiators invest enough time in relationship-building and in building the case for change.

➲ *Chapter 5, resources, 5.4, Dimensions of change, page 117*

What if …	Food for thought
… key actors do not want to get engaged, do not join the initial Container or the broader Container, and refuse to get involved?	• Rethink the stakeholder analysis • Design specific strategies to engage difficult actors, and be sure that you understand what makes them engaged or disengaged • Check if the timing for the initiative is right • Convey the goal but link it to the interest of the difficult stakeholder
… people change positions, drop out or send substitutes	• Accept that you may need to slow the process down and ensure that you get the new people on board • If the people attending meetings continuously change: try to engage superiors more consciously and explain how important it is that the same people attend consistently • Invest in relationship-building and invest time in getting people on board
… people do not understand the difference between a good Container and a formal committee or task force?	• Invest in relationship-building and building the case for change: inspiring information, inspiring people, supporting people's aspirations to make a difference, thinking in future possibilities rather than maintaining the status quo • Honor people's contributions and acknowledge their viewpoints • Create an atmosphere of creative and constructive exchange of ideas

5.11 Understanding the need to engage different stakeholder groups differently

Initiators of Stakeholder Dialogues sometimes overlook the differences of different stakeholder groups in their motivation to join and engage. It is helpful to keep in mind that each group may need to be treated in a different way to maintain interest. The following table is a reminder of what needs to be taken into account when engaging the three large societal stakeholder groups. Depending on the context, this may be even more complex: a stakeholder analysis helps to understand the motivations that can lead stakeholder groups to engage.

➲ *Chapter 6: 6.3 Stakeholder Analysis, page 168*

Aspects to be taken into account to engage the stakeholder group

Private sector	• Know that the private sector always has a busy schedule. • Involve private sector in the planning process. • Build a result-oriented process and create a flexible and practical environment. • Plan short meetings in a convivial setting. • Show the business case for change (help them to argue the business case for engagement). • Provide the opportunity to showcase their work and promote their image. • Take advantage of competitiveness to stimulate involvement and commitment.
Public sector	• Understand the power dynamics and hierarchical structures. • Recognize the importance of socio-cultural factors. • Be aware of formal, but also traditional, structures. • Ensure your knowledge of existing rules and regulations. • Always respect protocol. • Show the reputational case for change. • Consider supra-national and regional structures and their interests. • Highlight sustainability aspects. • Make reference and ensure conformity to international conventions.
Civil society	• Consider logistical support (i.e. funds, transport, accommodation, per diems etc.) for participation. • Ensure transparent and inclusive communication. • Be aware of their requirement to consult with their constituencies. • Respect the different mandates of different organizations. • Strengthen weaker representation (e.g. translation for community groups). • Respect and appeal to value-orientation. • Show the societal case for change. • Be prepared to address questions on impact–monitoring.

5.12 The role of communication in the four phases of Stakeholder Dialogues

5.12.1 Important elements of communication in Phase 1

➲ The goal of a successful communication process in Phase 1 is to set an engagement process in motion, which mobilizes the required energy for changing the status quo within the stakeholder system. Further, confidence and trust in the possibility of change and the potential for cooperation should be actively built up. In this phase, communication helps to explore the field of action and, at the same time, to build up constructive working relationships. Due to the complex nature and conflict-ravaged settings that Stakeholder Dialogues take place in, such trusting relationships are fundamental for overcoming difficult situations and frequent differences of opinion.

➲ *Chapter 5, resources, 5.9, Engageing stakeholders: building a Container for change, page 143*

During the first phase of **exploring and engaging**, it is important to understand the context in which the Stakeholder Dialogue is taking place. At this point, communication takes place on a more informal level. In the course of informal talks with the different stakeholders, it is crucial to clarify the issues as well as the different possibilities for dialogue. The urgency of an issue may also be communicated in these informal talks. Informal talks must be extremely well-prepared to win support from the actors and to be able to illustrate the benefits that individual stakeholders would gain by participating in the Stakeholder Dialogue.

At this point, it is imperative to pay special attention to the individual stakeholders and to be open to their views, opinions and interests. They must get the feeling that their needs and perspectives are being respected and tended to. Sufficient time and effort must be invested in initial contact with each stakeholder, and the setting of such meetings should be carefully chosen. This effort will pay off, because the stakeholder will develop interest in and commitment to the issue, and develop trust in the initiators. It is recommended to prepare these initial talks on the results of a stakeholder analysis thoroughly to take the actors' individual backgrounds, action fields and logic into account.

During informal talks, it will become clear who is interested in participating in the Stakeholder Dialogue and who has enough commitment for implementation. If it becomes clear who should become part of the core group, it is critical to provide these stakeholders with all essential information relating to the joint initiative and to create a comfortable working environment for these individuals. Communication plays a key role here as well, as does the outer framework. One must consider how to bring the members of the core group together as a team in a way that makes trusting collaboration possible swiftly. Transparent, honest and open communication between all members of the core group is essential to make this possible.

➲ *Chapter 2, Dialogic Change Model, Phase 1: page 55*

Very little should be communicated outwards during Phase 1 of a Stakeholder Dialogue. Only once key stakeholders have been engaged and successfully brought on board should discussion and planning be extended to a wider sphere.

5.12.2 Important elements of communication in Phase 2

> ➲ The goal of a successful communication process in Phase 2 is to build up a stable stakeholder system based on dialogue and cooperation, despite individual stakeholders' possible differences in approach. This means that stakeholders and stakeholder groups participating in the process must relate to the process's goals and components sufficiently.

➲ *Chapter 2, Dialogic Change Model,*

Phase 2: page 61

During the second phase of a Stakeholder Dialogue, building and formalizing, it is important for clarification of goals and resources to consolidate the relationships carefully built up during Phase 1. The group's interest in collaborating must be well–structured, and made formal. The *Container* must determine the appropriate form of communication for the decision-making process, the distribution of roles and the delegation of tasks. Phase 2 usually involves a larger group of stakeholders who meet for dialogue events. For example, stakeholders are invited to a workshop or a working meeting to set common goals, plan future communication strategies and lay the groundwork for the implementation phase.

It is important to determine well in advance what goals are to be pursued during a dialogue event and how these goals are best reached– be it in relation to end results, process-related issues or relationship-management. This means considering not only the event program and attendees, but also the kind of exchange taking place during the event, the style of moderation, the location, seating, and so on. All these details have a profound effect on the atmosphere during the event and have a direct influence on the type of communication taking place between the participants.

Initiators need to keep in mind that most of the participants outside of the core group will not have met before, and might be somewhat skeptical of one another due to diverging interests or imbalanced representation. An informal meeting, such as a welcome coffee before the event begins, can often be helpful in easing tensions between stakeholders. This way, they first meet as private individuals, and not in their official roles, which can have a positive effect on their openness to each others' views.

The objective of such a dialogue event is to discuss the present situation (e.g. a joint analysis of strengths and weaknesses), to clarify common goals, and, if possible, to work out initial agreements about the exact form of cooperation. Agreements and transparent communication within the stakeholder system are a deciding factor for creating and maintaining trust within the process. All stakeholders should be given equal opportunity to voice their opinions. If an individual stakeholder requires assistance in doing so, it is the core group's duty to guarantee each of the participants their right to express themselves fairly. This will insure that all stakeholders contribute equally and get the impression that it is a joint decision-making process.

For the further engagement process in the Stakeholder Dialogue, it is crucial to give each of the stakeholders the feeling that his or her needs, fears and interests are being taken seriously by all parties. This must be taken into account when planning the content and structure of a Stakeholder Dialogue event.

However, room must be left for healthy scepticism about the change initiative and its feasibility, which is, initially, almost unavoidable. At the same time, the core group must successfully communicate to all participants that such a stakeholder encounter is the first step in comparing and contrasting uncertainty with promising alternative solutions. Creating a coherent Stakeholder Dialogue is paramount to its success: only a coherent system can create a feeling of belonging and ensure continued cooperation, even in difficult times.

Furthermore, the stakeholders' cultural, political and work-related perspectives and traditions should be carefully taken into account when creating the agenda and workshop program.

5.12.3 Important elements of communication in Phase 3

> ➲ The goal of a successful communication process in Phase 3 is to push the dialogue process forward to make the implementation of agreements possible. It is central to this phase that all stakeholders are on board and that any additional stakeholders required are integrated in the process. Stakeholder engagement for the joint initiative should be well-maintained.

➲ *Chapter 2, Dialogic Change Model, Phase 3: page 68*

Internal communication in Phase 3, **implementing and evaluating**, should occur as transparently and regularly as possible to keep all parties equally informed. This could take the form of a short update, newsletter, event documentation, or progress report from the core group or a project secretariat, if there is one.

Agreements on communication, planning, frequency, or dialogue and expert workshops should be followed as closely as possible. Due to the fragile nature of Stakeholder Dialogues and the mistrust associated with many action areas, it is essential to establish and maintain trust through transparency and consistency within the dialogue system. For further dialogue events, the same important communication elements apply as were mentioned in Phase 2.

In Phase 3, the quality of communication occurring between individuals or institutions directly involved in the dialogue can be of utmost importance: the effort put forth by an individual stakeholder often legitimizes his or her participation. The responsibility for communication within the participating institutions lies with the respective representatives. However, the core group or a project secretariat can be of help here by offering to report on the form, content and results of the Stakeholder Dialogue directly to the involved institutions. Political supporters of the Stakeholder Dialogue must be regularly involved and informed.

In Phase 3, external communication becomes increasingly important. For more politically or implementation-oriented processes, the general public may also have a distinct interest in the results produced by the Stakeholder Dialogue. It may, therefore, become increasingly important to communicate results outside the group of participating stakeholders to raise awareness of an initiative's goals and approach. Communication with the media becomes especially interesting as soon as results become visible. Interaction with the media depends greatly on the type of Stakeholder Dialogue, its topic, as well as the degree of trust that exists between the participating stakeholders. In highly sensitive or political cases, it is extremely important to agree internally with stakeholders and institutions on the extent and content of press coverage. In political processes, sensibilities and formal procedures must also be taken into account.

In Phase 3, Stakeholders who do not participating directly in the Stakeholder Dialogue, but who are important to the process, must also be informed.

5.12.4 Important elements of communication in Phase 4

➲ The goal of a successful communication process in Phase 4 is to communicate the results of the process and prepare the scaling up, replication or institutionalization of the initiative. This may require integrating more stakeholders into the process, stakeholders who are not currently involved but who may represent an important addition to the dialogue for the future.

A Stakeholder Dialogue that is not concluded after the successful completion of Phase 3, enters into Phase 4, **developing further, replicating or institutionalizing**. To justify further development, it is important to make the results of Phase 3 public and explain the reasons for the replication, scaling-up or institutionalization of the Stakeholder Dialogue. The stakeholders involved must carefully agree upon the exact content of the information made public so that no misunderstandings result from the spread of possibly conflicting information by different stakeholders. It must also be clear to the stakeholders that the information made public will most probably be publicly criticized and brought into question, and that some may even attempt to discredit the results.

Further development implies that a new form of Stakeholder Dialogue is developed based on the results of the initial dialogue. This might mean a stronger formalization or institutionalization, the creation of a new institution, integration into an existing institutional system, or the repetition of the dialogue process in another region or on another topic. As was the case in Phase 1, new stakeholders must be brought on board with an extensive engagement process, and existing stakeholders need to be kept on board.

A further similarity to Phase 1 may be the need for fresh informal talks with relevant actors to build a new *Container*. Such talks will assist in recruiting new stakeholders to the cause in general, and also in finding new members for Stakeholder Dialogue's new driving team or core group. The same principles as in Phase 2 are valid for this Phase: goals must be clarified, participation must be organized authentically and agreements must be kept. If the implementation of the new Stakeholder Dialogue is taken over by a new group of people, a thorough handover that covers all central issues should be prepared by the outgoing core group.

➲ ***Chapter 2, Dialogic Change Model, Phase 4: page 73***

5.13 Principles of successful process designs for Stakeholder Dialogue events: Summary

Build a strong Container	A cross-sector core group committed to the goal and to conducting the Stakeholder Dialogue, a broader group of supportive actors
Build resonance for the goal and the Stakeholder Dialogue among actors that matter	Ensure high-level sponsorship and create resonance for the change through informal or formal conversations
Get the system into the room and into a conversation with itself	Microcosm represents macrocosm, ensure that participants can talk to each other in small groups, avoid conference-style meetings, allow space for task-related conversations among participants
Diagnose the current reality together	Allow a joint picture of the current reality to develop (e.g. through a SWOT Analysis[21], joint situational diagnosis, etc.)
Build relationships	Ensure that people get to know each other formally and informally, ensure that all voices are heard, create contact, encounter, meeting each other as human beings
Allow differences to emerge first, but in a structured way	Ensure that differences are listened to (and not swept under the carpet), make differences transparent through e.g. seating order of stakeholder groups, but also create space for commonalities, create opportunities for consensus-building, design a structured integration process if differences occur
Create task-orientation	When people work on a task together and achieve a joint result, they align and produce tangible outcomes more readily
Bring in expertise as needed	Ensure that all important facts are on the table (e.g. experts, task forces, etc.), allow space for participants to digest information in their own way, create opportunities to tailor information to the specific situation of participants
Find the common ground	Encourage participants to identify the common ground, ensure that facilitation keeps the common ground clear
Create expert groups or task forces	For content details or temporarily unresolvable issues, establish task forces and bring results from task forces back into the large group for further consideration
Keep the common goal clear	Remind stakeholders continuously of the larger issues at stake
Offer reliable structure	Create a handrail for the Stakeholder Dialogue process (program, working group instructions, road maps, planning) and be aware how space (relationships) and structure (from seating order to power relationships to mental models) affects action

[21] SWOT stand for the analysis of Strength, Weaknesses, Opportunities and Threads

TOOLS

TOOLS

The tools in this practical guide assist Stakeholder Dialogue facilitators in the structured planning and implementation of successful and result-oriented dialogic processes. On the basis of the conceptual chapters and the background resources they provide practical instruments that help initiators or members of core groups assess and design the process steps they need to move a Stakeholder Dialogue forward. Each section in this chapter focuses on a particular instrument with relevance to implementing Stakeholder Dialogues, as described in the previous chapters.

Note that tools should never be rigidly applied. They are not an end in themselves, but should only be used as supportive instruments in a conscious process design that requires a broader understanding of the purpose of Stakeholder Dialogues. As all tools they help to reduce complexity so that the complex and often controversial environment of Stakeholder Dialogues can be approached with more confidence and ease. In that way, they can guide action, cultivate reflection and function as early warning systems, if things become difficult. They raise awareness for the details that often require attention in Stakeholder Dialogues.

This compilation of tools is not a substitute for project-planning and management tools as they are widely available in private sector, public sector, civil society and development cooperation. These can be used as relevant or applicable. The chapter only provides tools that are specifically used for Stakeholder Dialogues.

6.1. Assessing the potential for Stakeholder Dialogues

➲ *Chapter 1: getting started, 1.2 Understanding different forms of Stakeholder Dialogues, page 32*

Stakeholder Dialogues are a methodological approach used to design cooperation and consultation processes that require the integration of relevant stakeholder groups. They should not, therefore, be used as a unilateral communication strategy in which certain groups are fed with information with the sole purpose of evoking the desired results. Conveying information about a specific topic to interest groups can be an important issue, but Stakeholder Dialogues go far beyond this. They are only appropriate if a common responsibility for changing the status quo is desirable and can be established. Depending on what needs to be achieved, Stakeholder Dialogues can take various forms.

Stakeholder Dialogues are recommended when the cause of problems needs to be explored and collectively designed solutions need to be reached. Integrating all stakeholders increases the chances of establishing a network of communication and cooperation between actors, a network that often continues to exist beyond the scope and timeframe of the Stakeholder Dialogue. This stimulates the development of network structures that help actors to take increased responsibility for the process and to create sustainable change.

➲ *Chapter 2: Getting active, 2.2.1 Phase 1: Exploring and engaging, page 55*

Assessing the potential for Stakeholder Dialogues can assist those who wish to initiate change to define what the involvement of different stakeholders can achieve. This tool can also help to determine if a Stakeholder Dialogue is the right approach for a particular project or initiative. If sufficient trust already exists between partners of, for example, a core group as a good Container, such an assessment can be carried out in the team of initiators.

➲ When does it make sense to consider using Stakeholder Dialogues?

- If implementing a goal requires the support of different groups of actors and decision-makers
- If the sustainable implementation of a project or initiative requires the acceptance of certain interest groups (those affected and those involved)
- If changing an issue's status quo is envisaged, but the key stakeholders needed for implementation do not see the need for change or cannot agree on goal and implementation modalities
- If many stakeholders see the need for change, but no actor takes the initiative
- If communication is intended to go beyond conveying information to stakeholders, but different perspectives are invited to be expressed and intended to be integrated

Certain pre-conditions need to be met to implement Stakeholder Dialogues successfully, build constructive relationships and achieve specific objectives. This is because Stakeholder Dialogues are complex communication and cooperation processes.

It is not always the case that all actors are prepared to commit fully to a particular cause at the beginning of the process – neither is this completely necessary. During the preparation phase, it is the initiators' job to win actors' support progressively for the approach to be taken in the process. Nevertheless, stakeholders need to have a basic interest in change for the dialogue to succeed. Each stakeholder's motivation to participate in bringing about this change may differ. This is why it is important to choose the right time and appropriate form for the Stakeholder Dialogue, and to invest sufficient time and resources in Phase 1.

If a Stakeholder Dialogue is officially established (Phase 2) before relevant stakeholders see the need for change and are properly engaged, the dialogue may fail in the long run. Important stakeholders may lose confidence in the possibility of jointly working toward the achievement of a goal, or even lose trust in the process initiators. To avoid this, informal talks as part of an engagement process in Phase 1 should be used to examine the stakeholders' potential interest and to understand their way of thinking. This can help the team of initiators to evaluate whether commencing with a Stakeholder Dialogue at that time is feasible.

➲ ***Chapter 2: Getting active, 2.2.1 Phase 1: Exploring and engaging, page 55, Chapter 5: 5.11, Understanding the need to engage different stakeholder groups differently, page 147***

A well-thought-out strategy for stakeholder integration (engagement process) and a corresponding project plan with sufficient personnel, expertise, time and financial resources are essential to plan and implement Stakeholder Dialogues successfully. However, the approach goes beyond the scope of regular project management. Stakeholder Dialogues are not limited to projects; they are part of an on-going global and societal development. Their innovative potential lies in their ability to integrate all relevant stakeholders into social, economic and environmental change processes beyond the boundaries of time-bound project plans.

➲ ***Chapter 2: Getting active, 2.2.2 Phase 2: Building and formalizing, page 61***

The **checklist on page 158** offers an overview of the criteria that should be considered before initiating a Stakeholder Dialogue. This tool is designed to support a joint reflection on the possible application of a Stakeholder Dialogue methodology, as well as to determine what needs to be done to create the proper conditions for such an approach.

➲ ***Chapter 5: Resources, 5.9 Engaging stakeholders: building a Container for change, page 143***

If, after carrying out the potential analysis, one or several criteria do not apply, it is recommended that facilitators identify the criteria that can be directly influenced by the initiators. Investing resources and abilities already present within the team of initiators can help to optimize the initial conditions for the launch of a Stakeholder Dialogue.

Criteria	*Yes*	*No*
Need for integration		
The envisaged change requires more than broad information, or the enforcement of rules and regulations		
The envisaged change will affect different stakeholders and require their consent		
The successful implementation of a project, initiative or consultation event requires involvement of and acceptance by different stakeholder groups		
The successful implementation of a project or initiative requires the active commitment of different stakeholders		
Formalized cooperation between different stakeholders is required to implement an agreed-upon change initiative		
Timing		
Key stakeholders see the need for change		
Key stakeholders are convinced that change requires dialogue and cooperation		
Conflicts between different stakeholders may exist, but do not keep stakeholders from their participation in a dialogue process		
The reputational risk of participating is low for most stakeholders		
Key stakeholders have confidence in the initiators		
Capacity		
The core group of initiators has sufficient time and resources		
The core group of initiators has adequate knowledge about, and/or experience in, integrating different stakeholders and conducting Stakeholder Dialogues		
The core group of initiators has sufficiently established relationships with all key stakeholders		
Commitment		
The Stakeholder Dialogue is supported by relevant decision-makers in the initiating institution(s)		
The core group of initiators is willing to steer a complex communication and cooperation process jointly		
The core group of initiators is able to respect different perspectives		
The core group is open to letting the goal be influenced or shaped by other stakeholders involved		

Need for integration

If any of the criteria in this category apply, it is worth considering a Stakeholder Dialogue approach. The topic and context determine which form of dialogue may be most appropriate. If none of the criteria apply, the initiators may choose a different approach to change and the initiators should think of different forms of implementation for the envisaged change. However, if aspects of implementation of a change initiative can only be successful with support from different stakeholder groups, it may be much more effective to implement the change by using a Stakeholder Dialogue approach.

● **Croatia** is a new member state in the EU. This requires the implementation of an **EU-Regulation on coastal zone management in the Mediterranean Sea**. The Croatian government is obliged to adopt the regulation, which makes discussing whether or not the stakeholders agree with it or not inconsequential. However, compliance with the regulation requires the understanding and cooperation of a variety of stakeholders. Supported by German development cooperation, the Croatian Ministry of Environment initiated a stakeholder consultation process to ensure that all relevant actors not only know about the regulation, but also develop their contribution to successful implementation beyond mere compliance enforcement. For this purpose, the project's core team organized a stakeholder workshop, where diverse interest groups from all levels and sectors were offered the opportunity to get to know each other and exchange ideas and experience on integrated coastal zone management.

Timing

If most or all criteria in this category apply, the timing is right for a Stakeholder Dialogue approach. If no criteria, or only a few criteria, apply, the initiators may need to explore in Phase 1 the extent to which they can create resonance for the change idea. They may also need to explore stakeholders' motivation for participating or not participating. If stakeholders do not see the benefit of a Stakeholder Dialogue approach, there may be different way of dealing with the complexity of the situation: initiators can avoid naming the approach Stakeholder Dialogue, but start the engagement process. If decision-makers do not see the need for cooperation or consultation at all, it may help to bring in examples from other projects, initiatives or countries to show the long-lasting benefits of consultative and cooperative approaches.

➲ ***Chapter 2: Getting active, 2.2.1 Phase 1: Exploring and engaging, page 55, Chapter 5: 5.11, Understanding the need to engage different stakeholder groups differently, page 147***

If stakeholders are in direct conflict, the situation may require a negotiation or conflict-management process before the Stakeholder Dialogue can begin.

Capacity

If any of the criteria in this category do not apply, it does not mean that initiators should abandon the idea of conducting a Stakeholder Dialogue. However, both financial resources and competence are an important factor for success. So, if criteria in this category do not apply, the initiators should think about how to put resources and capacity in place first. Alongside capacity-building for content issues, initiators may also consider offering capacity-building on how to work with Stakeholder Dialogues to key stakeholders. This may not only raise the interest in the methodology, but could also offer a platform for communication and cooperation while simultaneously equip stakeholders with skills to work together on an issue successfully.

Commitment

If not all aspects of "commitment" can be answered with yes, the initiators should carefully think about a stakeholder analysis and meticulously plan an engagement process as well as core group composition and Container building for the core group.

➲ ***Chapter 2: Getting active, 2.1 The Dialogic Change Model , page 55 , Chapter 6: Tools, 6.3 Stakeholder Analysis, page 168***

Initiators should find out why there is no commitment and how commitment can be developed. It helps to foster open communication among initiators about what they want the dialogue to achieve, and about how open they are to listening to a variety of perspectives on the issue. If decision-makers are not yet on board, this should gain sufficient attention in Phase 1.

6.2 Choosing the appropriate form of Stakeholder Dialogue

Because Stakeholder Dialogues can be once-off events or long-term dialogue and co-operation processes, it is important to consider which form of Stakeholder Dialogue is appropriate in a particular context and for a particular purpose. The form, however, cannot always be specified at the beginning of a dialogue process. But the overview of different forms of Stakeholder Dialogues can indicate which form would be most appropriate. The table below shows circumstances under which each different form would be recommended.

➲ *Chapter 1, 1.2 Understanding different forms of Stakeholder Dialogues, page 32*

It is important to keep in mind that Stakeholder Dialogues are processes, and that they might develop over time from consultation to cooperation processes. The table below and its examples, therefore, show how different forms can develop into each other or complement each other.

DIFFERENT FORMS OF STAKEHOLDER DIALOGUES

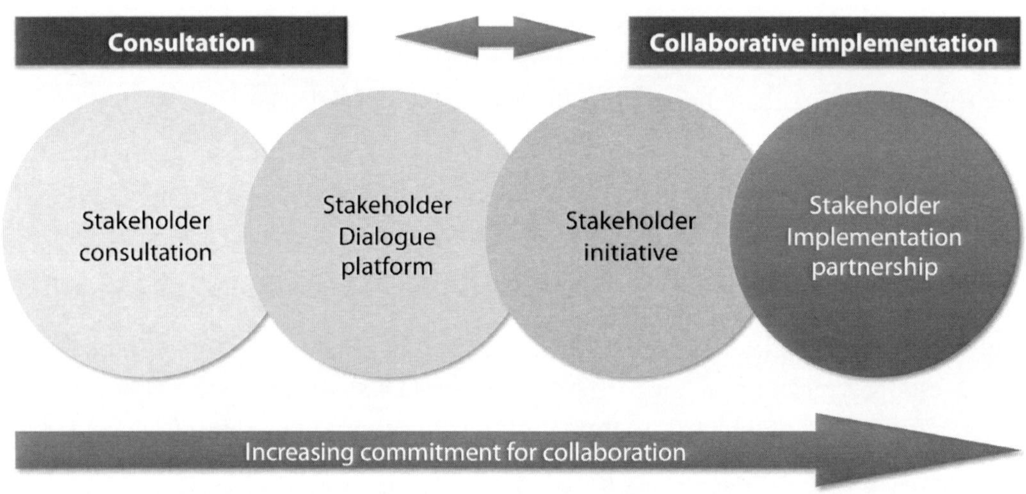

Singular Stakeholder Consultation

CONSULTATION	*Feature*	*Purpose*	*Recommended if:*
	Stakeholder event/workshop/ conference to get input from different stakeholders	To raise the interest in or awareness of stakeholders on a particular issue To get feedback from different stakeholders on a specific issue	• one stakeholder group requires input on an issue (project planning, policy development, strategy feedback, research feedback, etc.) from other stakeholder groups • an issue requires awareness of different stakeholder groups, or stakeholders' interest in a particular issues should be raised • no close or regular cooperation with different stakeholders is planned

Outlook

Should results from the singular stakeholder consultation prove helpful, the initiators may want to consider using this form of consultation regularly on particular issues. So, this form may develop into regular or even institutionalized consultation.

Consultation processes can increase the initiating stakeholder group's reputation or legitimacy.

Example:

Large multinational companies use this form to get feedback about specific strategic issues (e.g. implementation of their CSR strategy, or their sustainability report).

Example:

The public sector often uses singular consultations for environmental impact assessments, policy developments, or feedback about research results, for example.

Series of regular Stakeholder Consultations

CONSULTATION	*Feature*	*Purpose*	*Recommended if:*
	Consultative stakeholder events leading to a specific outcome	To let stakeholders participate in a development, decision-making process or exchange of experiences among stakeholders	• one stakeholder group requires the contribution or the feedback of different stakeholder groups for example for the acceptance of planning results, the introduction of new regulations, or simply for the legitimacy of the operations of an institution (public or private), • consultation is required in stages: at the beginning, during implementation or drafting, or at the end of a planning or policy-development process • an institution would like to develop a good relationship with otherwise critical stakeholders

Outlook

Should a regular stakeholder consultation prove helpful, and should stakeholders request to transform the form of consultation into a more structured and regular format, can the form of stakeholder consultation be institutionalized.

As a result of consultation processes (singular or regular), stakeholders may create a platform for regular exchange of progress, or even create a stakeholder initiative in which certain stakeholders come together to bring about change on particular topic.

Example:

Municipalities may decide to use regular stakeholder consultations for the development of their climate adaptation/mitigation strategies, and resolve to establish a more official stakeholder committee that has the function of overseeing the implementation of climate mitigation/adaptation measures.

Example:

A textile company that uses regular stakeholder consultations to improve social standards in their value chain may realize that the challenges it faces cannot be solved by them alone, and that these solutions require a consolidated effort of several companies. So, they may push forward a stakeholder initiative for the application of social standards.

Institutionalized Stakeholder Consultations

CONSULTATION	*Feature*	*Purpose*	*Recommended if:*
	Government-led stakeholder consultation embedded in regulations	To regulate input by stakeholders on certain issues of policy or planning development (as part of good governance)	• stakeholder input should be part of official procedures • the implementation of certain measures affects public goods

Outlook

Not all institutionalized Stakeholder Dialogues function well. The fact that they have become a procedural measure does not necessarily mean that the conductors understand their actual purpose and spirit. This can mean that institutionalized Stakeholder Dialogues are administered bureaucratically, losing their authenticity.

Example:

A provincial government may implement consultation between the private sector and civil society on development issues in a very formal way (e.g. written feedback to certain issues) without allowing stakeholders to get engaged in a content discussion across different stakeholder groups.

The challenge here lies in 'breathing life' back into the stakeholder consultation. This means ensuring proper participation of stakeholders, allowing for consultation events that spur the exchange of perspective, and giving the initiators a real picture of the different stakeholders' interests and concerns.

Stakeholder platform (exchange)

CONSULTATION	*Feature*	*Purpose*	*Recommended if:*
	Regular coming together of different stakeholders for an exchange of experience	To develop joint recommendations, to use the opportunity to meet different stakeholders, to ensure advocacy for stakeholder interests	• different stakeholders are looking for the possibility of a regular exchange with other stakeholders on a particular issue • a joint implementation of projects is not necessarily envisaged • stakeholders are looking for an opportunity for joint advocacy regarding a particular issue

Outlook

Creating a stakeholder platform can be advisable when different actors and experts intend to exchange experiences on their individual implementation of a certain issue, practice or methodology on a regular basis, for example. Such platforms often have a pull-effect: more and more interested stakeholders would like to join, and in that way they can contribute to the dissemination of certain practices, approaches, methodologies, etc.

Initiatives and partnerships can develop out of stakeholder platforms, as issues discussed raise the interest of different stakeholder groups, the platform strengthens communication and opens up opportunities for collaboration.

Example:

Often practitioner networks that include several stakeholder groups are organized as a stakeholder exchange platform.

Example:

Business associations that are oriented towards all levels of a value chain often include a variety of stakeholders. Their contribution to improved value-chain relationships can lead actors to cooperate in a different way or to start joint initiatives.

Stakeholder initiative

COLLABORATION AND IMPLEMENTATION	Feature	Purpose	Recommended if:
	Cross-sector initiative to solve complex problems, to develop joint policy and/or sustainability standards, or to achieve agreed-upon implementation objectives	To develop and implement new approaches, voluntary standards, new policies, or complex projects, jointly	• a new approach to change requires different stakeholders to align behind a goal to be implemented within an agreed-upon timeframe • different stakeholder groups can only find the solution to a problem together • different stakeholders intend to contribute jointly to change in a collaborative effort • stakeholders are prepared to commit to joint responsibility for the implementation of a change initiative • a goal or the solution to a problem cannot be mastered by one stakeholder group alone

Outlook

A stakeholder initiative is based on the participating stakeholders' different competencies. Complex stakeholder initiatives often require steering and governance structures as well as project secretariats.

In stakeholder initiatives that have been formed for a particular purpose, it may be necessary to consult with more stakeholders than those who are directly involved. So, these initiatives can use singular or regular stakeholder consultations for the initiation or implementation of the initiative.

Example:

Broad initiatives, such as those between internationally operating private-sector and development agencies, are often composed as strategic alliances with the intention of implementing specific approaches in different regions, countries or continents. Such initiatives can only be successful if they make use of structured consultation and engagement process in each country of implementation.

Stakeholder platform (implementation)

COLLABORATION AND IMPLEMENTATION	*Feature*	*Purpose*	*Recommended if:*
	Joint management of implementation of an issue of common concern	To ensure coordination and joint management of complex tasks by different stakeholders	• the implementation of a certain issue is ongoing and requires the continuous coordination of different stakeholders • joint management of an issue leads to improved implementation and service delivery • long-term collaboration between stakeholders is required

Outlook

A stakeholder platform (implementation) is the appropriate form if, for example, different stakeholders need to manage a common good like water resource management, and if this management requires optimal coordination and a thorough understanding of the issue by different stakeholders.

Stakeholder platforms for implementation often establish structures such as committees and secretariats. They may require the consultation of stakeholders who are not directly involved.

Example:

The management of a public good like water often requires well-coordinated collaboration between different stakeholders. This, ideally, can contribute to improved management of resources and improved service delivery. Stakeholder platforms in water management can conduct regular, broader stakeholder consultations to receive feedback from indirectly involved stakeholders.

Stakeholder partnership

COLLABORATION AND IMPLEMENTATION	*Feature*	*Purpose*	*Recommended if:*
	Cross-sector implementation project to achieve agreed-upon objectives	To achieve specific project results with complementary resources within a specific timeframe	• an agreed-upon project goal requires joint or complementary implementation • stakeholders are prepared to commit to shared responsibility for achieving results • for a specific timeframe, a collaboration between stakeholders is envisaged to lead to expected outcomes • stakeholders are prepared to enter into a formal agreement on joint implementation • stakeholders are willing to commit resources to a joint project

Outlook

Stakeholder partnerships require agreements that are more formal or less formal to collaborate. At the very least, they require jointly agreed project implementation plans, including monitoring and evaluation. Usually one can find typical project structures in stakeholder partnerships: financial and operational plans, staff allocation, and formally agreed-upon roles and responsibilities.

During their implementation phase, stakeholder partnership may require consultation processes with stakeholders that are not directly involved in the partnership.

Example:

Development partnerships between public-sector and private-sector companies, or between development agencies and private-sector companies, are often established as agreed-upon and time-bound projects to achieve specific results. To be successful, they often require the involvement of different stakeholders who are not part of the actual project agreement, in the form of both consultation and cooperation.

6.3 Stakeholder analysis

Stakeholder analysis is an important instrument that is used to identify and analyze all key actors who are relevant to a particular dialogic change initiative. It is best done in the team that intends to initiate and conduct the Stakeholder Dialogue. The purpose of applying this instrument is to develop a strategic view of the human and institutional landscape and the relationships between different stakeholders.

Although this instrument can be used throughout all phases of the Stakeholder Dialogue, it is crucial to conduct a stakeholder analysis at the outset of a dialogue initiative to have a clear understanding of the context as well as potential support or impediments. There are many methods for carrying out a stakeholder analysis. The following paragraphs show two different tools for conducting stakeholder analysis that have proven helpful in the preparation of Stakeholder Dialogues. They can be used individually or in combination.

The interest/influence grid

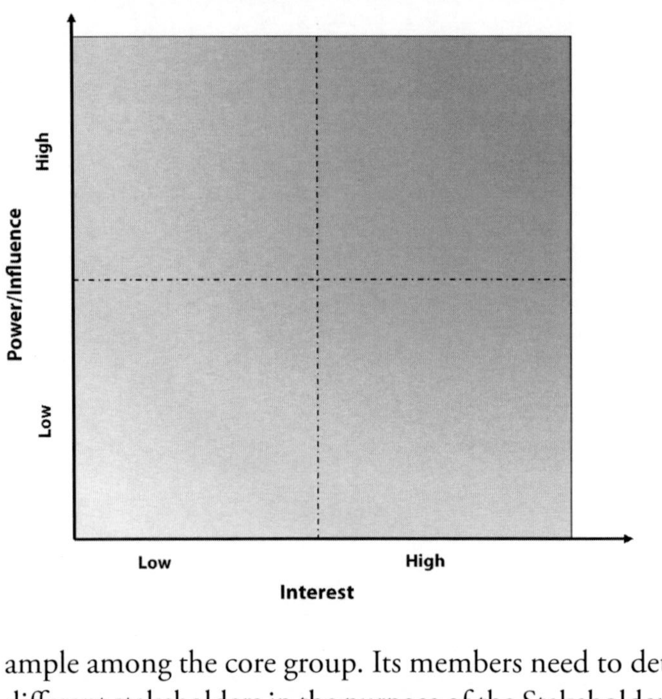

6.3.1 The interest/influence grid[22]

The use of the interest/influence grid is particularly helpful in determining what type of engagement process is required to create sufficient interest in the Stakeholder Dialogue. Stakeholders should be encouraged to incorporate their positions into the dialogue, and stakeholders' support (whether institutions or individuals) is imperative to the dialogue.

The instrument is a basis of a discussion process, for example among the core group. Its members need to determine the level of interest of different stakeholders in the purpose of the Stakeholder Dialogue (the larger common goal) and the level of influence they have in making the goal achievable.

[22] inspired by: ➲ www.changingminds.org/disciplines/change_management/stakeholder_change/interest_influence.htm

Step 1: ***Create a list of the stakeholders relevant to the success of the Stakeholder Dialogue initiative***	The first step is to create a general list of important stakeholders. These can be stakeholders already active in the field of work, in a dialogue process, or actors/organizations who are potentially interested in cooperation. There is no need to be overly comprehensive, but it is important to focus on the most relevant stakeholders (institutions or individuals) who can make the Stakeholder Dialogue succeed or fail.
Step 2: ***Assess stakeholders' influence and interest***	Categorize stakeholders according to their potential interest in and influence on the goal, and place them on the grid accordingly. It is important to make a realistic assessment of the current situation (do not place them where you think they should be, but where they are according to your assessment). Cross-check your results if you have placed most stakeholders in the high interest/high influence quadrant: is this the reality? When plotting stakeholders' positions on your grid, consider marking the stakeholders who you see as advocating or supporting your initiative in green, and those whom you expect to block or criticize your initiative in red.
Step 3: ***Consolidate and interpret your findings***	After discussing the results of your interest/influence grid, consolidate the conclusions. Consider the following questions related to the key stakeholders for the success of the Stakeholder Dialogue: • Are key stakeholders interested, or is there a need to raise their interest in the goal? • Are key stakeholders interested, but have little influence? • Are key stakeholders influential, but show little interest? • Are there key stakeholders you do not know enough about to be able to assess their interest or influence?
Step 4: ***Develop a good understanding of how best to engage the most important stakeholders***	Discuss the findings and explore, how your may have an influence on changing stakeholders' positions on the grid: • How can you raise the interest of stakeholders you need and whom you placed at low interest? • How could you convince powerful stakeholders to support you? • How can you support stakeholder with little influence, but high interest?

Develop your engagement process accordingly. Be aware that the key stakeholders you need to implement the Stakeholder Dialogue need to be in the right quadrants of high interest and low influence, or high interest and high influence. If not enough stakeholders are interested in the goal and the initiative, it may not make sense to continue. Once you understand stakeholder views, you can decide how best to engage them.

➲ ***Chapter 5: Resources, 5.9 Engaging Stakeholders, page 143***

Classification of the actors of a stakeholder system

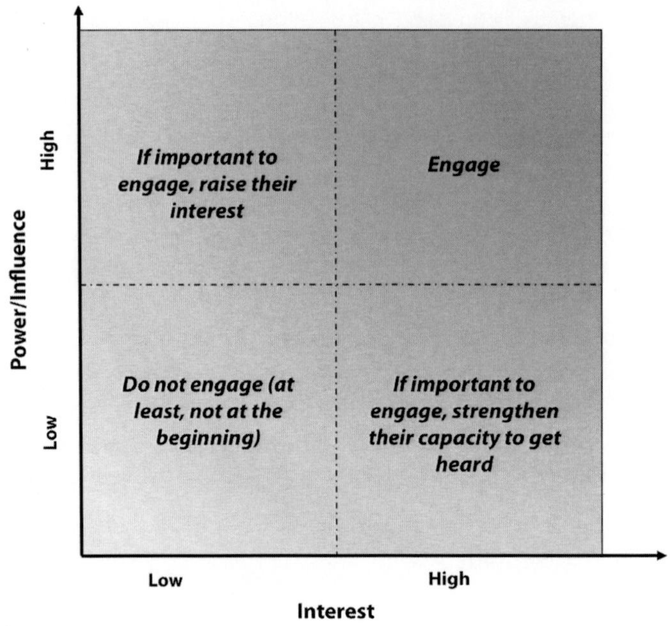

High-influence, high-interest stakeholders:

These are the people you must make the greatest effort to engage fully.

High-power, low-interest stakeholders:

Invest enough work into keeping these stakeholders informed at least. It is best to gain their interest, but do not overload them with information. Build good relationships if you do not need to involve them directly. If you need them in the dialogue process, make all efforts to raise their interest in the issue. How actively these stakeholders should be pursued needs to be driven by the importance of having them involved in the dialogue.

Low-influence, but interested stakeholders:

If these stakeholders' interest is high, there must be a reason. For example, they may be affected groups, or advocacy groups such as small businesses that are interested in a better business environment, communities, and so on. Often, these stakeholders have important information, perspectives or experiences. But they may lack the capacity to make their voices heard, so they need support in doing this. They may also be badly organized and need institutional strengthening to increase their influence. Stakeholders in this quadrant can become important supporters of the Stakeholder Dialogue. Engage them, support them, and keep them adequately informed to keep their level of interest in your initiative high. You must assess how important the point of view or experience of these actors is to the dialogue: this should be a criterion for actively involving them in the process

Low-influence, low-interest stakeholders:

Keep considering these stakeholders, but do not bore them with excessive communication. Do not involve them in the Stakeholder Dialogue, but review this approach periodically, because their status can also change.

It is important to use an inclusive and transparent approach in the stakeholder engagement process to build ownership and commitment. Stakeholders will be engaged in different ways in the various stages of the Stakeholder Dialogue: through gathering and providing information, consulting, dialogue, working together, and so on. If it is not possible to have all stakeholders involved from the outset, then a strategy for gradual involvement may be needed.

6.3.2 Mapping a stakeholder system landscape

In the first phase of stakeholder engagement, it can be extremely helpful to get a better understanding of the situation by creating a map or landscape of the collaborative system of relevant stakeholders. It is important to create a realistic picture of the current situation.

The purpose of mapping the stakeholder system is to:

- understand the system of stakeholders better;
- understand better where dialogue and collaboration is already happening;
- diagnose existing behavior or relationship patterns; and
- build a better basis for designing an engagement strategy.

MAPPING A STAKEHOLDER SYSTEM LANDSCAPE

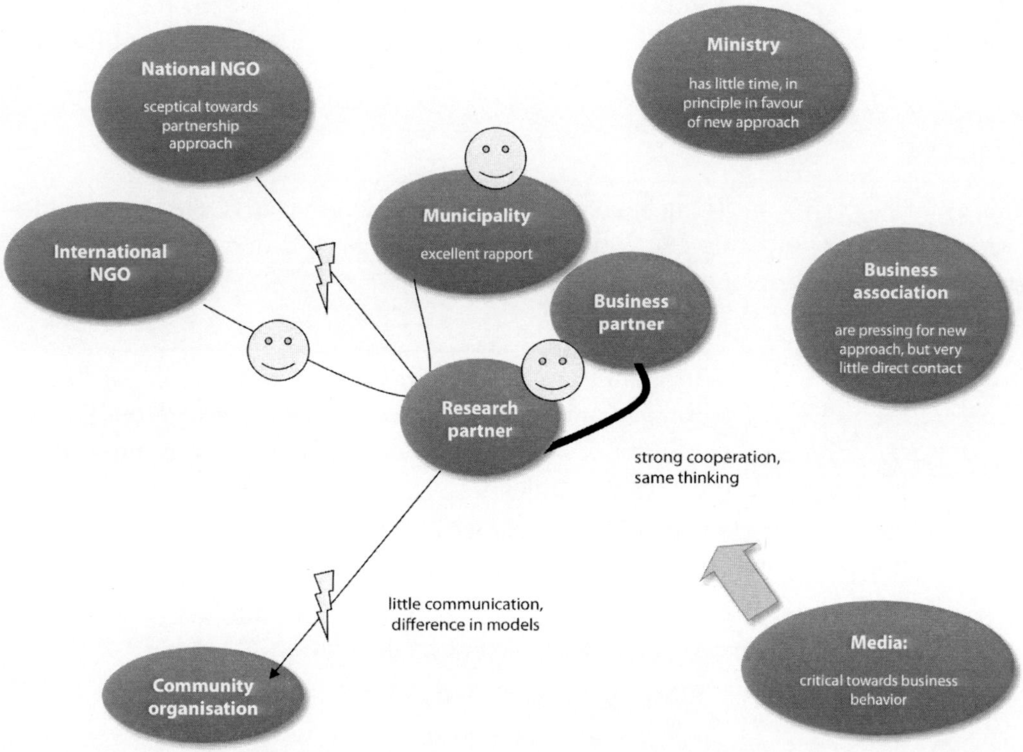

Step 1: Determine if the one carrying out the stakeholder analysis is part of the system	Determine whether you are acting as the initiator of a Stakeholder Dialogue; if you are just one actor among other stakeholders; or if you are an external actor supporting dialogue and collaboration in a system of stakeholders. In any of the cases, because you want to intervene in the system through initiative or leadership, put yourself in the center. If you are not part of the system, but you want to intervene at a later stage, determine the most important actor and start the map with this actor.
Step 2: Determine the stakeholders' relationships to the dialogue or cooperation initiative and to each other	Ask yourself: • What other important stakeholders are in the system? • What is our working relationship with them like? Draw the stakeholder actors one by one, assessing your working relationship with them by showing their distance from you, using thin or thick arrows; by showing one-way or mutual relationships; or by writing remarks about the relationships between you and the other actors.
Step 3: Determine which other actors can potentially influence the system	Think about the other actors in the system. Assess their importance to, and influence on, the possible success of what you plan to do.
Step 4: List external influences on the stakeholder system	Think about what other aspects or outside influences could have an effect on your initiative, and draw them into the picture.
Step 5: Evaluate the stakeholder mapping	When you have mapped the system, have a look at it from a distance and discuss your results and interpretation. Draw conclusions about whether, and how, you want to engage the different stakeholders. Some guiding questions here are: • How does the stakeholder system work? • Is dialogue and collaboration well established, or how is it malfunctioning? • What do you need to do to build outcome-oriented dialogue and collaboration? • Where is the energy for the purpose of the Stakeholder Dialogue in the system? • How could you expand this energy by engaging all relevant or important actors?
Step 6: Discuss intervention possibilities	Develop an intervention strategy on the basis of your map and decide on the next few steps to take. Then, review the process, review the map, and assess what has changed or what you see differently now. Revise your strategy.

6.4 Resource-mapping in Stakeholder Dialogues

Stakeholder dialogues often represent a cross-sector approach, involving diverse stakeholders from the major social sectors as partners in the initiative. This has the advantage of bringing in the necessary complementary skills and competencies to address and support the key issues for the initiative.

Resource-mapping is relevant to different forms of Stakeholder Dialogues, whether a consultation, a stakeholder platform, an initiative or a stakeholder partnership. Stakeholders bring different resources to any form of Stakeholder Dialogue. These resources can be technical, human, knowledge, physical, or financial resources.

The following diagram on **potential resources in Stakeholder Dialogue**,[23] illustrates the resources that different stakeholders can bring into a dialogue. These resources are diverse, and depend on the specific context of the initiative.

MAPPING THE RESOURCES WITHIN A STAKEHOLDER SYSTEM

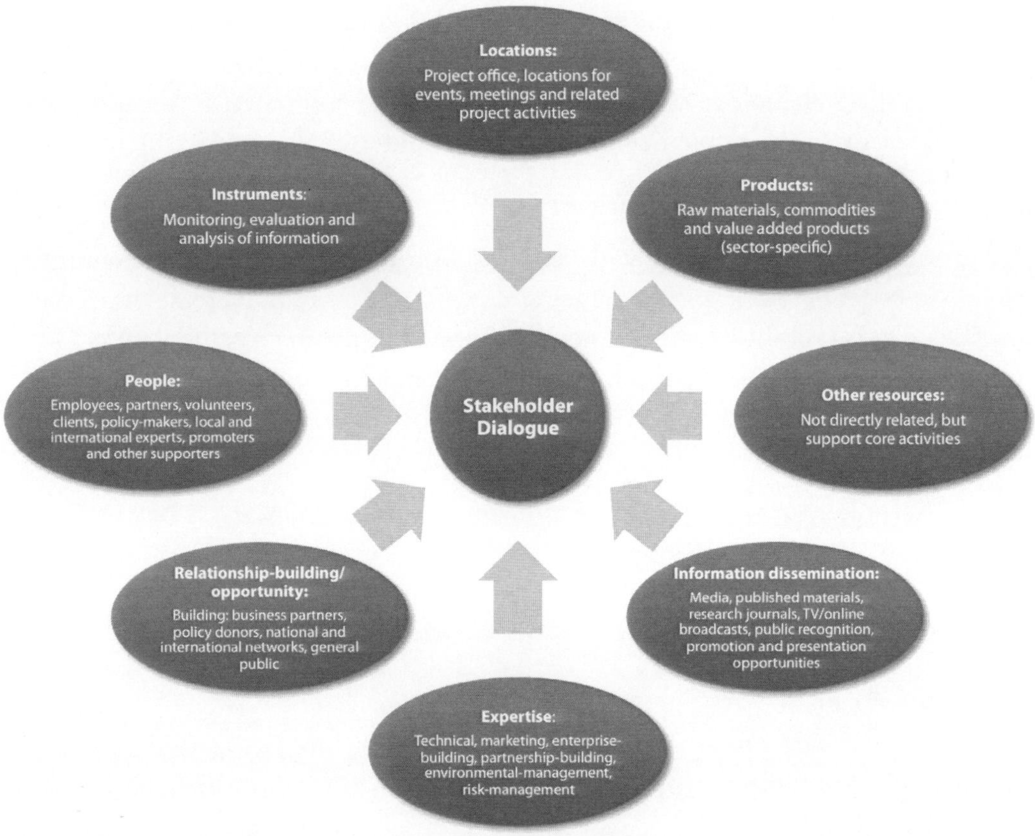

[23] inspired by and based on: The Partnering Initiative (2003): Partnership Toolbook:

➲ http://www.hepartneringinitiative.org/docs/tpi/pt/artneringToolbookEng.pdf

The following section briefly presents the resources that stakeholders from different sectors can bring to a Stakeholder Dialogue.

Business

Companies can provide valuable contributions by strengthening the stakeholders' dialogue-management capacity. Involving the private sector can bring in skills in business planning and cost-effectiveness, and can help the Stakeholder Dialogue to evaluate and consider the business environment and respective market possibilities. Private business partners can also contribute financially to the implementation of the Stakeholder Dialogue.

National and international public institutions

The presence of governments and international organizations brings a certain degree of legitimacy to a Stakeholder Dialogue. These bodies also provide much of the policy framework within which stakeholders operate.

Governments can create a positive enabling environment and use their political power to push an initiative forward. They can use their convening powers to bring potential partners to the table. They can also help by acknowledging and endorsing good business practices, or by promoting and helping to mainstream the learning from Stakeholder Dialogues across industry sectors. Through its presence, the public sector makes the Stakeholder Dialogue more visible. The public sector can also contribute financially to the implementation of Stakeholder Dialogues.

Donor institutions and foundations

These groups can help not only with funding but also by linking a Stakeholder Dialogue to wider networks of experience and expertise. This can increase the Stakeholder Dialogue's visibility. Foundations, for example, can also provide resources for research, advocacy, the participation of weaker stakeholder groups, and other crucial components of moving the Stakeholder Dialogue forward.

Civil society

Civil society organizations often have expertise in specific areas, access to and experience with certain target groups, and a well-developed network of critical or weaker stakeholder groups.

Communities

Communities can bring in an area's local and indigenous knowledge. This area can be thematic or geographical. They can also contribute to the knowledge-base in a specific sector or region.

Researchers and research institutions and networks

These groups provide knowledge and expertise about specific issues and can supply valuable information, scientific analysis and evaluations. They can also be potential publishers of best practices and insights that they have taken directly from the Stakeholder Dialogue, thus contributing to Stakeholder Dialogues' official recognition.

Trade unions

Trade unions and associations represent workers' interests, and have become increasingly active about environment and sustainable-development issues. Their participation contributes to the credibility of Stakeholder Dialogues, particularly if the private sector is involved.

Social groups

Social and gender-advocacy groups are an important resource that gives access to the viewpoints of less-organized target groups. They often also bring in grass-roots experience. This can ensure that the interests of weaker groups are protected and their rights secured. Women's groups, for example, can bring valuable perspectives and examples from their experiences to Stakeholder Dialogues.

It is very important to note that neither of the different stakeholder groups is homogenous, but that each group itself represents a range of perspectives and interests.

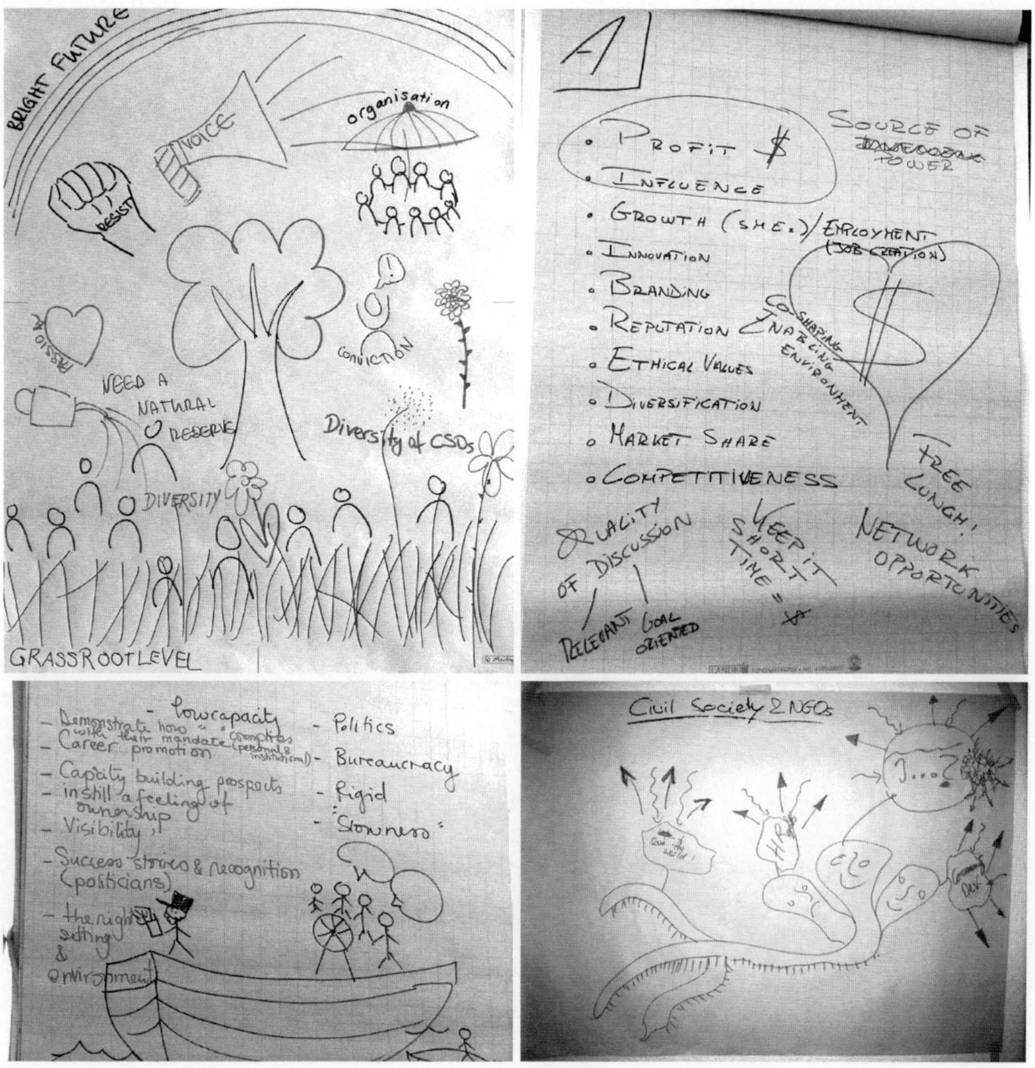

6.5 Checklist for the Dialogic Change Model – Implementing Stakeholder Dialogues in a result-oriented way

➲ *Chapter 2: Getting active, 2.1 The Dialogic Change Model , page 55*

The following checklist is a tool for planning Stakeholder Dialogues by following the four phases of the **Dialogic Change Model**. It includes the most important aspects involved in the planning of the individual phases. The checklist may also be used after you have completed one or more of the phases, as a tool for reflecting on the process. Initiators, implementers or the core group should use this checklist jointly as a group to reflect on its different aspects.

For the checklist the following answer categories can be used:

1	Strongly disagree
2	Mostly disagree
3	Partly disagree
4	Partly agree
5	Mostly agree
6	Strongly agree

If one or more of the questions in a particular phase are answered with number below 4, discuss which aspects of the phase require more emphasis or attention, need to be redone or can only be implemented with some delay.

Checklist for the Dialogic Change Model: Implementing Stakeholder Dialogues in a result-oriented way

PHASE 1: EXPLORING AND ENGAGING	*1*	*2*	*3*	*4*	*5*	*6*
1.1 Create resonance						
1.1.1 Have we invested sufficient time in creating bonds with all relevant actors and gathered their different opinions and points of view?						
1.1.2 Have we been able to get the idea across to potentially relevant actors through formal and informal conversations?						
1.1.3 Have we been able to convince relevant actors of the urgency of the initiative, and of having them take part in the shaping of the initiative's goals and objectives?						
1.1.4 Have we conducted small meetings with relevant actors to create resonance for affirming the initiative's common goals despite remaining unresolved questions?						
1.2 Understand the context						
1.2.1 Have all stakeholder groups that can provide us with a comprehensive view of the current situation and of possible future developments been consulted?						
1.2.2 Do we have all necessary information about the issue at stake?						
1.2.3 Have we conducted a Stakeholder Analysis and assessed what needs to be done for our engagement process?						
1.2.4. Are we well aware of the different factors or actors that may have an important influence on the initiative (positive or negative)?						
1.2.5 Are we aware of any results from similar initiatives elsewhere and have we evaluated previous experiences?						
1.2.6 Have we found out why change has not occurred earlier and what the impeding factors had been?						
1.2.7 Have we explored potential conflict situations that might arise?						
1.3 Build a Container or change						
1.3.1 Have we been able to convince and motivate the relevant stakeholders to become part of the core group to start the dialogue process?						
1.3.2 Have we invested sufficiently into Container-building for the core group and has this had the effect we envisaged?						
1.3.3 Are we maintaining a balance between developing internal plans or a structure for the initiative while preserving a certain degree of structural openness?						
1.3.4 Is the initiative's existing initial Container willing and able to consolidate the composition and role of its individual members?						
1.3.5 Is the core group as an initial Container sufficiently mandated?						
1.3.6 Have we obtained sufficient high-level sponsorship for the initiative?						
1.3.6 Have we promoted the Stakeholder Dialogue approach to various stakeholder groups relevant for or affected by the envisaged change system?						
1.3.8 Has the core group had the chance to understand the perspective of different stakeholders?						
1.3.9 Have we ensured that the core group and important actors are knowledgeable enough about the methodology of Stakeholder Dialogue?						
1.3.10 Have we assessed the need for expert information or capacity building regarding the issue at stake for relevant stakeholders including the core group and have we planned the necessary steps?						
1.3.11 Has a proper location and setting for the first Stakeholder Dialogue event been chosen in a way that the purpose of building stakeholder ownership and commitment can be fulfilled?						

Checklist for the Dialogic Change Model: Implementing Stakeholder Dialogues in a result-oriented way

2. PHASE 2: BUILDING AND FORMALIZING	*1*	*2*	*3*	*4*	*5*	*6*
2.1 Clarify goals and resources						
2.1.1 Have we sufficiently considered the motivation and requirements for participation of different stakeholder groups?						
2.1.2 Are the stakeholder invited to the first Stakeholder Dialogue event sufficiently representing the larger system of involved or affected actors?						
2.1.3 Have we done all necessary steps in preparing for the first Stakeholder Dialogue event ensuring the best possible engagement process?						
2.1.4 Have we engaged professional facilitation of the Stakeholder Dialogue event and agreed on an event format and program that fosters engagement?						
2.1.5 Have we taken all dimensions of change sufficiently into account (encounter, information, relationship building and event structure) ?						
2.1.6 Have we secured a sufficiently high-level opening for the event that shows high-level commitment to the process?						
2.1.7 Has the initiative been properly described so that all involved actors will feel adequately consulted/ cared for?						
2.1.8 Has the initiative been properly described so that all involved actors will feel adequately consulted/ cared for?						
2.1.9 Is the common goal of the initiative clear to all participating stakeholders?						
2.1.10 Does our engagement process promote the development of ownership for the initiative?						
2.1.11 Have the resources the various actors can contribute been explored/agreed upon?						
2.1.12 Are joint objectives, sub-objectives and interests defined in such a way that an initial planning and distribution of roles and responsibilities can be made formal among the stakeholders?						
2.2 Plan future together						
2.2.1 Are all relevant stakeholders sufficiently informed with respect to the initiative's area of action so that they can actively partake in consultation or collaboration efforts ?						
2.2.2 Have we provided the participating stakeholders with all necessary information and expertise required for shaping the future initiative?						
2.2.3 Have we, apart from bringing in information and expertise, planned the event in a way that participating stakeholders can jointly assess the current situation as a basis for shaping the future together?						
2.2.4 Do the steps taken in the process guarantee that the involved stakeholders feel their opinions and comments are taken seriously, causing them to stay committed to the advancement of the dialogue process?						
2.2.5 Is the planning process designed in such a way that stakeholders feel supported in their willingness to shape the future together?						
2.2.6 Has enough room for encounter, exchange of experience, exposure to each other's perspective and joint learning been given?						
2.2.7 Is further consultation or collaboration planned in such a way that synergies can be achieved quickly and visible results can be attained?						

2.3 Consolidate agreements and establish structures						
2.3.1 Does the initiative's form and implementation of the project goals (agreements, memorandum of understanding, project plan, press release, implementation plan etc.) support stakeholder identification with the shared objectives?						
2.3.2 Does the form of the agreements made guarantee the credibility and reliability of the said agreements?						
2.3.3 Have realistic milestones been jointly agreed upon?						
2.3.4 Have roles and responsibilities been accorded for further collaboration?						
2.3.5 Has a realistic timeframe been agreed upon?						
2.3.6 Is there sufficient attention on early results to be showcased as success stories for all participating stakeholders to witness?						

Checklist for the Dialogic Change Model: Implementing Stakeholder Dialogues in a result-oriented way

3. PHASE 3: IMPLEMENTING AND EVALUATING	*1*	*2*	*3*	*4*	*5*	*6*
3.1 Ensure transparency and communication						
3.1.1 Has the communication structure been established that permits a good internal communication and information flow within the initiative?						
3.1.2 Are all of the initiative's major implementation areas sufficiently transparent in their planning?						
3.1.3 Are advancements in implementation recognized and accordingly communicated to the participating stakeholders?						
3.1.4 Is the core group functioning as a good Container supporting the constant, active participation of the stakeholders?						
3.1.5 Are we leaving enough freedom for providing feedback and integrating it into the process constructively?						
3.2 Create results and celebrate success						
3.2.1 Are we picking the 'low-hanging fruits' sufficiently?						
3.2.2 Have all relevant actors in the sector been duly informed of successes?						
3.2.3 Are opportunities to learn from one another and from successes being exploited?						
3.2.4 Have successes in the dialogue process been recognized as such and duly celebrated?						
3.2.5 Do we reliably follow the agreed upon plan or process design?						
3.2.6 Has an agreement been reached about how successes should be communicated to the public in a way that avoids misunderstandings?						
3.2.7 Is the general public properly informed and are communication channels that are important to the progress of the initiative being used constructively?						
3.2.8 Have we sufficiently involved high-level sponsorship into the celebration of successes?						
3.3 Establish learning mechanisms						
3.3.1 Has the core group in its function as a good Container developed the introspection and self-awareness to determine if we are on the right track?						
3.3.2 Is feedback from stakeholders being sufficiently integrated into the process to give them a feeling of participation in the process?						
3.3.3 Do stakeholders still feel their input is being taken seriously?						
3.3.4 Does an internal monitoring and evaluation system exist, which benefits the process?						
3.3.5 Do we regularly assess the quality of our process?						
3.3.6 Does an internal system for strategic learning exist that all key stakeholders are part of?						

Checklist for the Dialogic Change Model: Implementing Stakeholder Dialogues in a result-oriented way

4. PHASE 4: Developing further, replicating or institutionalizing	*1*	*2*	*3*	*4*	*5*	*6*
4.1 Build the next-level Container						
4.1.1 Is there a need to scale-up or replicate the initiative?						
4.1.2 Have current strategies and procedures been reviewed and, if needed, adapted for the next implementation phase?						
4.1.3 Does this up-scaling, replicating or institutionalizing of the Stakeholder Dialogue require new stakeholders to participate, and have they been identified?						
4.1.4 Has a strategy been developed for creating a wider involvement of stakeholders?						
4.1.5 Are stakeholders who have been identified as important messengers for the advancement of the initiative been sufficiently coached/ integrated into the Container (if they were not already in it)?						
4.1.6 Are alliances required for the initiative's advancement being adequately sought after/supported/ identified?						
4.1.7 Is the ownership and commitment of existing stakeholders being safeguarded in any way?						
4.2 Create management structures						
4.2.1 Has the potential extended field of action been sufficiently explored and is the potentially new or changing context well enough understood to properly plan the next steps?						
4.2.2 Are all key actors aware of the requirement of adequate management structures and has this been discussed with key stakeholders?						
4.2.3 Has enough time been planned for preparing institutionalization, replicating or scaling-up?						
4.2.4 Has a structural/organizational form been identified, which the initiative's next implementation phase will require?						
4.2.5 Is the new Container well-poised to withstand difficulties and balance this transitional phase?						
4.3 Establish governance and learning systems						
4.3.1 Have financial support and capacity-building needs for scaling up been identified?						
4.3.2 Have the structures for learning and proper reflection been preserved, despite increased management structure and the integration of new key actors?						
4.3.3 Has the correct design been identified for the continuation of the joint dialogue process, allowing for the adequate form of structure, professionalization and openness required by further expansion?						
4.3.4 Has the wider system of stakeholders been informed about successes from the past process so that they can become supportive of the next level development?						
4.3.5 Have monitoring and evaluation systems been installed?						
4.3.6 Have governance system been established that follow the form of stakeholder participation of the past process?						
4.3.7 Is the new structure or set-up of the initiative assessed as sustainable in the long-run?						

6.6 Seating orders for Stakeholder Dialogue events: a brief overview

The setting of a meeting has a more decisive influence on the results of a meeting than we may be aware of. The structure of a seating order often determines to a great extent the way people communicate with each other. The following paragraphs briefly highlight advantages and disadvantages of certain seating orders for Stakeholder Dialogue events.

6.6.1 The conference setting

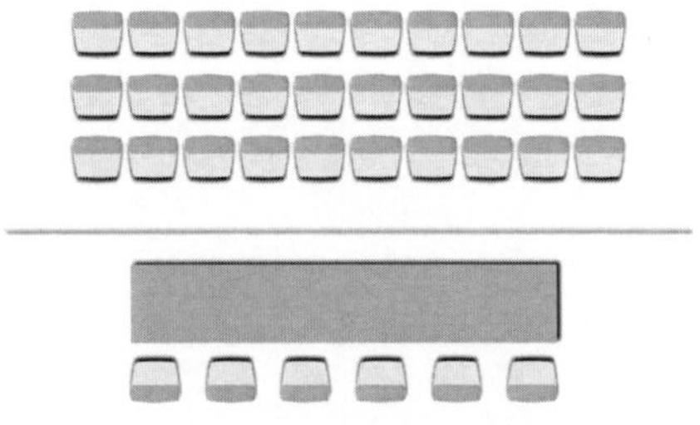

In a formal conference setting there is usually a panel at the front of the room, or a speaker's podium, and the meeting facilitator stands in front of a row of chairs. People, most of the time, silently listen to the speakers, the panelists or presenters, while occasionally having the chance to ask a question or make a short statement on a particular issue.

Advantage:

The setting allows for a large number of participants. High-level supporters and speakers are given sufficient respect and feel acknowledged.

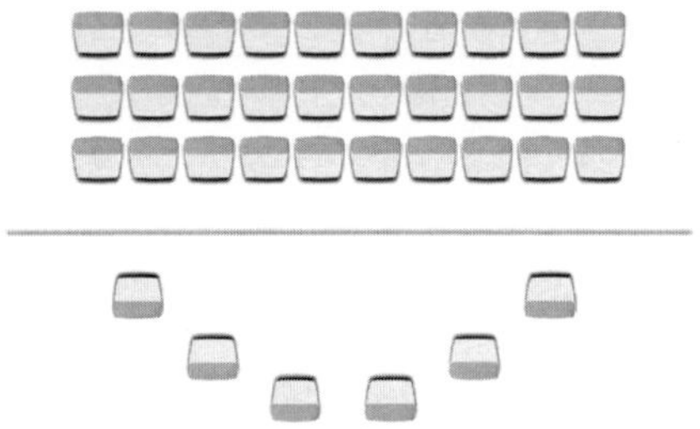

Disadvantage:

The setting creates a barrier between the more important people and the rest of the participants; it therefore emphasizes the hierarchy between speakers and listeners.

Most commonly only a few individuals in the front, the speakers, will talk, while others may only comment occasionally. Quite often opposition will be raised in the form of statements, disguised as a question. There is, for the most part, a unilateral flow of communication. No real dialogue between speakers and listeners can emerge, and there is practically no communication between the participants.

Even a panel discussion does not easily allow for a conversation between the panel and the audience, who are likely to resort to making statements. This setting does not promote discussion, insight, encounter or experience.

Conclusion:

The setting is not suitable for any Stakeholder Dialogue event that claims to authentically engage different stakeholders' perspectives and consider their contributions. It is also incapable of bringing stakeholders into an exchange with each other – which is a prerequisite for a successful dialogue processes.

6.6.2 The U-shape setting

In a formal Stakeholder Dialogue setting people often resort to this type of seating order as it is the most commonly used form for round table discussions which include different stakeholders. In this setting, the possibility for high quality communication among different stakeholder also depends on the mandated facilitator. In hierarchical settings where protocol plays an important role, the highest person in charge often chairs such meetings. This may not always be a person skilled in ensuring that dialogue can take place. Such meeting settings can also be facilitated by professional moderators, which can improve the likelihood of an equal contribution by all participating stakeholders.

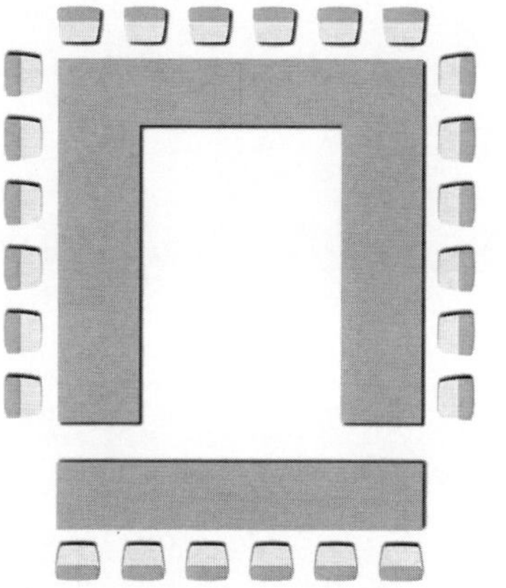

Advantage:

This seating order allows for a limited number of stakeholders to enter into a close exchange of perspectives and positions. This setting is known to most stakeholders from the public sector, private sector and civil society and therefore does not provoke irritation when used for Stakeholder Dialogues. For stakeholders who are already familiar with each other and have well established and communicative relationships, this setting can foster good results.

Disadvantage:

The U-shape seating order also establishes a hierarchy between the important people in the front and the other participants. The setting, unless facilitated by a very skilled professional moderator, (or unless stakeholders know each other very well) will invite participants into conveying statements rather than entering into a conversation with each other. One can expect a communicative pattern of serial monologues (move/move), a debate (move/oppose), or, in very hierarchical settings, compliant communication (move/follow). This will rarely lay the ground for developing ownership and collaboration. Participants will tend to defend their positions and territories. In some cultures, opposition may not be raised openly at all. This setting makes group work impossible, unless the facilitator plans for break-out sessions.

Conclusion:

For a kick-of event of a Stakeholder Dialogue the settings is not particularly suitable, as it rarely achieves a shift in communicative or relational patterns or permits participants to encounter each other in smaller working or discussion groups. It does, however, keep the hierarchy safe, and may therefore be considered a first starting point for Stakeholder Dialogue. At the beginning of a Stakeholder Dialogue, it may even be impossible to convince decision-makers to use a seating order other than a U-shaped one. If there is no alternative, Stakeholder Dialogue facilitators should stay aware of the fact that this seating order can do little in achieving encounter, relationship building and a sense of collaboration. They must therefore find other ways of bringing these elements into the Stakeholder Dialogue process.

6.6.3 The round-table setting

In general, the round table setting (alternatively: small square tables) serve Stakeholder Dialogues very well as they make it possible to combine input and exchange and conversation between stakeholders who sit at the same table. In order to create an intimate atmosphere and to give participants the opportunity to engage in conversation, the number of people at the table should be at maximum eight, and the diameter of the table should allow for conversations across the table.

However, it also matters who sits around which table with whom. The key to success for Stakeholder Dialogue events is a careful selection of table groups and therefore part of the preparation and the process design. It is advisable to orchestrate the seating in the beginning to make certain people meet certain other people, as this can create openness to change. Depending on what needs to be achieved, facilitators may compose tables of

- homogenous stakeholder groups, when it is important to show differences between stakeholder groups. This usually feels safer and is suited to letting stakeholder groups elaborate a joint position, or
- mixed tables with different stakeholder groups sitting at the same table, when getting to know each other and integration of perspectives is more important. This can be fruitful for exchange of views, and for working on solutions or recommendations etc. that are acceptable to all.

The round table seating order only makes sense, if during part of the Stakeholder Dialogue event, the table groups are tasked to discuss certain issues among themselves, work on a specific task together or reflect together on issues presented. The setting requires, particularly if the stakeholder group is large, a very structured facilitation, and a focus on table related group work rather than plenary discussion.

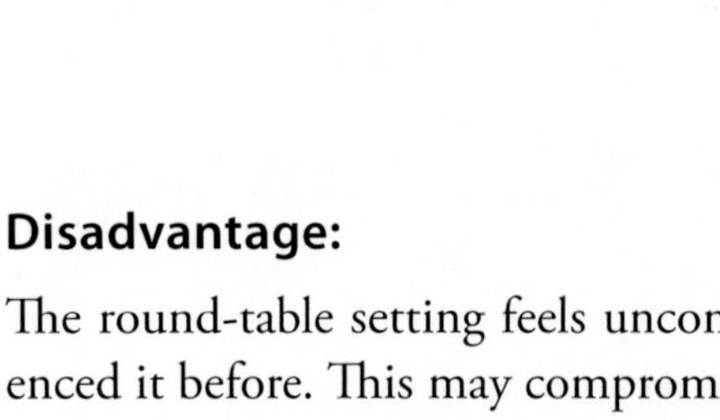

Advantage:

The round-table setting creates a level of intimacy that helps stakeholders connect with each other as people and across differences. It also saves facilitators time as small working groups can take place at the tables and there is no need for break-out sessions that often compromise timing in events.

This setting can host a large number of people (up to 100, depending on the size of the room).

Disadvantage:

The round-table setting feels uncomfortable to stakeholders who have not experienced it before. This may compromise their willingness to engage and this needs to be counteracted by a very conscious event design that allows them to get to know each other right at the outset of the event.

More important people, e.g., decision-makers, may have reservations towards such a setting as they do not have a distinguished seating position. Such a problem can be alleviated by creating an opening panel with important speakers at the beginning of a Stakeholder Dialogue event, and by letting officials announce the dialogue in a more informal working session.

Conclusions:

The round-table setting is the ideal seating order for Stakeholder Dialogue events as it can ensure that stakeholders get into a closer communication with each other, listen to different perspective from different tables but are still able to follow speakers and presenters. The round-table setting requires professional facilitators who are familiar with the setting and know how to balance interaction, presentation and working groups.

6.7 Agreements in Stakeholder Dialogues

The unique value of Stakeholder Dialogues lies in the contribution that all stakeholders can make to the process. While Phase 1 in a Stakeholder Dialogue is characterized by informal working structures, it is important in Phase 2 that the commitment to dialogue and collaboration is consolidated in a more formal agreement. This can be a formal document that shows the scope of the commitment, such as a strategy paper, a documented joint statement of the current situation and the way forward, or a declaration of a joint interest in the goal. Agreements formalize and consolidate the results of the more informal building up of engagement in Phase 1. They strengthen further co-operation and dialogue, offer guidance and support in the case of unavoidable conflicts, and serve as an orientation in the complex environment of the Stakeholder Dialogue. So, they are important for fostering the cohesion among collaborating stakeholders.

Stakeholder agreements:

- require those who are involved in the drafting and signing to have a clear mandate (this mandate can be acquired by a single organization or by the larger system);
- need to be developed jointly and consensually among key stakeholders;
- should reflect the form of dialogue and cooperation, whether formal or informal;
- should be based on mutual respect and the principles of equality between different stakeholders;
- do not need to be legally binding, but show and convey the commitment;
- can (but do not need to) develop from less to more formal agreements, such as from a declaration of interest to a memorandum of understanding or a formal contract;
- are based on voluntary commitments; and
- should, if they formalize structures, ensure optimal representation of stakeholder interests (which has to be reflected in all temporary working structures such as steering committees, task forces or working groups).

The type of agreement suitable for a Stakeholder Dialogue depends on the form of the dialogue. The more the dialogue moves towards collaboration and joint implementation, the more detailed and comprehensive agreements will be necessary. This means formalizing working structures, internal and external communication, roles and mandates, finances, or other contributions. It also requires setting a timeline for implementation. The more binding the agreements, the more important it is to have them approved by senior management in the institutions involved.

Agreements must be worded well to be easily and correctly understood by all stakeholders. Typical legal language should be avoided as much as possible. The formal nature of agreed-upon conditions and commitments regarding the cooperation can be increased step by step during the course of a dialogue. Very formal agreements should only be made, if Phase 1 (exploration and consultation) of Stakeholder Dialogue has been completed, which means sufficient trust has been built and stakeholders are prepared to cooperate.

The following list shows examples of agreement types, in ascending order of formality. Most of these forms of agreements are not specific to Stakeholder Dialogues, but are also used in other forms of cooperation.

Declaration of interest:

Often used by private-sector stakeholders to show their interest in dialogue and collaboration pragmatically.

Agreement on next steps:

In complex or fragile Stakeholder Dialogues, this is a good way of consolidating and agreeing jointly on the next meeting and the process ahead.

Commented documentation of stakeholder workshop results

Where more formal agreements may still be too contentious, documentation sent around to all stakeholders for comments can serve as a form of agreement that makes meeting results transparent.

Minutes of meetings

In smaller Stakeholder Dialogue rounds, meeting minutes are a pragmatic form of process- and results-documentation that creates commitment and cohesion.

Declaration of membership

Particularly for stakeholder platforms, this form of agreement is a typical way of showing commitment to both the group of stakeholders and the public. It is sometimes preceded by an agreement on membership rules.

Joint declaration of cooperation

This is particularly for stakeholder initiatives. It is a way of showing, internally and externally, the commitment to collaborate and achieve results. A declaration of cooperation should include important elements of the implementation of the results. Such a declaration can, depending on the context and goal of the Stakeholder Dialogue, be made public, or just communicated among the participating stakeholders.

Joint project plan or plan of operations

Stakeholder Dialogues with emphasis on implementation require joint and agreed planning of the dialogue and cooperation process. This can include roles and responsibilities, activity planning and forms of monitoring.

Agreements on steering structures or governance mechanisms

Steering structures are important for implementing complex Stakeholder Dialogues. They are used in stakeholder initiatives, and sometimes in stakeholder partnerships. Agreements here define the terms of reference for steering structures and representation of stakeholders in the structure. These terms includes selection procedures, sequence of meetings and a definition of decision-making responsibilities.

Memorandum of Understanding

A Memorandum of Understanding (MOU) is a form of consolidating cooperation commitment between two or more stakeholders. It can include detailed paragraphs on the form of cooperation.

TOOLS

Joint press statement

A joint press statement makes the dialogue or cooperation known to the public. This can be a way of showing commitment to each other, but also to the public, in Phase 2 or 3. These are only issued when the first results of the process have been achieved.

Cooperation contract

A legally binding contract specifying roles and responsibilities, resource contribution and allocations, duties and obligations. Most often used in stakeholder partnerships.

Possible agreements in the different forms of Stakeholder Dialogues

Form of Stakeholder Dialogues		*Examples of agreements*
Stakeholder Consultation	In **stakeholder consultation** there is usually one stakeholder group (e.g. public sector, private sector) taking the lead in integrating the results of the consultation into its strategic and operational activities. Agreements here display the lead agency's commitment to using the consultation results in an appropriate way and the commitment of participating stakeholders to contribute their input.	• Time plan showing how and when the results from consultation will be integrated • Agreements on form and sequence of further consultation • Agreements on time and form of review meetings • Agreements on the form of further communication with or among stakeholders
Stakeholder Platforms	**Stakeholder platforms** can have varying degrees of formality, depending on who is the convener and who is involved. Some stakeholder platforms are very open, inviting whoever is interested to join. Others only function by invitation, or may develop criteria for membership and rules of participation.	• Open membership • Membership regulations • Rules of participation
Stakeholder initiative	**Stakeholder initiatives** require more formal arrangements, as there is a joint responsibility for success. This suggests the establishment of structures and the allocation of roles and responsibilities. The contribution is usually also formalized in an agreement, be it a financial, in kind or in any other form.	• Memorandum of understanding • Strategy documents • Project plans • Rules of participation • Rules for internal and external communication • Agreements on roles and responsibilities • Agreements on steering structures • Agreements on contributions
Stakeholder partnership	**Stakeholder partnerships** often require formal arrangements such as binding contracts. All stakeholders that are directly part of the partnership are obliged to follow agreed-upon plans, and contribute the agreed-upon resources.	• Binding contracts for cooperation including financial or other contributions • Project and activity plans • Strategy documents • Rules for internal and external communication • Agreements on roles and responsibilities • Agreements on steering structures

6.8 Steering and implementation structures

Steering and implementation structures are most relevant to Stakeholder Dialogues that have a focus on collaboration and implementation. Stakeholder platforms for implementation, stakeholder initiatives and stakeholder partnerships require transparent and stakeholder-composed steering, implementation or governance mechanisms.

The construction of such structures should only begin after a consolidated and successful Phase 2 and should follow the purpose of the Stakeholder Dialogue: the initiation and implementation of change. Lean and non-bureaucratic structures are recommended, but this depends on the type and context of the Stakeholder Dialogue. Too much structure can create an administrative or political advocacy culture in Stakeholder Dialogue with too little emphasis on results. Too little structure can endanger the implementation capacity of a dialogue process.

The steering structure is an important contribution to the legitimacy of the Stakeholder Dialogue, and the implementation structure is a prerequisite for delivery and outcome-orientation. There is no blueprint for the establishment of steering and implementation structures in Stakeholder Dialogues, but the following list shows possibilities that have proved effective.

High level sponsorship:

This secures high-level commitment and can have degrees of formality. A formal arrangement of high-level sponsorship would be an officially announced patronage. Less formal arrangements can include the endorsement of content, goal and process of a Stakeholder Dialogue by the respective hierarchy in the institutions of the participating stakeholders.

Steering committees:

Steering committees need to be composed of the different participating and/or affected stakeholders. Members of a steering committee need to be enabled to take ownership of the process and results. The selection of members for the steering committee depends on the context of the Stakeholder Dialogue, and may include official representatives selected by the different stakeholder groups. It is important that members of the steering committee are sufficiently engaged. Mere official representation, with little interest in results, can jeopardize a Stakeholder Dialogue. In complex Stakeholder Dialogues, it may be helpful to introduce 'rapporteurs'. These are 'speakers' selected from the steering committee members by each group of stakeholders. They manage the communication between the stakeholder group, the implementation structures (and project secretariats) and steering committees.

(Project) secretariats/process management teams:

(Project) secretariats facilitate implementation and communication among stakeholders, and between the steering committees and the implementing institutions. They can, but do not need to be, composed of different stakeholders. Emphasis here is on professional management of implementation, but they need to earn the trust of all stakeholders and of the steering committee. Secretariats guarantee reliability of processes and transparency of communication, they prepare and document all stakeholder meetings, and they push implementation forward. They follow agreed-upon planning and reporting procedures. Members of secretariats must be authentically service-oriented, interested in the goal and neutral among the different interests of stakeholders. External facilitators can support secretariats.

Task forces or expert working groups:

Many complex Stakeholder Dialogues require content work on specific issues, be it research, preparation of decisions or recommendations to the steering committee. Task forces are often composed of different stakeholders to ensure that the expertise and interests of different stakeholder groups are represented. Expert working groups do not necessarily need to be composed of different stakeholders, but often require specific, sometimes external, expertise. Task forces and expert working groups should be endorsed by steering committees.

Advisory groups:

Complex stakeholder groups with contentious or politically sensitive content often establish advisory groups. These can be composed of non-participating stakeholders who have an interest, but no stake, in the issue. Examples are funder representatives, interested research organizations, representatives from other stakeholder initiatives, and so on.

Experts:

In addition to members of expert working groups Stakeholder Dialogues can, particularly in Phase 1 and Phase 3, involve external experts on certain issues. All expert input should be carefully planned, particularly in Stakeholder Dialogues with low trust among stakeholders. The project secretariat should take care of the way in which expert input is presented so that participating stakeholders do not feel bullied or manipulated.

STEERING AND IMPLEMENTATION STRUCTURES

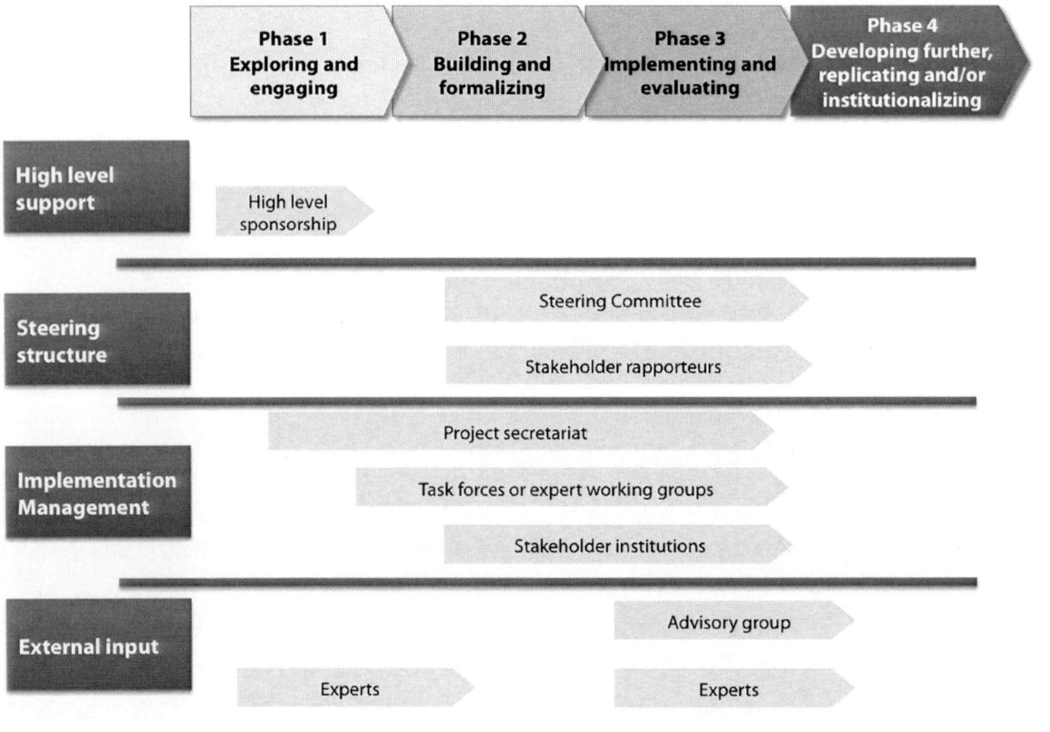

6.9 Managing difficulties in Stakeholder Dialogues

Difficulties and conflicts in Stakeholder Dialogues are normal side-effects of contrasting points of view and different, or even opposing, interests. They can cause disagreements and misunderstandings, and can complicate implementation. If a Stakeholder Dialogue is not given enough attention in preparation and process design, it runs the risk of going stagnant or failing altogether. Many difficulties can be prevented by applying careful planning, adhering to the principles of successful engagement processes and conducting events that take the dialogic practices into account.

➲ *Chapter 2, Getting active, 2.1 The Dialogic Change Model , page 55, Chapter 5: Resources, 5.9 Engaging Stakeholders, page 143, 5.10 Pitfalls in engagement processes, page 146, 5.11 Understanding the need to engage different stakeholder groups differently, page 147*

However, Stakeholder Dialogues are complex processes and will always need to overcome difficulties at some stage. This makes it important to be aware of difficulties and conflicts when they arise and to deal with them properly. It is not possible to avoid them completely during the course of a Stakeholder Dialogue; however, it is possible to avoid the escalation of such difficulties through good communication and relationship-management.

The following table offers possible responses to the different types of difficulties that may arise during a Stakeholder Dialogue. A timely, thought-through response can ensure the continuation of the dialogue. If or when specific types of difficulties arise in a Stakeholder Dialogue depends greatly on the overall conditions and general atmosphere between the actors involved in the dialogue.

Possible responses to difficulties in Stakeholder Dialogues

The situation occurring	*Possible responses*
Some stakeholders do not have the willingness to communicate or talk with each other	• Create a platform to solve the conflict outside the formal Stakeholder Dialogue; • Engage actors individually and informally; • Hold bilateral conversations to clarify objectives and topics and to explain the methodology of Stakeholder Dialogues; • Clarify the participants' needs; • Get a bilateral commitment to staying in the process; and • Allow time for informal conversations (e.g. coffee breaks, etc.).
Hierarchy or authorities feel they have not been sufficiently involved, and question the dialogue	• First, engage hierarchy or authorities actors informally on an individual basis, and then engage them officially and integrate them into the process; • Inform the hierarchy using a report, and, through this, gain interest for the process; and • Agree on regular communication
"Territorial" conflicts occur: the Stakeholder Dialogue covers topics that are considered to be the territory of other individuals or institutions	• Make yourself aware of territories before the Stakeholder Dialogue starts; • Clarify conflicting boundaries beforehand • Engage in bilateral conversations and start genuine dialogue with stakeholder separately on synergy effects

The dialogue's initiators are not supported because they have no official mandate	• Explore the possibilities of getting a clear mandate; • Get high-level sponsorship for Stakeholder Dialogues and carefully compose a core group with the consent of high-level sponsors; • Promote the benefits of Stakeholder Dialogues; • Explain the initiator's role to important stakeholders; • Communicate the benefits that could result from the dialogue better; • Underline the initiator's goal of bringing about positive change and demonstrate that there is no hidden agenda; • Interact neutrally with stakeholders but with a clear engagement towards the dialogue's goal; • Offer service orientation; and • In Phase 1, build the core group as an initial Container including different stakeholders.

Possible responses to difficulties in Stakeholder Dialogues

The situation occurring	***Possible responses***
Clashes of interest/ideological differences/hidden agendas occur	• Understand the system: conflict-mapping, early stakeholder analysis; • Use good process-design; • Clarify what is in it for all parties; • Clarify underlying interest (bilateral); • Acknowledge differences, and integrate them into process-design; • Let parties state their differences; • Discuss with them what is at stake if no solution is found; and • Seek support from other important actors, if necessary.
Stakeholder complain about a lack of transparency	• Ensure comprehensive information about the process; • Make sure that issues of communication and information are agreed upon by the stakeholders involved; • Address stakeholders' perceived lack of transparency individually and informally
Power differences become obvious	• Ensure that all voices are heard; • Ensure that weaker stakeholder groups remain in the process or enter into the process; get support for this • If necessary, address power issues with stakeholders separately and talk about their effects; remind more powerful stakeholders of their impact and discuss the impact on the Stakeholder Dialogue • Ensure that process architecture is agreed upon and stick to it; and • Support weaker groups with capacity-building and advocacy.

There is a lack of willingness to come to an agreement	• Find out about stakeholders' willingness to engage and to come to a solution separately and informally; • Re-analyze the situation or re-do a stakeholder analysis, consider the possibility that some stakeholders may benefit from a conflict or disagreement or the continuation of the status quo; re-do Phase 1 • If no willingness exists, postpone the Stakeholder Dialogue; • Explore the possibility of conducting the Stakeholder Dialogue without the stakeholders in question
There is a lack of resources to conduct a Stakeholder Dialogue	• Promote the result-orientation of Stakeholder Dialogues; and • Advocate for resources with potential sponsors
Stakeholders do not understand or agree with the objective of the Stakeholder Dialogue	• Integrate content-related capacity building into the process design • Re-address goal alignment as part of the engagement process.

Possible responses to difficulties in Stakeholder Dialogues

The situation occurring	***Possible responses***
Stakeholders do not understand the Stakeholder Dialogue methodology/There is a lack of professional capacity to contribute to the Stakeholder Dialogue	• Integrate capacity building for Stakeholder Dialogues' as a methodology into the process design of Phase 1 and 2 • Specifically build the capacity of the core group in conducting Stakeholder Dialogues
The core group perceives a lack of leadership or initiative by participating stakeholders, there is no sense of collective responsibility	• Adhere to the principles of an engagement process, strengthen the initial Container, then build the broader Container and gradually involve more stakeholders • Reflect in the core group adjustments in process design • Insist on the importance of each stakeholder's contribution; • Promote the idea of taking leadership for cooperation-management and participation; • Focus on the benefits of result-orientation; • Improve full understanding of the problem; and • Look beyond the obvious situation and explore the reasons for lack of leadership with all key stakeholders

A sense of ownership is lacking among participating stakeholders	• Review process-design; • Address in informal conversations what would create the feeling of ownership; • Go back to clarifying the context (Phase 1); • Ensure honest participation; • Apply dialogic practices; • Clarify relevance of the problem for all participants; • Create a clear vision with all participants; • Clarify that the Stakeholder Dialogue participants are the ones responsible for the problem's solution; and • Build commitment through careful engagement and Container building
Differences in the "languages", decision-making logics, or reporting requirements between the public and private sector occur (e.g. clash of organizational cultures)	• Make an understanding of "languages", decision-making structures, reporting requirements and cultures/ rationales of different stakeholder groups part of an integrated capacity-building into the process design • Clarify the rationale of the different institutions • Explore the needs for reporting with different stakeholder groups
Roles and responsibilities are unclear	• Re-address Phase 2 issues; • Re-clarify roles, structures and responsibilities; • Re-clarify the mandate, making it transparent; • Address issues of engagement that lead to a sense of ownership

Possible responses to difficulties in Stakeholder Dialogues

The situation occurring	***Possible responses***
There is the perception of deteriorating or absent trust	• Re-think the process–design; • Ensure that dialogic practices are implemented; • Engage in one-on-one conversations; • Ensure that the initiator/facilitator is a living example of trustworthiness; • Ensure transparency; • Keep agreements; • Keep to the agreed process-design; • Truly engage and involve; • Do not make false promises; • Work informally and in a structured way on relationship–building; • Conduct events in a way that allows for good conversations and frequent interaction among participants (round tables, coffee break, etc.); • Create face-to-face situations in communications; and • Create and celebrate common successes (success must be tangible)

6.10 Process-monitoring in Stakeholder Dialogues: self-assessment

The purpose of process-monitoring is to keep track of the quality of the process design and of the key success factors for Stakeholder Dialogues. It helps to check if the Stakeholder Dialogue is leading towards the expected outcome regularly – a commitment to progress. Guiding questions are:

- What is the quality of process design and management of the Stakeholder Dialogue?
- Does the process we have designed lead to the expected result and effect?

Process monitoring is best done in the form of a self-assessment. It is never a completely objective measurement, but rather a subjective assessment of a Stakeholder Dialogue's current status. The result may serve as a starting point for a future learning process, and initiate a dialogue concerning success-oriented process management between the core group members or involved stakeholders. The self-assessment tool below, when used throughout the entire process of a Stakeholder Dialogue implementation, can provide interesting documentation of the process, and show learning, adjustment, progress and the overcoming of setbacks.

It is important to make sure that those using this tool understand its key factors, and, if necessary, that they adapt them to each specific Stakeholder Dialogue. The basis for the following self-assessment tool are the key factors for successful Stakeholder Dialogues described in Chapter 4.

The critical success factors are interrelated and mutually supportive. They are interrelated and mutually supportive, and can be seen as lenses through which a group of initiators or conveners can look at the quality of their Stakeholder Dialogue process and review areas that require attention. None of the factors is entirely distinct from another – they influence each other, but they all are leverage points for the improvement of process quality and, subsequently, leverage points for the effect that a Stakeholder Dialogue can have. The amount of attention that each of these factors needs depends on the form and purpose of the Stakeholder Dialogue.

1	Absent
2	Very little in place
3	Not sufficiently in place
4	Somehow in place, but with room for improvement
5	Almost fully in place
6	Fully in place

TOOLS

How can the process monitoring self-assessment be used?

Option 1:	• Everyone participating in the self-assessment should be familiar with the key factors for successful Stakeholder Dialogues. • Then use the spider chart and jointly assess the factors on a scale of 1 to 6. • Initiate a discussion about why the situation is assessed as it is and what can contribute to an improvement.
Option 2:	• Everyone participating in the self-assessment should be familiar with the key factors for successful Stakeholder Dialogues. • Go through the questionnaire and check the list of relevant indicators for the key factors in the different phases. • Assess individually and let individuals mark their own spider charts on a scale of 1 to 6. • Bring the results together and initiate a discussion about why the situation is assessed as it is. • Explore the differences in assessments. • Discuss what can contribute to an improvement. Agree on action to take.

KEY FACTORS FOR SUCCESSFUL STAKEHOLDER DIALOGUES

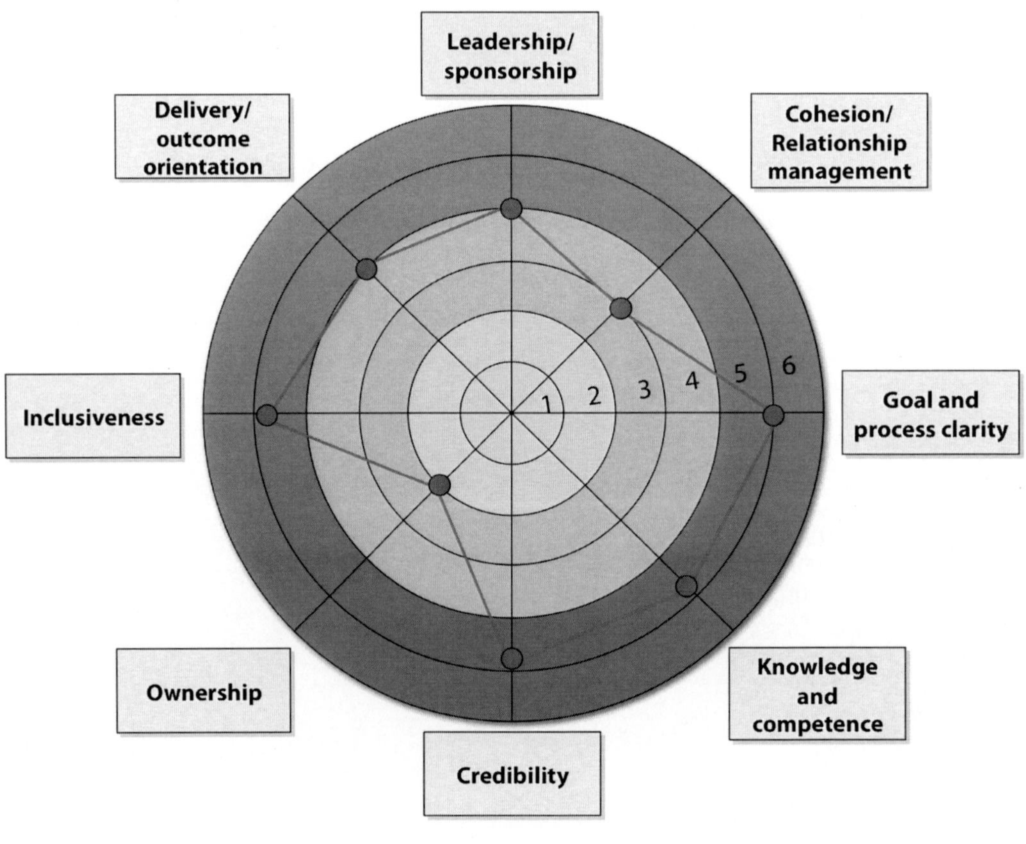

6.10.1 Process-monitoring assessment and indicators

Key factors and guiding questions for assessment	*1*	*2*	*3*	*4*	*5*	*6*
Leadership/sponsorship						
• There is a strong and committed core group functioning as a good Container and representing the collaborating actors.						
• There is appropriate high-level sponsorship for the Stakeholder Dialogue.						
• There are enough committed participants beyond the core group. High-level management in the collaborating institutions is committed to goal and process.						
Cohesion/relationship-management						
• Relationship-management gets sufficient attention. People can meet as people and feel fully respected.						
• Informative and inspiring communication is in place.						
• The relationship between participating stakeholder representatives and their respective institutions gets sufficient attention.						
Goal and process clarity						
• The contribution of the Stakeholder Dialogue to an overall goal is clear to all stakeholders.						
• Participating stakeholders are sufficiently aligned behind the overall goal.						
• Process designs and participation patterns are transparent and reliable.						
Knowledge and competence						
• Knowledge and information about all necessary content areas is available and sufficiently distributed. Content capacity building is built into the process design.						
• Capacity building for the methodology of Stakeholder Dialogues is built into the process design.						
• Sufficient resources for the Stakeholder Dialogue process and implementation are available.						
Credibility						
• Initiators, the core group and/or a process-management team have a sufficient mandate and are trusted by all stakeholders.						
• All relevant stakeholders are adequately represented.						
• Decision-making procedures are transparent, agreed upon by stakeholders (if possible), adequately efficient, and take into account different stakeholders' organizational cultures.						
Inclusivity						
• Weak stakeholder groups are adequately integrated into the process. Stakeholder Dialogue meetings and events are conducted in a way that ensures that all voices are heard.						
• There is an agreed-upon procedure in place on how to deal with critical voices and complaints. Critical voices are either integrated, or good relationships with them are maintained.						
• Stakeholders with high influence have become sufficiently interested in, and integrated into, the Stakeholder Dialogue.						

Key factors and guiding questions for assessment	*1*	*2*	*3*	*4*	*5*	*6*
Ownership						
• The relevance of goal, objectives and outcomes is regularly reviewed with all main stakeholders.						
• All stakeholders contribute their points of view and/or decision-making input equally. Decision-making takes place on the basis of consensus building.						
• The contributions of different stakeholders are sufficiently acknowledged.						
Delivery and outcome-orientation						
• Stakeholder meetings are designed to allow collaborative task completion and always have meeting results reviews. Decisions made in the Stakeholder Dialogue are implemented collectively or by the participating stakeholder institutions.						
• Clear roles and implementation, or steering structures, are in place.						
• Stakeholders have agreed on implementation-monitoring and progress-review procedures. Progress reviews take place regularly.						

6.10.2 The role of process-monitoring in the four phases of the dialogic change model

How can the process-monitoring tool be used in the different phases?

Phase 1: ***Exploring and engaging***	• Introducing the success factors into the core group at an early stage helps to keep the focus on the need for good process design. • The self-assessment can be used to review the process design and review meetings among initiators/core group, a joint assessment supports Container building and a sense of ownership
Phase 2: ***Building and formalizing***	• The self-assessment can be used regularly in the core group or the secretariat/process-management team, inspiring a continuous learning discussion about factors that have contributed to success and to difficulties. • The success factors can also be introduced to a wider group of participating stakeholders as part of capacity building for Stakeholder Dialogues.
Phase 3: ***Implementing and evaluating***	• The self-assessment can further be used in the core group or secretariat/process-management team, inspiring a continuous learning discussion about factors that have contributed to success and to difficulties. • When the Stakeholder Dialogue system is stable enough, and all stakeholders are familiar with the success factors, the self-assessment tool can be introduced as a regular reflection on where the dialogue stand, in addition to activity- and result-monitoring. • This should inspire reflective dialogue on strengths and weaknesses, and should lead to an agreement on action to be taken. • A process-management team can also use the self-assessment as a feedback from stakeholders on their work. • Assessment results should be commented on, and should enhance a reflective dialogue on possible improvements. • If all stakeholders agree, external evaluators can use the assessment tool in conversation with the different stakeholders. Results should be discussed in the framework of a stakeholder meeting.
Phase 4: ***Developing further, replicating and/or institutionalizing***	• The self-assessment can be used regularly in the core group or secretariat/process-management team. However, as Phase 4 involves re-entry into a new engagement process, new stakeholders should be carefully introduced to the principles and key factors for successful Stakeholder Dialogues and not be overwhelmed in the beginning with monitoring. • If a Stakeholder Dialogue develops into a more institutionalized structure, it may require reviewing the relevance of the key factors and creating a new set of factors as a basis for a continuous learning approach.

6.10.3 Indicators for good process-design in the four phases of Stakeholder Dialogues

Leadership/sponsorship

Key factor	*Indicators of good process-design*			
	Phase 1	***Phase 2***	***Phase 3***	***Phase 4***
There is a strong and committed core group functioning as a good Container and representing the collaborating actors.	A small, ideally cross–sector, core group has developed good working relationships and leads the process collectively.	All stakeholders to carry the process forward mandate the core group or secretariat/process-management team.	The core group, a secretariat/process-management structure or an implementation team is committed to delivery and feels accountable to all stakeholders.	A new or widened, committed Container leads the process into institutionalization, replication or scaling-up.
There is appropriate high-level sponsorship for the Stakeholder Dialogue.	High-level support by people whom all stakeholders respect has been obtained.	High-level sponsors endorse goals, objectives and agreements and/or implementation plans.	High-level sponsors are regularly informed about progress and stay interested.	High-level sponsorship is renewed and adjusted for next-level development.
There are enough committed participants beyond the core group. High-level management in the collaborating institutions is committed to goal and process.	Core group members have embedded goals and process objectives of the Stakeholder Dialogue in their respective institutions.	The management of collaborating institutions endorses agreements and implementation plans for the Stakeholder Dialogue, and adequate resources are provided.	Participating key actors regularly report progress to their institutions and integrate feedback into the implementation process, and resources are adequately adjusted.	The management of collaborating institutions endorses further development.

Cohesion/relationship management

Key factor	*Indicators of good process-design*			
	Phase 1	***Phase 2***	***Phase 3***	***Phase 4***
Relationship-management gets sufficient attention. People can meet as people and feel fully respected.	The core group has built good and trusting working relationships. They understand each others' concerns and aspirations.	Collaborating stakeholders respect each other despite differences, and they have had the chance to meet 'people as people'.	Collaborating stakeholders have developed strong informal and formal communication and working relationships.	Stakeholders are prepared to integrate new participants actively.
Informative and inspiring communication is in place.	The core group has set up an internal communication system and agreed on how to engage stakeholders actively.	The wider stakeholder group has agreed upon internal and external rules of communication.	The core group, a secretariat/ process-management team keeps all stakeholders regularly updated about implementation progress. Positive results and success stories are celebrated in an agreed-upon way (rituals of celebrating success).	Communication about further development of the Stakeholder Dialogue. has been agreed by all main stakeholders
The relationship between participating stakeholder representatives and their respective institutions gets sufficient attention.	The core group takes care of mutual relationship-building and one-on-one relationship-building in the engagement process of stakeholders.	Stakeholder meetings and events are designed in a way that stakeholder representatives can discuss progress and agreements with their respective hierarchy.	The core group has a good sense of how to support stakeholder representatives in informing their hierarchy about the progress of the dialogue.	The core group and all stakeholders take care of integrating new stakeholders in a systematic engagement process.

Goal and process clarity

Key factor	*Indicators of good process-design*			
	Phase 1	***Phase 2***	***Phase 3***	***Phase 4***
The contribution of the Stakeholder Dialogue to an overall goal is clear to all stakeholders.	The core group has agreed that the Stakeholder Dialogue approach is the best possible way to achieve the overall goal and short-term objectives.	On the basis of a joint situational analysis, stakeholders have jointly reviewed goal and objectives. Roles, structure, agreements and plans are transparently developed with reference to the overall goal.	The contribution of achievements to the overall goal is regularly reviewed.	All stakeholders, including newly engaged stakeholders, review the goal for further development.
Participating stakeholders are sufficiently aligned behind the overall goal.	The core group is in full agreement regarding the overall goal.	Despite differences in the operationalization of objectives, all stakeholders have agreed on the overall goal.	The overall goal is kept clear and implementation progress reports refer to the goal in internal and external communication	New stakeholders are engaged in a way that they can subscribe to the overall goal.
Process designs and participation patterns are transparent and reliable.	The core group has agreed on a process design and a sequence of actions.	Agreed-upon road maps, sequences of meetings and implementation plans are adhered to.	Implementation plans are regularly reviewed and transparently adjusted. Any changes in stakeholder participation are agreed upon and/or made transparent.	The procedure of integrating new stakeholders is made transparent.

Key factor	*Indicators of good process-design*			
	Phase 1	*Phase 2*	*Phase 3*	*Phase 4*
Knowledge and information about all necessary content areas is available and sufficiently distributed. Content capacity building is built into the process design.	The core group has carried out a sufficient situational analysis (see phase 1); a joint SWOT[24] with core team has taken place. Capacity building needs are identified.	Sufficient information from the situational analysis is integrated in goal development; a joint SWOT with a larger stakeholder group has become the basis for goal adjustment, agreements and implementation planning. Capacity building on content is integrated into the process.	A mechanism of information dissemination on content issues and progress is integrated into implementation planning. Capacity building for implementation takes place as required	Information about institutionalization or scaling-up requirements is available, new stakeholders or new staff receives sufficient capacity building in content areas
Capacity building for the implementation of Stakeholder Dialogues is built into the process design.	The core group has carried out an initial assessment of capacity building needs for the upcoming Stakeholder Dialogue	Capacity building needs regarding stakeholder management are transparently discussed during the first stakeholder workshop	If required Capacity building on stakeholder Dialogues continues.	New stakeholders receive capacity building in Stakeholder Dialogues, capacity needs for scaling-up, replication or institutionalization are identified
Sufficient resources for the Stakeholder Dialogue process and implementation are available.	The core group has identified and secured required resources for process management, process consultancy, training needs, etc.	The larger stakeholder group has secured sufficient resources for process management and capacity building	Review of resources for process management and capacity building is integrated into implementation monitoring	Sufficient resources for scaling-up, replication or institutionalization have been secured

[24] SWOT stand for the analysis of Strength, Weaknesses, Opportunities and Threads

Credibility

Key factor	*Indicators of good process-design*			
	Phase 1	*Phase 2*	*Phase 3*	*Phase 4*
Initiators, the core group and/ or a process management team have a sufficient mandate and are trusted by all stakeholders.	A cross-sector core group agrees upon the process design for phase 1. The core group is mandated as Stakeholder Dialogue initiator or facilitator by their respective hierarchies	The core group or a process management team is trusted or mandated by all stakeholders	There is a feedback mechanism in place for the work of the core group or process management team. In an agreed upon mechanism stakeholder representatives review progress and implementation.	Management mechanisms are agreed upon
All relevant stakeholders are adequately represented.	The core group is seen as adequately representing the stakeholder system and capably to initiate the dialogue.	All relevant stakeholders take part in larger stakeholder meetings.	The larger stakeholder group regularly convenes to review progress	Rules for representation are part of agreed upon governance or institutionalization procedures.
Decision-making procedures are transparent, if possible agreed upon by stakeholders, adequately efficient and take into account different stakeholder's organizational cultures.	The core group has agreed on a decision-making procedure for the preparation phase.	An agreement states the decision-making procedures respecting the role and internal procedures of different stakeholders.	The larger stakeholder group convenes with agreed upon representation to review progress and adjust plans	Representation of stakeholders and, if required integration of new stakeholders, is agreed as part of governance mechanisms

Inclusivity

Key factor	*Indicators of good process-design*			
	Phase 1	*Phase 2*	*Phase 3*	*Phase 4*
Weak stakeholder groups are adequately integrated into the process.	During context analysis, weak stakeholder groups are identified and strategies are designed to include their voices.	Weak stakeholder groups have the opportunity to form their views before meetings (e.g. stakeholder pre-meetings, organizational support for weaker stakeholder groups).	Process management ensures continuous participation of weaker stakeholder groups.	Formal mechanisms are designed to ensure the participation of weaker stakeholder groups.
There is an agreed-upon procedure for how to deal with critical voices and complaints. Critical voices are either integrated or good relationships are maintained.	The core group ensures structured listening to critical voices	The larger stakeholder group agrees on how to deal with external and internal critical voices.	An agreed-upon complaint mechanism is implemented.	The complaint mechanism is part of the governance mechanism.
Stakeholder Dialogue meetings and events are conducted in a way that ensures that all voices are heard.	The core group ensures that all voices are sufficiently considered in context analysis and informal preparatory meetings or conversations.	Stakeholder Dialogue meetings ensure that all voices are heard equally and provide professional facilitation, if required.	Stakeholder Dialogue meetings ensure that all voices are heard equally and provide professional facilitation, if required.	Stakeholder Dialogue meetings ensure that all voices are heard equally and provide professional facilitation, if required.
Stakeholders with high influence have become sufficiently interested in, and integrated into, the Stakeholder Dialogue.	The core group has secured participation of influential stakeholders.	Influential stakeholders are actively engaged, but do not dominate the results.	Influential stakeholders have an important role in implementation.	Influential stakeholders support further development, replication or scaling-up.

Ownership

Key factor	*Indicators of good process-design*			
	Phase 1	***Phase 2***	***Phase 3***	***Phase 4***
The relevance of goal, objectives and outcomes is regularly reviewed with all main stakeholders.	The idea for the Stakeholder Dialogue is reviewed with a cross-sector core group and further tested in informal conversations or small pre-meetings.	All stakeholders can give their inputs and contributions to the situational analysis, goal and objectives.	The relevance of goals and objectives is reviewed regularly during progress-review meetings with all stakeholders.	A redefinition of goals and objectives for scaling-up or replication takes place with all relevant stakeholders.
All stakeholders contribute their points of view and/or decision-making inputs fairly. Decision-making takes place on the basis of consensus-building.	The core group operates non-hierarchically, ensuring input from all members.	The larger stakeholder group operates non-hierarchically, ensuring that all stakeholders can contribute their perspectives fairly.	The larger stakeholder group operates non-hierarchically, ensuring that all stakeholders can contribute their perspectives fairly.	New stakeholders are integrated following the principles of equal contribution.
The contributions of different stakeholders are sufficiently acknowledged.	The core group has become a good Container and agrees on content and process unanimously.	All methodologies towards decision-making are based on consensus-building.	All methodologies towards decision-making are based on consensus-building.	Governance mechanisms regulate the procedures of consensus-building.

Delivery and outcome-orientation

Key factor	*Indicators of good process-design*			
	Phase 1	*Phase 2*	*Phase 3*	*Phase 4*
Stakeholder meetings are designed in a way that they allow collaborative task completion and always have meeting results reviews. Decisions made in the Stakeholder Dialogue are implemented collectively or by the participating stakeholder institutions.	The core group is committed to convey decisions made among stakeholders into their institutions effectively.	The purpose of the Stakeholder Dialogue is sufficiently embedded in the management of participating institutions, and there is a good information flow between the Stakeholder Dialogue participants and the management of participating institutions/organizations.	The progress made in the Stakeholder Dialogue is regularly reported back to the management of the participating institutions.	The participation in institutionalization or scaling-up is sufficiently anchored in the management of participating institutions.
Clear roles and implementation or steering structures are in place.	The core group has agreed on roles and process design for preparation.	An implementation plan, a meeting schedule or a road map is agreed upon by all stakeholders, and involved stakeholders have agreed upon a mechanism of process steering and the representation of different stakeholder groups.	A process management team reviews implementation progress and reports back to the larger stakeholder group or steering structure.	Scaling-up, replication or institutionalization is agreed upon with operational plans and timelines. Steering and management structures are agreed upon.
Stakeholders have agreed on implementation-monitoring and progress-review procedures. Progress reviews take place regularly.	The core group, or the secretariat/process management team has designed an internal progress review mechanism (e.g. self-assessment of process and progress).	The larger stakeholder group has decided on forms of monitoring and progress reviews.	Monitoring (process and results) is implemented by a secretariat/process management team and transparently reviewed by a larger stakeholder group or steering structure.	Learning, including monitoring, has become part of agreed-upon governance mechanisms.

LINKS AND LITERATURE

LINKS AND LITERATURE

CHAPTER 7

This chapter is dedicated to helping you, the reader, continue your journey on the path towards collective leadership by providing you with a list of informative and inspiring literature on many of the topics discussed in this book. For your convenience, we have clustered these books, articles and websites into the following 5 thematic groups:

1. Stakeholder engagement, dialogic change and cross-sector partnerships
2. Collective leadership, leadership for sustainability and sustainable (organizational) change
3. (Cross-sector) partnership initiatives and the partnership approach
4. Websites on Stakeholder Dialogues
5. Further Links

7.1 Selected literature on stakeholder engagement, dialogic change and cross-sector partnerships

Corporate Social Responsibility. Balancing Tomorrows Sustainability and Today's Profitability
David E. Hawkins (2006), Palgrave Macmillan, New York.

With this book, David E. Hawkins deals with the necessity of balancing short-term economic results with a strategy oriented towards sustainability. He underlines his thoughts by showcasing different examples relevant for business men and women, such as risk management, ethical trade, entrepreneurship, eco-efficiency, resource distribution or community relations. This book offers thought-provoking impulses for alternative approaches within entrepreneurship as well as for strategies for the integration of economic goals in long-term societal needs.

The New Broker: Beyond Agreement. Brokering Partnerships for Development
Michael Warner (2003), Overseas Development Institute, London.

The New Broker offers its readers an introduction into the "art and science" of partnership-brokering: Chris, an employee at an oil-drilling company, visits a goldmine in South America. Here he witnesses efforts to negotiate a partnership agreement between the mining company and different actors on local governance level, civil society and private business. Written in the style of a novel, this book points out negotiation techniques and possible in partnership agreements. Thereby Warner demonstrates the complex challenges partnership brokers face and fleshes out theoretical approaches with a real human background.

LINKS AND LITERATURE

A turning point for responsible supply chain management in the coffee sector: The Case of the Common Code for the Coffee Community – an international multi-stakeholder partnership for sustainable coffee, Petra Künkel, Stanislava Cholakova and Vera Fricke (2007), in: Enhancing the Effectiveness of Sustainability Partnerships
Editors: The National Research Council of the National Academies (2009), The National Academies Press, London
Or: ➲ **www.collectiveleadership.com**

After a 4-year stakeholder process in the coffee sector, in 2006 producers, roasters and traders from the coffee sectors agreed on the "Common Code for the Coffee Community (4C)", a basic quality standard and verification system for the entire value chain of the coffee mainstream-market. Petra Künkel accompanied the process as a consultant and process facilitator. In this article she pinpoints decisive factors for the coming about and success of multi-stakeholder partnerships. The authors furthermore delineate how a very complex and fragile stakeholder initiative benefits from a careful and thoughtful process design.

Open Space Technology. A User's Guide
Owen Harrison (1997), Berrett-Koehler Publishers, San Francisco.

Owen Harrison, founder of the *Open Space Technology* (OST), in this handbook documents background, procedures and preconditions for the application of the interactive OST. He describes in detail the logistical and material requirements for the implementation of an OST event. The book offers checklists for practical application. Furthermore, Harrison examines the situations where the OST can be applied and offers a guideline assisting in the decision for or against the use of this method in individual working or group processes.

Putting Partnerships to Work
Michael Warner und Rory Sullivan (2004), Greenleaf Publishing, Sheffield

Showcasing various practice examples, *Putting Partnerships to Work* illustrates how partnerships with the private sector can be established and implemented efficiently. The book is based on the work of the secretariat of the Natural Resources Cluster of Business Partners for Development, project-based initiative set up to study, support and promote strategic examples of cross-sector partnerships worldwide (www.bpdweb.com). Along with the positive results from established partnerships and insights from this program, the authors also depict risks and cost that can occur with this form of cooperation. The book furthermore features an implementation tool for the establishment and monitoring of partnerships.

The Necessary Revolution
Peter Senge (2008), Doubleday, New York.

In *The Necessary Revolution,* Peter Senge tackles innovative approaches of individuals and enterprises striving to deal with current social and ecological challenges in a sustainable manner. By means of practice examples he points out how enterprises can design their performance in a more sustainable manner. The book contains a number of strategies for developing visions and competencies with regard to more social, economic and ecological sustainability.

Multi-Stakeholder Processes for Governance and Sustainability. Beyond Deadlock and Conflict.
Minu Hemmati (2002), Earthscan Publications, London.

Multi-Stakeholder Processes for Governance and Sustainability is a guideline for the organization and implementation of multi-stakeholder processes. In order to meet the complex challenges of sustainable development, Hemmati and her co-authors explain how actors of integrative stakeholder processes equally provide space for social, economic and ecological aspects and how they can deal with risks in a constructive manner. This book contains detailed examples as well as suggestions for designing Stakeholder Dialogues.

Enhancing the Effectiveness of Sustainability Partnerships
Editors: The National Research Council of the National Academies (2009), The National Academies Press, London

The Round Table "Science and Technology" of the National Academies targets the mobilization of science and research practices that promote sustainable development. One of the working focuses lies on the effectiveness of multi-sectoral partnerships in linking academic knowledge with concrete action for sustainable development. In the context of a symposium in 2008, a group of experts of the round table discussed 11 showcase examples on stakeholder partnerships for sustainability. *Enhancing the Effectiveness of Sustainability Partnerships* is a summary of this symposium and contains excerpts of these showcases as well as highlights of the discussion rounds during the event.

Solving Tough Problems.
Adam Kahane (2004), Berrett-Koehler Publishers, San Francisco.

In *Solving Tough Problems,* Adam Kahane delineates strategies for solving complex and conflict-bearing problems beyond conventional paradigms. People often out of habit chose to solve problems by consulting handed-down knowledge and best-practice examples. According to Kahane, in the case of more complex problem situations such an approach can lead to a stalemate. He explains how an environment allowing for profound dialogue, constructive action and creative solutions can evolve.

The World Cafe: Shaping Our Futures Through Conversations That Matter
Juanita Brown and David Isaacs (2005), Berrett-Koehler Publishers, San Francisco

The *World Café* is a method for bringing groups into a cooperative and constructive dialogue. Enterprises, government bodies, communal institutions and NGOs increasingly make use of this procedure to work on questions and issues relevant for a various stakeholder groups. Juanita Brown and David Isaacs, the founders of the World Café method, illustrate the core principles of the method and its practical implementation by means of showcase examples and selected café -dialogues.

On Dialogue
David Bohm (1996), Routledge, New York. London

David Bohm, former Emeritus professor at the University of London, describes dialogue as a multi-facetted process beyond conventional ideas of conversational parlance and exchange. In this piece, he defines his notion of "dialogue", presenting a working manual for those engaging in dialogue and a theoretical foundation for reflection about the dialogic world view.

7.2 Selected literature on collective leadership, leadership for sustainability and sustainable (organizational) change

Leading Change. The Argument for Value-Based Leadership
James O'Toole (1995), Ballantine Books, New York

Management theorist James O'Toole proposes a vision of leadership based on values and respect, targeted at the welfare of their followers. He furthermore depicts why this approach to leadership is effective in complex organizational set-ups and how leaders can constructively deal with individuals resisting fresh and open approaches to change.

The Leader of the Future. New Visions, Strategies, and Practices for the Next Era.
Editors: Frances Hesselbein, Marshall Goldsmith, Richard Beckhard (1996), Jossey-Bass Publishers, San Francisco.

The Leader of the Future features numerous essays by lead executives, consultants and renowned authors on organizational development and change management. They share their vision, insights and ideas on, amongst others, how leaders emerge, how leadership roles fostering change are defined, how leaders can motivate their followers and how leaders can lead their organization into a sustainable future.

Leadership and Spirit. Breathing new Vitality and Energy into Individuals and Organizations.
Russ S. Moxley (2000), joint publication by Jossey-Bass Publications, San Francisco and Center for Creative Leadership, Greenboro.

Where individuals feel uninspired in their jobs, leaders are required to provide space for their followers to gain perspective, release their very individual strengths, commitment, creative and development potential. In his book, Moxley explains how leadership and spirit must and can be linked in order to foster committed and creative workforce. He underlines his explanations by analyzing prevalent leadership practices that cause the needed spirit in leadership to wither.

Spiral Dynamics. Mastering Values, Leadership, and Change.
Don Edward Beck and Christopher C. Cowan (1996), Blackwell Publishing, Malden, Oxford, Carlton.

Spiral Dynamics presents a framework for understanding the dynamic forces in human interaction, be it at work, education, personal lives or geopolitics. It is based on bio-psychological system concepts and provides a toolkit for managing differences in people for more productive and sustainable organizations, communities and living together.

Global Leadership: Portraits of the Past, Visions of the future.
Editors: Michael Harvey and JoAnn Danelo Barbour (2009), The James MacGregor Burns Academy of Leadership, Maryland.

Global leadership contains numerous essays by different contributing authors on past and future leadership models, in different thematic and cultural contexts. The book is a volume in the International Leadership Association series "Building Leadership Bridges".

Leadership is Global – Co-Creating a More Humane and Sustainable World
Editors: Walter Link, Thais Corral and Mark Gerzon (2006), Global Leadership Network.

Leadership is Global comprises of 21 essays on sustainability-oriented leadership. The focus lies on how to optimize cooperation between individuals, organizations and cultures and overcome conflict constructively. During many years, the authors have gained experience in the fields of governance, civil society empowerment, education and learning, economic development as well as cross-sector and cross-cultural partnerships. Based on their experiences, they share their view on how leadership can promote integration and sustainability in a globalised world.

The Dance of Change. The Challenges of Sustaining Momentum in Learning Organizations.
Peter Senge et al. (1999), Nicholas Brealey Publishing, London

The Dance of Change addresses managers and executives of every level and every sector. It outlines how leaders can cooperate to anticipate the challenges that profound, true organizational change and how to build needed personal and organizational capacities.

The Change Handbook
Peggy Holman, Tom Devane, Steven Cady and Associates, Berrett-Koehler Publishers (2007), San Francisco

This manual features profiles of more than sixty methods such a World Café, Appreciative Inquiry, Future Search, Six Sigma and many more. The different authors illustrate approach and application of each method and flesh out the theory with case studies. A comparative chart provided assists in the selection of the appropriate method, additional chapters describe how to best mix, match and sustain results.

LINKS AND LITERATURE

Primal Leadership. Realizing the Power of Emotional Intelligence.
Daniel Goleman, Richard Boyatzis, Annie McKee (2002), Harvard Business School Press, Boston.

A leader's emotions and attitude, as the authors argue, are contagious and have determining influence on energy and enthusiasm of their co-workers and thus on an organization's success or flounder. Showcasing the examples of different leaders, they illustrate how emotional intelligence in leadership leads to sustainable organizational and business results. Doing so, they highlight six leadership styles and methods (i.e. coaching, pacesetting) that leaders can employ to connect to their followers establishing better relationships and motivation at the workplace.

The Sustainability Champion's Guidebook. How to Transform your Company.
Bob Willard (2009), Ney society Publishers, Gabriola Island (British Colombia)

The Sustainability Champion's Guidebook is an easy to use manual presenting seven items helpful for enterprise leaders, such as change processes, sustainability practices, possible derailers and organizational change methods. Each item is broken down into seven implementation steps or seven methodological examples, making them easily applicable for practitioners.

Mind and Heart. Mapping your Personal Journey Towards Leadership for Sustainability.
Petra Künkel (2008), Books on Demand, Norderstedt.

Mind and Heart leads the reader to the aspects of leadership that need to form and emerge out of the very selves of us. Künkel delineates how leaders can use life and leadership experience to actively shape their contribution to sustainability - their personal leadership journey. Building on her own leadership journey and intensive conversations with 14 leaders from 8 different countries, she demonstrates how to develop one's own humanity as a gateway to leadership for sustainability.

The Art of Thinking Together: a pioneering approach to communicating in business and in life. William Isaacs, (1999), Crown Business, New York

Modern conversation is a lot like nuclear physics, argues William Isaacs. Lots of atoms zoom around, many of which just rush past each other. But others collide, creating friction. Even if our atomic conversations don't turn contentious, they often just serve to establish each participant's place in the cosmos. One guy shares a statistic he's privy to, another shares another fact, and on and on. Each person fires off a tidbit, pauses to reload while someone else talks, then fires off another. In Dialogue and the Art of Thinking Together, Isaacs explains how we can do better than that.

Theory U: Learning from the Future as It Emerges
Otto Scharmer (2009), Berrett-Koehler Publishers, San Francisco

In this ground-breaking book, C. Otto Scharmer invites us to see the world in new ways. What we pay attention to, and how we pay attention is the key to what we create. What often prevents us from 'being present' is what Scharmer calls our blind spot, the inner place from which each of us operates. Becoming aware of our blind spot is critical to bringing forth the profound systemic changes so needed in business and society today.

7.3 Selected online resources on (cross-sector) partnership initiatives and the partnership approach

The Partnering Initiative

➲ **www.thepartneringinitiative.org**

The P*artnering Initiative,* a program of the International Business Leaders Forum, promotes cross-sector partnerships in the field of sustainable development. The website furnishes an introduction into the benefits and risks of cross-sector partnerships and an overview of relevant definitions. Furthermore, a number of publications are available for download: tool books e.g. for the effective planning and implementation of partnerships or the role of partnership brokers, case studies about successes and challenges of various partnership initiatives: as well as background papers on different aspects of cross-sector partnerships. The publications are currently available in 13 languages.

The SEED Initiative

➲ **www.seedinit.org**

SEED is an initiative founded in 2002 by IUCN, UNEP and UNDP supporting cross-sector partnership initiatives in developing countries. SEED awards particularly promising partnerships and promotes them also financially. The website features learning material, tools, case studies, further links and publications on different thematic clusters. Additionally, practitioners can access the partnership cycle, a toolkit for planning partnership initiatives effectively and sustainably. These are accessible as online tools under

➲ **www.entrepreneurstoolkit.org/index.php/Main_Page** and

➲ **www.empowering-partnerships.org/**

Business Partners for Development

➲ **www.bpd-waterandsanitation.org**

The international cross-sector network *Business Partners for Development (BPD) Water and Sanitation* works for the improvement of the access to clean water and sanitation facilities in marginalized communities. The website suggests publications as well as links to project partners working specifically on water and waste water management, cross-sector partnerships and public-private partnerships. The handbook for dialogue with enterprises in the field of wastewater management available for download illustrates strategies and examples of sustainable wastewater management systems. The website is available in English, Spanish and French.

The Centre for Partnership Studies

➲ **www.partnershipway.org**

Based on a holistic partnership approach, the *Centre for Partnership Studies* conducts research, develops and teaches regarding the relationship between institutions, humans and nature. On their website, they offer methods for structuring institutions and interpersonal relationships with view to a sustainable dealing with nature. Numerous articles, audio- and video files are available in English and Spanish.

7.4 Selected websites on Stakeholder Dialogues

Democratic Dialogue Network

➲ **www.democraticdialoguenetwork.org**

The *Democratic Dialogue Network* is an initiative of the regional office for Latin America and the Caribbean of the United Nations Development Program (UNDP). It offers support to government and civil society actors in establishing Stakeholder Dialogues, democratic dialogues and capacity building measures. As a methodological tool, a handbook for the systematic establishment and implementation of Stakeholder Dialogues is available for download in French, English and Spanish. The entire Website is available in English and Spanish.

Collective Leadership Institute

➲ **www.collectiveleadership.com**

The *Collective Leadership Institute* (CLI) e.V. supports the design and result-oriented implementation of cross-sector partnerships and Stakeholder Dialogues. Alongside process-oriented research for the further development of the stakeholder approach the CLI offers competence development for the implementation of partnership processes for public, private and civil society as well as for organizations working in international development. The website, available in German and English, features publications on Stakeholder Dialogues for download.

Global Knowledge Partnership

➲ **www.globalknowledge.org**

The multi-stakeholder network *Global Knowledge Partnership* concentrates on knowledge management and ICT for development. Main focus of their programs and activities is education, poverty reduction and resource mobilization. Numerous publications on Stakeholder Dialogues and case studies on i.e. partnership initiatives using digital technology are available on their site.

Synergos

➲ **www.synergos.org**

The *Synergos Institute* works on cross-sector cooperation with view to poverty reduction and social progress. Geographic focus of their work is the developing world. The Synergos website is furnished with many multimedia features such as videos, photo galleries. The online library is sorted according to countries and thematic areas. Additionally, a comprehensive selection of links leads to further thematically related organizations and programs.

AccountAbility

➲ **www.accountability21.net**

AccountAbility is a network of institutions of different sector collaborating to promote sustainability on global markets through responsible competition, good governance and cross-sector cooperation and Stakeholder Dialogues. The Accountability tools and concepts (i.e., the AA1000 Standard for Stakeholder Dialogues and sustainability) are accessible in up to 8 languages. The entire website is available in English, Spanish and Chinese.

Future Search
➲ **www.futuresearch.net**

The worldwide network *Future Search* offers information on the innovative planning tool of the same name, which brings together people of different institutions and sectors into a dialogue-oriented process. The approach has been tested in many countries and cultural contexts, case studies are available for download. On top of that there are reading suggestions and videos i.e. ion a UNICEF project in South Sudan.

7.5 Selected further links

Theories on and approaches to participation, conflict resolution and leadership

- Association for Conflict Resolution
  ➲ **www.acresolution.org**
- Bohm-Dialog
  ➲ **www.infed.org/archives/e-texts/bohm_dialogue.htm**
- Ideas and Tools for Community Change
  ➲ **www.everyday-democracy.org/en/index.aspx**
- Eldis Participation Resource Guide
  ➲ **www.eldis.org/participation/index.htm**
- Conflict Resolution Information Source (CRinfo)
  ➲ **www.crinfo.org**
- Leader to Leader Institute: Strengthening the leadership of the social sector
  ➲ **www.druckerinstitute.com**
- Dialogue on Leadership
  ➲ **www.dialogueonleadership.com**
- Search for Common Ground
  ➲ **www.sfcg.**
- Resiliency in Action
  ➲ **www.resiliency.com**
- Innovations in democracy
  ➲ **www.democrcyinnovations.org**
- International Institution for Public Participation
  ➲ **www.aip2.org**
- Citizens Juries
  ➲ **www.jefferson-center.org**
- The Alliance for International Conflict Prevention and Resolution
  ➲ **www.aicrp.org**
- International Conflict Research Institute (INCORE) of the Ulster University, UK
  ➲ **www.incore.ulst.ac.uk**
- America Speaks - 21st Century Town Meeting
  ➲ **www.americaspeaks.org**

LINKS AND LITERATURE

Concepts and methods for conflict management and stakeholder processes

- Sustainable Development Gateway / Multi-Stakeholder Processes
  ➲ **www.sdgateway.net/topics/265.htm**
- Berghof Center for Constructive Conflict Management, Germany
  ➲ **www.berghof-center.org**
- The World Café
  ➲ **www.theworldcafe.com**
- The Program on Intergroup Relations
  ➲ **www.igr.umich.edu/**
- Center for Partnership Studies (Riane Eisler)
  ➲ **www.partnershipway.org**
- Mediation
  ➲ **www.mediate.com**
- Citizens Choicework
  ➲ **www.publicagenda.org/public-engagement-nmaterials/citizen-choicework-technical -assistance**
- National Association for community Mediation
  ➲ **www.nafcm.org**
- Stakeholder Research associates - **Consultancy**
  ➲ **www.stakeholderresearch.com**
- Peacebuilding Portal (UNDESA, UNDP, African Union)
  ➲ **www.peacebuildingportal.org**
- One World Trust/Global Accountability Project
  ➲ **www.oneworldtrust.org**
- The Co-Intelligence Institute
  ➲ **www.co-intelligence.org**
- The Diplo Foundation
  ➲ **www.diplmacy.edu**
- Global Partnership for the Prevention of Armed Conflict (GPPAC)
  ➲ **www.gppac.net**
- Public Conversations Project
  ➲ **www.publicconversations.org**
- South African Truth and Reconciliation Commission
  ➲ **www.joj.za/trc**

Process tools and practice examples

- Open Space Technology
  ➲ **www.openspaceworld.org**
- The Water Dialogues: Multi-Stakeholder Dialogues on Water and the Private Sector
  ➲ **www.waterdialogues.org/index.htm**
- Diversophy: A Game Designed to Develop Global and Local Competence
  ➲ **www.diversophy.com/index.htm**
- Dialogos
  ➲ **www.dialogos.com**

- Appreciative inquiry
  ➲ **www.appreciative-inquiry.org**
- Conversation Café
  ➲ **www.conversationcafe.org**
- The Sustainable Food Laboratory
  ➲ **www.sustainablefoodlab.org**
- Sustained Dialogue
  ➲ **www.sustained dialogue.org**
- The Environment Council UK
  ➲ **www.the-environment-council.org.uk**
- Intractable Conflict Knowledge Base Project
  ➲ **www.beyondintractability.org**
- UNDP on governance
  ➲ **www.undp.org/governance**

Exchange networks on group methods and multi-stakeholder processes

- Web Lab's Small Group Dialogue
  ➲ **www.weblab.org/**
- Society for Organizational Learning
  ➲ **www.solonline.org**
- Portal on Multi-Stakeholder Processes of the University of Wageningen, The Netherlands
  ➲ **http://portals.wi.wur.nl/msp/**
- International Association of Facilitators
  ➲ **www.iaf-world.org**
- A Gateway for Capacity Development
  ➲ **www.capacity.org/en/content/view/full/2#**
- Generative Change Community
  ➲ **www.gc-community.net**
- National Coalition for Dialogue and Deliberation (NCDD)
  ➲ **www.thataway.org**
- Ideas, Thinkers, Practice
  ➲ **www.infed.org**
- National Issues Forums
  ➲ **www.nifi.org**
- Social Standards Round Tables
  ➲ **www.coc-runder-tisch.de/coc-runder-tisch/**

DEFINITIONS

Stakeholder Dialogue: Stakeholder Dialogues are a methodology for designing and implementing consultation and cooperation in complex change processes that require different interest groups to be included and integrated. Well-structured Stakeholder Dialogues can create and cultivate ownership of change towards sustainability.

Stakeholder: Stakeholders are people or institutions that have an interest in a particular course of development, or a particular decision, either as individuals or as representatives of a group. This includes people who influence a decision, who are key players in implementation, or who are affected by the development.[25]

Container: The term 'Container' refers to the function and relational quality of an initiating team or core group of interested actors in Stakeholder Dialogues. A good container exists, if actors are dedicated to the change envisaged, emotionally engaged with future possibilities and if they are committed to initiating and implementing the intended change jointly. A good Container creates a holding space for the planned change, an emotional home for the joint initiative and an initial pattern of the envisaged dialogue or cooperation.

Initial Container: A group of people who initiate change- in this context in the form of a Stakeholder Dialogue. The cross-sector core group can be such an initial Container.

Broader Container: The broader Container is composed of people who the core group begins to engage, and who are supportive of the Stakeholder Dialogue. They may get involved in promoting the Stakeholder Dialogue and can take the dialogue process beyond those who form the initial Container.

Involved Stakeholder System: These are usually those actors who participate in one or several Stakeholder Dialogue events, such as consultation meetings, workshops, planning meetings, etc.

Wider affected system: These are the directly involved stakeholders or other actors who may be affected by the change initiative.

Core Group: The group of actors initiating the Stakeholder Dialogue. Ideally a core group already represents the different stakeholder groups involved. In Phase 1 members of the core group will engage high-level sponsors, decision-makers who are crucial to the success of the Stakeholder Dialogues, but it also aim to get into conversations with selected key stakeholders, most often in a more informal way (e.g. in bilateral meetings or small focus-group meetings). Ideally the core group remains in place throughout all phases.

Project secretariat/Process management team: Project secretariats are mandated teams who facilitate the implementation of a Stakeholder Dialogue as well as the communication among stakeholders, for example between the steering committees and the implementing institutions. Project secretariats or process management teams can be, but need not necessarily be composed of different stakeholder groups. But they need to be trusted and mandated by all stakeholder involved.

[25] ***Hemmati 2002: 2***

Capacity Building: In the setting of international cooperation, capacity building stands for the further development of both individual and organizational competencies through e.g., training, coaching, or professional development support, which enable one to more successfully work towards and accomplish a particular mission or objective.

Process design/ Process architecture: Process architecture refers to the design of the overall preparation, implementation and review process of a Stakeholder Dialogue.

Engagement process: An engagement process starts with establishing and cultivating the initial Containers of commitment in which people who are critical to achieving the goal can take a stand together on the dialogue's behalf.

Collective Leadership: Collective Leadership for sustainability is the capacity of a group of leaders to contribute to a more sustainable future through assuming joint and flexible leadership in service of the common good. It takes place by various individuals on a collective scale towards the larger and integrated goal of economic, social and environmental sustainability At the core of collective leadership is the human capacity to dialogue and transform differences into progress: it enables the transcendence of self-centered views – a pre-requisite to successfully addressing the challenges of globalization and sustainability.

Result monitoring: The purpose of result monitoring is to keep track of the activities agreed upon and to assess the results achieved.

Impact monitoring: The purpose of impact monitoring is to look beyond activities and results, and to assess if the Stakeholder Dialogue has had the effect it was expected to have.

Process monitoring: The purpose of process monitoring is to keep track of the quality of the process design and key factors for success. It helps to check if the Stakeholder Dialogue is leading towards the expected outcome – a commitment to progress.

BIBLIOGRAPHY

Bohm, David, 1996: On Dialogue, edited by Lee Nichels, Routledge, London and New York

Connelli, Dianne M., 1986: All sickness is homesickness, Centre for Traditional Acupuncture, Columbia, Maryland

Collective Leadership Institute, 2009: Fieldguide "Working with Stakeholder Dialogues", Potsdam, internal document

Guajardo, Francisco, 2009: Geo 2010 National Conference: Insights on Collective Leadership, From vulnerable to powerful

Hemmati, Minu, 2002: Multi-Stakeholder Process for Governance and Sustainability, Beyond deadlock and conflict, Earthscan, London

Isaacs, William, 1999: Dialogue. The Art Of Thinking Together, *A Pioneering Approach to Communicating in Business and in Life, Crown Business, New York*

Kantor, David 1997: DIALogos, Fieldguide, The Art of Thinking Together, Cambridge, internal document

Kellogg Foundation, 2007: A collective leadership framework,

➲ **http://www.wkkf.org/~/media/E64C59A377E34AA99515B5C293E4B0C6.ashx**

Kuenkel, 2005: A turning point for responsible supply chain management in the coffee sector, Collective Leadership Institute, Potsdam,

➲ **www.collectiveleadershipinstitute.com**

Kuenkel, Petra, 2008: How to make multi-stakeholder initiatives work: the Case of "The Common Code for the Coffee Community" – an international strategic alliance for sustainable coffee, Collective Leadership Institute, Potsdam

Kuenkel, Petra; Fricke, Vera and Cholakova, Stanislava, 2007: Case Study – The Common Code for the Coffee Community (4C). In: Enhancing the Effectiveness of Partnerships for Sustainability. National Research Council. Washington, DC: National Academies Press

Kuenkel, Petra, 2008: Mind and Heart, Mapping Your Personal Journey Towards Leadership For Sustainability, BoD, Norderstedt

Kusek & Rist, 2004: Ten Steps to Result-Based Monitoring and Evaluation System, The World Bank, Washington, D.C

Ramdas, Kavita. 2010: Global Fund for Women: Why collective leadership matters, Recognizing Collective Leadership as a Model,

➲ **http://www.globalfundforwomen.org/**

Scharmer, Claus Otto, 2000: Presencing. Learning From the Future As It Emerges, Paper presented at the Conference on Knowledge and Innovation, May 25-26 2000, Helsinki School of Economics, Finnland

Scharmer, Claus Otto, 2009: Theory U: Learning from the Future as It Emerges, Berrett-Koehler Publishers, San Francisco

Senge, Peter, 2000: The Dance of Change, The Challenges Of Sustaining Momentum In Learning Organizations, Nicholas Brealey Publishing, London

Vahlhaus & Thomas (GIZ), 2000: Guidelines for Impact Monitoring in Economic and Employment Promotion Projects with Special Reference to Poverty Reduction Impacts, Deutsche Gesellschaft für Internationale Zusammenarbeit (GIZ), Eschborn

Wheatley, Margaret, 1999: Leadership and The New Science, Discovering Order In A Chaotic World, Berrett-Koehler Publishers, San Francisco

Wilber, Ken, 2003: Introduction to Integral Theory and Practice, Integral Institute, Louisville

ONLINE

Deutsche Gesellschaft für Internationale Zusammenarbeit (GIZ) GmbH

➲ **www.giz.de**

Isaacs, William

➲ **http://www.dialogos.com/index.html**

Kantor, David

➲ **www.davidkantortheory.com**

OECD (Organisation for Economic Co-operation and Evaluation) Journal of Australasia, 2002 "Glossary of Key Terms in Evaluation and Results-Based Management." Paris: OECD/DAC

OECD: Capacity Development:

➲ **http://www.oecd.org/document/42/0,3343,en_2649_34565_42393642_1_1_1_1,00.html**

Straker, David (2008): Changing Minds, In Detail, Syque Press

➲ **www.changingminds.org/disciplines/change_management/stakeholder_change/interest_influence.htm**

Tennyson, Ros, 2003: The Partnering initiative, Partnership Toolbook

➲ **http://www.thepartneringinitiative.org/docs/tpi/pt/PartneringToolbookEng.pdf**

Rapp, Schwägerl &Traufetter, 2010: The Copenhagen Protocol: How China and India Sabotaged the UN Climate Summit

➲ **http://www.spiegel.de/international/world/0,1518,692861-3,00.html**

THE COLLECTIVE LEADERSHIP INSTITUTE

Who we are

The Collective Leadership Institute (CLI) is an internationally operating non-profit organization based in Germany (Potsdam) and South Africa (Cape Town). It was founded 2005 and is an independent initiative supporting stakeholders from the private sector, the public sector and civil society in creating and implementing collaborative change initiatives for innovative and sustainable solutions to global, societal and local challenges.

Our Vision

As an international non-profit organization we are an anchor for a spirit of **collective leadership for sustainability** globally and a catalyst for dialogic change. We inspire and enable people to build sustainable futures together and help them achieve tangible results in their collective initiatives.

Our Mission

With the focus on capacity development in collective leadership, we are building competence for sustainability in cross-sector collaboration, Stakeholder Dialogues, sustainable business practices, personal leadership and conflict transformation. The Collective Leadership Institute thus makes a vital contribution to the realization of profound global change towards a sustainable future.

What we stand for

The Collective Leadership Institute (CLI) stands for **sustainable acting, thinking, communicating and leading**. Hence, process competence in sustainability engagement is the principal concern and interest of our work. Central to our approach is creating a climate of collective leadership. This is an important premise for implementing profound and complex change initiative. It enables a group of committed leaders to share responsibility and collectively contribute to sustainable development, by respecting difference and diversity and cultivating the individual and collective identification with sustainability.

Who we support

In Germany and Europe, Asia, Africa and South America, we work with leaders, project managers and change agents from

- corporations,
- small and medium sized companies,
- development agencies,
- the public sector and
- civil society organizations.

What we offer

Our **educational programs** in Stakeholder Dialogues and collective leadership integrate knowledge building, personal mastery and the actual work reality of participants. We offer open seminars and tailor-made courses.

Based on key conceptual content our **educational programs** incorporate the actual work reality of participants. We strive to deliver knowledge that can be implemented in day to day business. Participant's feedback helps us to continuously improve.

Our **process support** for cross-sector collaboration projects combines advisory and capacity building: this way we enable people to develop their own competence according to their specific challenges.

Our **leadership development** for sustainability fosters change in thinking and practical implementation through knowledge building, reflection and exposure.

Our **research** is designed as a learning process for sustainability helping people move quicker towards new action.

Our **networking** connects people from different sectors in order to help bridge gaps and create new opportunities for sustainability engagement.

Our **collaboration projects** are piloting new approaches to cross-sector learning and engagement for sustainability.

Our work is based on the principle of Collective Leadership

Collective Leadership for sustainability is the capacity of a group of leaders to deliver their contribution to a more sustainable future through assuming joint and flexible leadership in service of the common good. At the core of collective leadership is the human capacity to dialogue and transformation differences into progress: it enables the transcendence of self-centered views – a pre-requisite to successfully addressing the challenges of globalization and sustainability.

Our **educational programs** in Stakeholder Dialogues and collective leadership integrate knowledge building, personal mastery and the actual work reality of participants. We offer open seminars and tailor-made courses.

The programs are designed to help build strategic abilities and implementation skills in cross-sector cooperation, Stakeholder Dialogues and leadership for sustainability. Participants can exchange experience, gain insights, knowledge and practical skills to build consensus-building stakeholder relationships, convene networks for high impact solutions, and create the space for learning and collaborating with different stakeholders.

The program **'Working with Stakeholder Dialogues'** is experience-based and focuses on understanding success factors in Stakeholder Dialogues. It also develops participants' competencies to assess the applicability of Stakeholder Dialogue approaches and enhances your skills to successfully initiate and implement such dialogue processes. It introduces key elements and their application in the preparation and implementation of Stakeholder Dialogues.

The program **'Leading Change Through Stakeholder Dialogues'** is an advanced practitioner program focusing on the application of success factors in stakeholder cooperation and consultation. It enhances participants competence to design successful process architectures and broadens skills to achieve consensus, commitment for implementation and outcome-orientation among all stakeholders. It equips participants with methodologies for large systems change and helps to review and adjust strategies for the application in the preparation and implementation of Stakeholder Dialogues.

"Creating a Culture of Collective Leadership" is an experience-based leadership development course and focuses on understanding both the individual and the collective leadership contribution to sustainability initiatives and complex cooperation projects. It develops your competence to map your own developmental path as a leader and enhances your ability to successfully initiate and implement collective change processes.

Through our programs we build bridges between strengthening individual self-mastery and collective capacity to implement collaborative change towards sustainability.

For more information, visit ⊃ **www.collectiveleadership.com**